AND NOW FOR SOMETHING COMPLETELY DIFFERENT

AND NOW FOR SOMETHING COMPLETELY DIFFERENT

Critical Approaches to Monty Python

Edited by Kate Egan and
Jeffrey Andrew Weinstock

EDINBURGH
University Press

Edinburgh University Press is one of the leading university presses in the UK. We publish academic books and journals in our selected subject areas across the humanities and social sciences, combining cutting-edge scholarship with high editorial and production values to produce academic works of lasting importance. For more information visit our website: edinburghuniversitypress.com

© editorial matter and organisation Kate Egan and Jeffrey Andrew Weinstock, 2020, 2022
© the chapters their several authors, 2020, 2022

Edinburgh University Press Ltd
The Tun – Holyrood Road
12(2f) Jackson's Entry
Edinburgh EH8 8PJ

First published in hardback by Edinburgh University Press 2020

Typeset in 10/12.5 pt Sabon
by IDSUK (DataConnection) Ltd

A CIP record for this book is available from the British Library

ISBN 978 1 4744 7515 0 (hardback)
ISBN 978 1 4744 7516 7 (paperback)
ISBN 978 1 4744 7517 4 (webready PDF)
ISBN 978 1 4744 7518 1 (epub)

The right of Kate Egan and Jeffrey Andrew Weinstock to be identified as the editors of this work has been asserted in accordance with the Copyright, Designs and Patents Act 1988, and the Copyright and Related Rights Regulations 2003 (SI No. 2498).

CONTENTS

List of Figures vii
Acknowledgements viii
Notes on Contributors ix

    'It's . . . The Introduction' 1
    Kate Egan and Jeffrey Andrew Weinstock

PART ONE   SITUATING PYTHON

1. Six Comics in Search of a . . . : Monty Python and
   Absurdist/Surrealist Theatre 23
   Rick Hudson

2. 'None shall pass' and 'The skull beneath the skin':
   Monty Python, the British Class System and Death 39
   Gina Wisker

3. Der Ver Zwei Peanuts: Depictions of a Distant War in
   Monty Python's Flying Circus 57
   Anna Martonfi

PART TWO   PYTHON'S PRACTICES, FORMS AND MEDIUMS

4. The Royal Philharmonic Goes to the Bathroom:
   The Music of Monty Python 75
   James Leggott

5. The Disruptive Metamorphoses of an Impish God:
    Gilliam's Satiric Animation   91
    Paul Wells

6. Figures Traced in Shite: The Scribe, The Illuminator and
    Monty Python's *Holy Grail*   107
    Ewan Wilson

PART THREE   CONTEXTS AND REPRESENTATIONS

7. Grannies from Hell, Daring Bicycle Repairmen, Upper-Class
    Twits and 'Make Tea Not Love': *Monty Python's Flying Circus*
    and 1960s British (Popular) Culture   125
    Caroline Langhorst

8. The Parrot, the Albatross and the Cat: Animals and
    Comedy in Monty Python   141
    Brett Mills

9. 'Political Correctness', Reversal and Incongruity:
    Dynamics of Humour in *Life of Brian*   155
    Kathleen J. Cassity

PART FOUR   CULT, FANDOM AND PYTHON

10. Philosophy, Absurdity, Waste and *The Meaning of Life*:
    A Cult Film, of Sorts   173
    Ernest Mathijs

11. In Praise of Silliness: The Cult of Python   189
    Jeffrey Andrew Weinstock

12. Memories of Connecting: Fathers, Daughters and
    Intergenerational Monty Python Fandom   207
    Kate Egan

Index   227

FIGURES

I.1 Michael Palin's 'It's' Man: *Monty Python's Flying Circus* (1969–74)   2
I.2 Cleese shows Undertaker Chapman his mother in the sack: *Monty Python's Flying Circus*, episode 26 (1970)   6
10.1 *Monty Python's The Meaning of Life* (1983) and *The Rocky Horror Picture Show* (1975): *joie de vivre éclatante*   179
10.2 Hyperbole and waste at work in *The Meaning of Life*   183
10.3 The end of *The Meaning of Life*: A solid rant on entertainment today   186
11.1 Just a flesh wound: *Monty Python and the Holy Grail* (1975)   197
11.2 Møøse control: *Monty Python and the Holy Grail*   201
11.3 Arthur confronts the Knights Who Say Ni: *Monty Python and the Holy Grail*   202
12.1 The higher percentage of 18–35-year-olds in the 'Dad Memories Group' compared to the *Monty Python Memories* database as a whole   210
12.2 The higher percentage of female respondents in the 'Dad Memories Group' compared to the *Monty Python Memories* database as a whole   211

ACKNOWLEDGEMENTS

We would like to thank everyone at Edinburgh University Press, particularly Gillian Leslie and Richard Strachan, for their guidance and investment in this book project, and Ernest Mathijs for suggesting that we work together as editors on a book on Monty Python!

Kate would also like to thank Sian Barber, Martin Barker, Beck Edwards, Russ Hunter, Stephanie Jones, Paul Newland, Tim Noble, Lisa Richards, Jamie Sexton and Justin Smith for their feedback and encouragement.

NOTES ON CONTRIBUTORS

Kathleen J. Cassity holds a PhD in English from the University of Hawaii-Manoa in Honolulu, Hawaii, USA. She currently serves as Dean of the College of Liberal Arts and Sciences and Professor of English at Western Oregon University in Monmouth, Oregon, USA. Dr Cassity has published and presented several papers and book chapters relating to humour, including a recent article on *Life of Brian* published in the *Journal of Religion and Film*. She is also co-editor of an anthology of Anglo-Indian writing, *Curtain Call: Anglo-Indian Reflections*. Her scholarly interests include liberal arts advocacy, writing pedagogy, life writing/memoir and Anglo-Indian narrative.

Kate Egan is Senior Lecturer in Film and Media at Northumbria University, UK, and the author of *Trash or Treasure? Censorship and the Changing Meanings of the Video Nasties* (2007), *Cultographies: The Evil Dead* (2011) and (with Martin Barker, Tom Phillips and Sarah Ralph) *Alien Audiences* (2015). She is also co-editor (with Sarah Thomas) of *Cult Film Stardom* (2012). She is currently conducting research on the local censorship of *Monty Python's Life of Brian* throughout the UK in the late 1970s and early 1980s, and is writing up her findings from an international audience project on audience memories of Monty Python.

Rick Hudson has written professionally since leaving school and has had his fiction not only broadcast by the BBC, but widely published in collections and professional magazines. He has written experimental literary fiction, popular genre fiction and work that sits somewhere between these two poles. Rick also works in game design and has produced game materials for computer game companies and table-top role-playing games. In addition, Rick is an English Literature academic who lectures on fantasy/SF and horror fiction, TV and film. His previously published academic work includes chapters in: Christopher Shaberg (ed.) *Deconstructing Brad Pitt* (2014) and Lynn Whitfield, Paul N. Reinarch and Robert G. Weiner (eds) *Python Beyond Python* (2016).

Caroline Langhorst holds a BA in Film Studies and British Studies and a MA in Film Studies from the University of Mainz, Germany. She is currently working on her PhD thesis on male rebellion and rebellious actors in 1960s British cinema at the Cinema and Television History Research Institute (CATHI), De Montfort University Leicester, UK. Her main research interests include British and American cinema, television, popular music and culture, gender studies, star studies and acting/performance studies as well as the 'long' 1960s and the counterculture.

James Leggott is Senior Lecturer in Film and Television at Northumbria University, UK. He has published on various aspects of British film and television culture. He is the author of *Contemporary British Cinema: From Heritage to Horror* (2008), and the co-editor of *No Known Cure: The Comedy of Chris Morris* (2013), *British Science Fiction Film and Television: Critical Essays* (2011) and *Upstairs and Downstairs: British Costume Drama Television from The Forsyte Saga to Downton Abbey* (2019). He is also the principal editor of the *Journal of Popular Television*.

Anna Martonfi completed her PhD at the University of East Anglia, UK, examining transnational aspects of Jewish humour in British and Hungarian films in the inter-war era. Her research interests include British radio, television and film comedy, transnational humour, Hungarian comedies of the inter-war era, and Jewish comedy; and she has also published on how the translation and transcreation of audiovisual texts, including animation, impacts the cultural complexities of interpretation. She currently works as Lecturer at the Vrije Universiteit Amsterdam, and as Visiting Lecturer at Universiteit Leiden.

Ernest Mathijs is a Professor in Film and Media Studies at the University of British Columbia, Canada. He researches cult film, genre cinema and European film. He has written on the reception of digital cinema and fantasy (*The Hobbit* and *The Lord of the Rings*), on Belgian cinema, *The Room*, and on the activism and acting of Delphine Seyrig. He has also published *100 Cult Films, Cult*

Cinema, The Cult Film Reader and *Alternative Europe*, among others. He is the author of monographs on David Cronenberg and *Ginger Snaps*, and the co-producer and co-writer of the two-part documentary *The Quiet Revolution* (2019), on Canadian genre film since the 1970s. His most recent book is *The Routledge Companion to Cult Cinema* (co-edited with Jamie Sexton).

Brett Mills is Professor of Media and Culture at the University of East Anglia, UK. He is the author of *Television Sitcom* (2005), *The Sitcom* (2009) and *Animals on Television: The Cultural Making of the Non-Human* (2017), and co-author of *Creativity in the British Television Comedy Industry* (with Erica Horton, 2017) and two editions of *Reading Media Theory: Thinkers, Approaches, Contexts* (with David M. Barlow, 2009/2012). His funded research projects include 'Make Me Laugh: Creativity in the British Television Comedy Industry' (Arts and Humanities Research Council, 2012–15) and 'Multispecies Storytelling: More-Than-Human Stories about Place' (with Professor Claire Parkinson; Arts and Humanities Research Council, 2019–21).

Jeffrey Andrew Weinstock is Professor of English at Central Michigan University, USA and an associate editor for the *Journal of the Fantastic in the Arts*. He is the author or editor of twenty-three books. These include *The Monster Theory Reader* (2020), *The Cambridge Companion to the American Gothic* (2018), *Critical Approaches to Welcome to Night Vale: From the Weather to the Void* (2018), *The Works of Tim Burton: Margins to Mainstream* (2013), *The Vampire Film: Undead Cinema* (2012), *Scare Tactics: Supernatural Fiction by American Women* (2008), *Taking South Park Seriously* (SUNY, 2008), *The Rocky Horror Picture Show* (2007) and *Spectral America: Phantoms and the American Imagination* (2004). Visit him at JeffreyAndrewWeinstock.com

Paul Wells is a Professor of Animation at Loughborough University, UK, and Director of the Animation Academy, a research group dedicated to cutting-edge engagement with animation and related moving-image practices. Paul is an internationally established scholar, screenwriter and director, and has written and directed numerous projects for theatre, radio, television and film. His books include *Understanding Animation* (1998), *The Horror Genre: From Beelzebub to Blair Witch* (2001), *Animation: Genre and Authorship* (2002), *The Fundamentals of Animation* (2006) and *The Animated Bestiary: Animals, Cartoons and Culture* (2009). His work also embraces collaborative texts, including *Drawing for Animation* (2008) with master animator, Joanna Quinn, and *Re-Imagining Animation* (2008) with Johnny Hardstaff, leading graphic designer and filmmaker with Ridley Scott Associates. He is Chair of the Association of British Animation Collections (ABAC), a collaborative initiative with the BFI, BAFTA and the National Media Museum.

Ewan Wilson has recently submitted a PhD thesis entitled 'A New Archaic Avant-Garde?: Tradition and Experimentation in the Neo-Mediaeval Cinema of Terry Gilliam, Derek Jarman, and John Boorman' to the University of Dundee. He has published work on the similarities between the stop-motion animation of Jan Švankmajer and the Brothers Quay and the aesthetics of kinetic sculpture in *Animation: An Interdisciplinary Journal*, and has presented papers on Gilliam's *The Fisher King* as a cathartic project, his filmmaking process as represented in *Lost in La Mancha*, and *Time Bandits* as a modern dream vision. Ewan's research interests include, but are not limited to, European and British cinema, cinematic medievalism, production design and animation.

Gina Wisker currently works at the University of Bath, UK in the International Centre for Higher Education Management. She was previously Professor of Higher Education and Contemporary Literature at the University of Brighton, UK and prior to that at Anglia Ruskin University in Cambridge, UK. She specialises in contemporary women's writing, and postcolonial, Gothic and popular fictions. Her books include *Horror Fiction* (2005), *Key Concepts in Postcolonial Writing* (2007), *Margaret Atwood: an Introduction to Critical Views of Her Fiction* (2012) and *Contemporary Women's Gothic Fiction* (2016), and she is currently completing *Contemporary Women's Ghost Stories* (2020). Gina teaches and researches in learning, teaching, postgraduate study supervision and academic writing. She chaired the Contemporary Women's Writing Association, the Heads of Education Development Group, SEDA Scholarship and Research committee, and is chief editor of SEDA journal, *Innovations in Education and Teaching International*, dark fantasy online journal *Dissections* and poetry magazine *Spokes*.

'IT'S ... THE INTRODUCTION'

Kate Egan and Jeffrey Andrew Weinstock

On 5 October 1969, a new sketch comedy programme premiered on BBC1. The episode, with a title, 'Whither Canada?' designed to confound critics and reviewers, opened with a bedraggled, half-drowned man (Michael Palin) emerging from the ocean and collapsing exhausted on the shore, where he uttered one word: 'It's...' His thought was then completed by a sedate narratorial voice revealing the unlikely name of the programme, '*Monty Python's Flying Circus*', backed by John Philip Sousa's 'The Liberty Bell' march and against surreal, stylised animation of exploding heads, naked ladies and characters squashed by a giant foot. Following the opening credits, Wolfgang Amadeus Mozart (John Cleese) considered ridiculously inaccurate famous deaths in history as rated by a panel of judges; a British language instructor (Terry Jones) attempted to teach Italian to native speakers; a commercial was presented for butter touted as indistinguishable from a dead crab; a talk show host (John Cleese) interviewed a famous director (Graham Chapman) but failed to get past trying to establish the director's name; another talk show host (Eric Idle) interviewed one of the world's 'leading modern composers' (Terry Jones) but, again, focused on the composer's name; news coverage was offered of a bicycle race in which the participants were all twentieth-century artists; and the history of a joke so funny that to hear it was to die immediately from laughter was pursued in the form of a documentary. In between segments, pigs squealed and animated bits featured absurd and suggestive manipulations of photographs. The episode then ended with the same bedraggled man who had opened the episode laboriously returning to the ocean.

Figure I.1 Michael Palin's 'It's' Man: *Monty Python's Flying Circus* (1969–74).

The premiere episode of *Monty Python's Flying Circus* was audacious, erudite and irreverent. With parts filmed in front of a studio audience and parts on location, and mocking different media formats including the documentary, news broadcast, talk show and game show, the episode combined dazzling wordplay (Cleese's litany of contemporary artists during the 'Picasso/Cycling Race' segment stands out) with absurdist animation, sophisticated references to art and history with unapologetic silliness, and original sketch comedy with parody. It was also not particularly well received.

The first episode premiered at just shy of 11pm on a Sunday, with *Flying Circus* replacing a religious devotional programme for clergymen that had received lacklustre ratings (Hewison 1981: 7). According to Robert Verkaik, the first episode captured only a 3 per cent share of the British viewing population – about 1.5 million people – the lowest ratings for any 'light entertainment show' for the week (Verkaik 2009). Even more alarmingly, BBC management expressed concern about the content of some of the sketches. As reported by Verkaik:

Aubrey Singer, the head of the BBC's features group, told the meeting that he had found parts of the programme 'disgusting' while the controller of BBC1 [Paul Fox] complained the show had 'gone over the edge of what was acceptable'. (Ibid.)

Audience response, however, appears to have been a bit more positive. The *History of the BBC* 'Monty Python at 50' website reports that '[w]ithin a week of Monty Python's first episode, BBC Audience Research had undertaken one of its regular Audience Research Reports. The results overall were positive – amusing, entertaining, goon-like, and "outrageous" being some of the comments' (BBC n.d.a). Fortunately, enthusiasm for the series on the part of viewers and critics built over the course of the first series' thirteen-week run, and the series went on to run for four seasons – a total of forty-five episodes, plus two recorded specifically for German television.

Looking back from a vantage point of over fifty years after the series' premiere, it is clear that both the BBC executives and the viewing audience intuited correctly what was happening as the Pythons 'tore up the rule book of comedy grammar, conventions and traditions' (BBC n.d.a). That which is new and innovative is invariably received as threatening by the standard bearers of the status quo and those invested in not ruffling feathers, and the goal of the Pythons was never adhering strictly to established standards of good taste. The yardstick against which success was measured was instead simply: is it funny? And, as Hewison notes, '[t]he Pythons were quick to exploit the humorous possibilities of bad language', as well as sex and 'comic violence' (Hewison 1981: 14). But *Monty Python's Flying Circus*, of course, did more than that. As Wilmut proposes and Landy develops at length in her book devoted to the programme, the series 'mock[ed] the techniques of television' (Wilmut 1980: 198). No wonder BBC executives were perturbed! Audiences, however, increasingly appreciated what the Pythons were doing, first on their television show and, later, in their films as they rewrote the rules of television comedy with humour that could be, in the words of *Encyclopaedia Britannica*, 'simultaneously sarcastic, scatological, and intellectual'. Television, notes the entry, 'had never broadcast anything so surreal, daring, and untraditional as *Monty Python*, and its importance to television is difficult to overstate' (*Encyclopaedia Britannica* n.d.).

And yet, while popular appreciation of the Pythons has swelled to truly impressive proportions – as attested to by the fact that tickets for the 2014 reunion show sold out in forty-three seconds, leading the troupe to quickly announce more shows (Dex 2013) – and as the Pythons have been justly honoured and fêted for their achievements, scholarly appraisal of their artistry and accomplishments (as is often the case with scrutiny of popular culture) has lagged behind. The purpose of this collection then, on the occasion of the fiftieth anniversary of the premiere of *Monty Python's Flying Circus*, is to contribute to the surprisingly slim – although growing – body of scholarship on Monty Python. With this in mind, we will first offer a brief recapitulation of the troupe's history and output, before considering what made them so ground-breaking.

How to Recognise Monty Python from a Long Way off

The history of Monty Python – of the coming together of the troupe, the development of the *Monty Python's Flying Circus* television series, and of the subsequent films, including *Monty Python and the Holy Grail* (1975), *Monty Python's Life of Brian* (1979) and *Monty Python's The Meaning of Life* (1983) – has been exhaustively detailed in a number of book publications, frequently as narrated by the troupe members themselves, including *Monty Python Speaks!* (1999) and *The Pythons: An Autobiography by the Pythons* (2003). For that reason, this Introduction will limit itself to a concise historical overview. Terry Jones and Michael Palin met at Oxford University, where they performed together as part of a comedy group called the Oxford Revue. Graham Chapman, John Cleese and Eric Idle similarly met at Cambridge University as part of the Cambridge University Footlights dramatic club, and Chapman, Cleese and Idle then met American Terry Gilliam in New York City while on tour with the Footlights (Landy 2005: 6–13). From 1964 to 1969, the six future-Pythons collaborated in various capacities and combinations on a variety of different British radio and television shows. All five British Pythons worked on the satirical television show *The Frost Report*, which broadcast from 1966 to 1967 and featured Cleese as a cast member and writer, and Idle, Palin, Chapman and Jones as writers (BBC n.d.b). Idle, Jones and Palin – together with Gilliam, who was brought in as an animator – went on to work on the quirky British television series *Do Not Adjust Your Set*, which aired from 1967 to 1969 (Wilmut 1980: 181), and Jones and Palin also created and starred in the six episodes of *The Complete and Utter History of Britain* in 1969 (see Eggers 2006). Cleese and Chapman, for their part, served as cast members and writers for the programme *How to Irritate People* in 1968 (Cleese *et al.* 2003: 128) and then as writers for *Doctor in the House* in 1969 (McCall 2014: 5).

There appear to be two different origin stories for *Monty Python's Flying Circus*. As told by Cleese in *The Pythons: An Autobiography by the Pythons*, the *Flying Circus* found its beginnings in Cleese and Chapman's admiration for *Do Not Adjust Your Set*. 'Graham and I used to watch *Do Not Adjust Your Set*', recalls Cleese. 'We would finish early and watch that because it was the funniest thing on television. I said to Graham, "Why don't we ring the guys and see if they want to do a show with us?"' (Cleese *et al.* 2003: 126). Idle, Jones, Palin and Gilliam had in fact been offered a contract by Thames Television to create their own late-night comedy series, but the production company wouldn't have a studio available until the summer of 1970 – some year or eighteen months later – so, according to the official Monty Python website, Monty Python was born in May 1969 when the six sat down together at a tandoori restaurant in Hampstead, London ('Pythons' n.d.). Television producer Barry Took remembers it differently in *Monty Python Speaks*. According to his recollection, the germ of the programme was his conversation with British actor and comedian Marty Feldman. Took had been working with Palin and Jones on *Do Not Adjust Your Set*, while Feldman had worked with Chapman and Cleese on *The Frost Report* and, again, on *At Last the 1948 Show*. According to Took, he said to Feldman, 'I'll put my two Oxford chaps [Palin and Jones] against your two Cambridge chaps [Cleese and Chapman]', which was meant as a joke but later struck him as a good idea. He ran the idea past Palin, but Palin would only agree if he could bring Gilliam and Idle along. Took then ran the idea by Cleese and Chapman, who also agreed, and Took brought the idea to the BBC (Morgan 1999: 22–3).

As Wilmut explains, choosing a title for the programme had been difficult since the troupe did not wish to give away content. Various silly names were considered, including *Owl Stretching Time* and *A Horse, a Spoon, and a Bucket*, before the group settled on *Monty Python's Flying Circus* as suitably ridiculous (Wilmut 1980: 195–6). The programme was certainly influenced by other important comedy series, including *The Frost Report* and Spike Milligan's ground-breaking series *Q5*. Milligan, who had earlier starred in the comedy radio programme, *The Goon Show*, eschewed the typical sketch comedy format on *Q5*, preferring instead a more stream-of-consciousness approach with a surreal element. Michael Palin recalls that 'Terry Jones and I adored the Q ... shows. ... [Milligan] was the first writer to play with the conventions of television' (Ventham 2002: 157). Jones extends on this, noting that Milligan 'totally ripped up all form and shape – and there we'd been writing three-minute sketches with beginnings, middles and ends – and Milligan started a sketch, and then it turned into a different sketch, then it turned into something else' (quoted in Wilmut 1980: 197). John Cleese, too, notes the influence of Spike Milligan and *Q5*, explaining in *The Pythons Autobiography by the Pythons* that

> we [Cleese and Terry Jones] both happened to watch Spike Milligan's *Q5*, and one or the other of us phoned up and said kind of jokingly but also rather anxiously, "I thought that's what we were supposed to be doing?" And the other one said, "That's what I thought too." We felt that Spike had got to where we were trying to get to ... [I]n a way that fact that Spike had gone there probably enabled us to go a little bit further than we would have otherwise gone. (Cleese *et al.* 2003: 131)

Despite these anxieties concerning influences, the style of *Monty Python's Flying Circus* was quite different from its predecessors and, as we will go on to outline, the group broke new ground through its sketches and episodes that targeted the banalities and idiosyncrasies of British life as the troupe experimented with and parodied the conventions of television. As noted above, their humour was not always considered appropriate for the television of the period, leading to increasingly heated clashes with the BBC during the series' run (and then larger concerns following the release of *Monty Python's Life of Brian* in 1979), as Robert Hewison chronicles in *Monty Python: The Case Against*. Notable in this regard is the notorious 'Undertakers' sketch – the final sketch of the second series' final episode (episode 26, 'Royal Episode 13') – in which John Cleese's character takes his dead mother to an undertakers' office and her youthful appearance suggests to the undertaker (Chapman) the possibility of cannibalism. Cleese's character is initially shocked, but then admits to 'feeling a bit peckish'. The outcry concerning this sketch was predictable and in December 1989 John Cleese would eulogise Chapman, who suggested the final line of the sketch, 'All right, we'll eat her, but if you feel bad about it afterwards, we'll dig a grave and you can throw up into it', with the characterisation, 'Anything for him but mindless good taste' (Cleese 1989).

Figure I.2   Cleese shows Undertaker Chapman his mother in the sack: *Monty Python's Flying Circus*, episode 26 (1970).

While the 'Undertakers' sketch, which was wiped from the master tape of the episode, was not rebroadcast until 1987, the Pythons were brought back for a third season, which aired from October 1972 to January 1973 – under a more watchful eye from the BBC (Wilmut 1980: 214). As Hewison notes, by the spring of 1972, the troupe had been producing material without much respite for two years and tensions had developed. Cleese had expressed his desire to leave after the end of the second series, but had been persuaded to continue, 'although in his opinion the search for new ideas was making them thrash about, exploiting the strange and violent rather than the funny' (Hewison 1981: 23). By the third series, Cleese felt that they were just rehashing earlier sketches (Cleese *et al.* 2003: 225) and left at the conclusion of the series. The 'Python style', however, continues Hewison,

> had been perfected, and the idea of what a comedy series was supposed to be totally changed. In three years, they had moved from minority cult to acknowledged mastery of the School of British nonsense. The term "pythonesque" was firmly established in the language. (Hewison 1981: 23)

The remaining Pythons produced a shortened fourth series consisting of six episodes, with the final episode broadcast on 5 December 1974.

Even during the original run of *Monty Python's Flying Circus*, the troupe did not restrict themselves to television, but expanded into other media, including records, books and film. Between 1970 and 1974, the Pythons released four records consisting of recordings of sketches and songs: *Monty Python's Flying Circus* (1970), *Another Monty Python Record* (1971), *Monty Python's Previous Record* (1972) and *The Monty Python Matching Tie and Handkerchief* (1974). The group subsequently released album versions of their films (*The Album Version of the Soundtrack of the Trailer of the Film of Monty Python and the Holy Grail* in 1975, *Monty Python's Life of Brian* in 1979 and *Monty Python's The Meaning of Life* in 1983), live albums (*Monty Python Live at Drury Lane* in 1974 and *Monty Python Live at City Center* in 1976), and multiple singles and compilation albums.

In the world of print, they published *Monty Python's Big Red Book* (a book with, of course, a blue cover) in 1971. Edited by Idle, the book consists mostly of material that expands on sketches from the first two series of the television programme. This was followed in 1973 by *The Brand New Monty Python Bok* (*sic*). The dust jacket for this one was printed with realistic fingerprints on the front, which Michael Palin recalled fooled some into thinking their copy was used, but a bit more surprising to many was the fake cover beneath the dust jacket: 'a mock soft-core magazine, featuring lots of bare-bottomed ladies beneath the title: "Tits and Bums, a Weekly Look at Church Architecture"' (Palin 2006: 136). As Robert Hewison (1981: 29) notes, this play with the print medium recast the forms of subversion they had employed in the television medium. And this medium-specific irreverence also extended to their albums, with, for instance, *The Monty Python Matching Tie and Handkerchief* indulging in diegetic play with the sounds of vinyl crackle and scratched records in 'The Record Shop/First World War Noises' sketch. Many further books followed, including expanded reissues of the first two, film scripts and television transcripts, oral histories and autobiographies by the members.

And then there were the films. The first film, *And Now for Something Completely Different* (1971), consisted of recreations of sketches from the first two television series without an audience, and was intended for an American audience unfamiliar with the series. Cleese appears occasionally between sketches in different positions (such as being roasted on a spit or on a desk in a pink bikini) to deliver the now-iconic line, 'And now for something completely different'. The film was first released in America in 1972, but had little success at the time – likely because, at that point, the American public had had no real exposure to Monty Python. As Jeffrey Miller reports, Python records and books had begun to 'trickle in', and those near the Canadian border could view the programme via the Canadian Broadcasting Company, which began to air it in 1970 (Miller 2000: 128), but Monty Python was far from being a household name. Python began to take hold in America in 1974 when the Public Broadcasting Station KERA in Dallas began broadcasting the *Flying Circus*. Other PBS stations followed suit, and a re-released version of *And Now for Something Different* in 1974 performed much better. Noting the growing popularity of *Monty Python's Flying Circus*, ABC (American Broadcasting Company) began to air selected episodes of the series in mid-1975 on its late-night *Wide World of Entertainment* programme. ABC, however, re-edited and censored the episodes, altering their flow and continuity (Hewison 1981: 43). The Pythons took ABC to court, ultimately gaining control over subsequent US broadcasts (see ibid.: 54–6).

Despite the success of the *Flying Circus*, both in the UK and abroad, Monty Python is, however, perhaps best known today for the troupe's three feature-length original films, *Monty Python and the Holy Grail* (1975), *Monty Python's Life of Brian* (1979) and *Monty Python's The Meaning of Life* (1983). *Holy Grail*, conceived during the hiatus between the third and fourth series of *Flying Circus*, drew upon and parodied Arthurian legend. Mostly shot on location in Scotland, the film cast Chapman as King Arthur, Cleese as Sir Lancelot, Gilliam as Arthur's servant, Patsy, Idle as Sir Robin the Not-Quite-So-Brave-as-Sir-Lancelot, Palin as Sir Galahad and Jones as Sir Bedevere. Each of the Pythons also played a variety of other roles. While reviews of the film were mixed, the film today is widely considered to be a cult classic.

Monty Python and the Holy Grail was followed four years later by *Monty Python's Life of Brian*. Directed by Jones and written collectively by the

Pythons, the film tells the story of Brian Cohen (Chapman), a young Jewish man mistaken for the Messiah. Controversial from the moment of its inception, funding for the film was withdrawn by EMI Films days before production was scheduled to begin; financial backing was then organised by Python fan George Harrison through the formation of his company, HandMade Films (Rainey 2011). Containing elements of religious satire, the film was characterised as blasphemous by some religious groups and banned in certain parts of the UK and some other countries. The film was nevertheless – or likely because of the controversy – a box office success. It was the fourth highest grossing film in the UK for 1979 and the highest grossing British comedy film in American history at the time of its release (ibid.).

In 1982, the Pythons released *Monty Python Live at the Hollywood Bowl*, a recording mostly of sketches from *Flying Circus*, but incorporating material predating *Flying Circus* – notably, the 'Four Yorkshiremen' sketch from 1967's *At Last the 1948 Show*, which features four men attempting to outdo each other with tales of their humble origins. *Hollywood Bowl* also features inserted material dubbed into English from the Pythons' two episodes of *Flying Circus* prepared specifically for German television and aired in 1972 (IMDb n.d.).

Hollywood Bowl was then followed a year later by the last Python film to feature all six original members: *Monty Python's The Meaning of Life* (1983). While both *Holy Grail* and *Life of Brian* had coalesced around a single somewhat coherent story, *Meaning of Life* returned the troupe to its roots in sketch comedy as it is loosely structured around a series of scenes addressing different stages of life. Although not as successful as *Holy Grail* and *Life of Brian*, the film did win the Grand Prix at the 1983 Cannes Film Festival (Chilton 2014). It would be another thirty-one years before the remaining Python members would perform together as part of the *Monty Python Live (Mostly)* events in 2014.

It's a Living

Following the conclusion of the *Flying Circus*, the individual Pythons all pursued different projects, many of which were Python-adjacent in the sense of relating back to the programme and/or involving other members of the troupe. Eric Idle, for example, appeared in Terry Gilliam's film, *The Adventures of Baron Munchausen*, and, in 2004, created *Spamalot*, a musical comedy based on 1975's *Monty Python and the Holy Grail*. The 2005 Broadway production, which starred Tim Curry as King Arthur, received fourteen Tony Award nominations, winning in three categories including Best Musical (*New York Times* 2005). Idle was also the creator and director of the live show *Monty Python Live (Mostly)*, which took place at London's O2 Arena between 1 and 20 July 2014, and joined fellow Python John Cleese in 2015 and 2016 for the 'John Cleese and Eric Idle: Together Again at Last . . . For the Very First Time' tour of venues in North America, Australia and New Zealand. For his part, Cleese went on to have a very successful career in comedy, television and film, including co-writing and starring in the comedy series *Fawlty Towers*. In 1988, he wrote and starred in *A Fish Called Wanda* – a film that also featured Michael Palin.

After *Flying Circus* ended, Palin collaborated with Terry Jones on the comedy series *Ripping Yarns* (BBC 2014) and starred as Dennis the Peasant in Gilliam's 1977 film *Jabberwocky*, with whom he also co-wrote the 1980 film *Time Bandits*. Palin and Gilliam teamed up again in 1984 when Palin appeared in Gilliam's film *Brazil*. After *A Fish Called Wanda*, Palin again worked with Cleese on 1997's *Fierce Creatures* – a successor (if not a direct sequel) to *Wanda*, co-written and starring Cleese. After a small part in *The Wind in the Willows* in 1996, a film written and directed by Terry Jones, Palin stepped back from film, focusing instead on a series of travel documentaries. In 2019, he received a knighthood for 'services to travel, culture and geography' (BBC 2019).

Following the end of *Flying Circus*, Terry Gilliam, as the overview above suggests, focused his energies and talents on screenwriting and directing, often involving other Pythons in his projects. His films include *Jabberwocky* (1977), *Time Bandits* (1981), *Brazil* (1985), *The Adventures of Baron Munchausen* (1988), *The Fisher King* (1991), *12 Monkeys* (1995), *Fear and Loathing in Los Vegas* (1998), *The Imaginarium of Doctor Parnassus* (2009) and *The Man Who Killed Don Quixote* (2018). Terry Jones, who had co-directed *Holy Grail* with Gilliam and served as sole director of *Life of Brian* and *Meaning of Life*, went on to direct *Erik the Viking*, involving Cleese, in 1989, and *The Wind in the Willows* in 1996. In 2015, he directed the comedy *Absolutely Anything*, which featured the voices of the five remaining Pythons. Jones also went on to author a number of books and screenplays, including works on medieval history.

Graham Chapman alone did not survive to see the twenty-first century or to appreciate the full extent of contemporary Python adoration. Following *Flying Circus*, he moved to Los Angeles and wrote and starred in a pirate film called *Yellowbeard* (1983) that featured appearances by, among others, Cleese, Idle, Marty Feldman and Spike Milligan. Chapman reunited with the other Pythons for *The Meaning of Life* and then appeared again with them one last time for a spot that was included in November 1989 in a televised, BBC-produced *Flying Circus* twentieth-anniversary special called *Parrot Sketch Not Included – 20 Years of Monty Python*, hosted by Steve Martin. Chapman died on 4 October 1989 – before the anniversary special was broadcast.

In 1988, Monty Python received a BAFTA award for Outstanding British Contribution to Cinema (BAFTA n.d.); ten years later, they received an American Film Institute star award (McCall 2014: 203). The five living Pythons gathered for the premiere of Idle's *Spamalot* in 2005, a musical which, as noted, won the 2004 Tony Award for Best Musical. In 2005, PBS in the United States aired the entire run of *Monty Python's Flying Circus* and added new one-hour specials focusing on each group member. Each episode was written and produced by the individual on which the episode was focused, with all five remaining Pythons collaborating on Chapman's. In 2009, to commemorate the fortieth anniversary of the debut of *Flying Circus*, a six-part documentary, *Monty Python: Almost the Truth (Lawyer's Cut)*, was released, featuring interviews and excerpts from the show. They also received a special BAFTA award in 2009 for their 'outstanding contribution to film and television' (BAFTA 2009).

Celebration of the Pythons' achievement then culminated in the long-awaited 2014 reunion, *Monty Python Live (Mostly): One Down, Five to Go*, which was live broadcast in cinemas worldwide. In 2018, Netflix purchased the rights to the majority of the Pythons' film and television catalogue, ensuring its continued circulation, and is reportedly looking to commission new content from the remaining Python members (see Lynch 2018). As we completed work on this book, Terry Jones sadly passed away at the age of seventy-seven, leaving behind an incredible body of work and creative legacy. As their last act with Jones, the Pythons marked the fiftieth anniversary of the premiere of *Monty Python's Flying Circus* in November 2019 by releasing a country and western version of their song 'I'm So Worried' – retitled 'I'm (Still) So Worried'. Originally written by Terry Jones for the *Monty Python's Contractual Obligation Album* in 1980, Jones apparently sang on the recording: as Gilliam reported, 'He can no longer speak but he can still sing' (*Chortle* 2019).

Archaeology Today

In their 2017 edited collection, *Python beyond Python*, Reinsch, Whitfield and Weiner focus on 'the creative endeavors of Python members, alone and in smaller groupings', arguing that – in contrast to 'the canonical Monty Python texts' – this work has been 'neglected or misread' (Reinsch *et al.* 2017: 2). While studying the work of individual Python members outside of the Python canon is clearly valuable, this argument assumes that Monty Python's canon of work has already been well covered and explored within academic scholarship. To some extent this is the case, with academic writing on Python stretching from the chapter on *Flying Circus* in Frank Krutnik and Steve Neale's *Popular Film and Television Comedy* (1990), to Adam Whybray's 2016 article on the uses and meanings of drag in Python's work. However, our book returns to analysis and investigation of the Monty Python canon without apology, and with an acknowledgement of the fact that (as we will go on to outline) there is an array of approaches and questions of crucial importance to considering and reflecting on the initial impact and continued popularity of Monty Python that have yet to be brought to bear on Python as a set of comedy texts, as a comedy team of creative individuals, and as a multi-media comedy phenomenon.

Our book is indebted, however, to the – largely excellent – scholarly work that has already been published on Python, which, we would argue, can be loosely grouped into four strands in terms of theme and chronology. Between 1990 and 2005, work by Krutnik and Neale, Stephen Wagg, and Marcia Landy laid the groundwork for scholarly investigations of Monty Python within television and media studies, through its mapping of the key influences, contexts, features and themes of Python's comedy, with particular focus on the groundbreaking nature of *Monty Python's Flying Circus*. This work offers a number of key forms of knowledge and insight. Firstly, it has focused on identifying and outlining 'the show's British (indeed English) antecedents, sociocultural context, and institutional base' (Neale 2001: 64), contextualising Python's style and techniques within the '1960s satire boom' (Mills 2014: 126) and Oxbridge revues and in relation to, on the one hand, contemporaneous comedy such as *Beyond the Fringe* and *Q5*, but, on the other, the influence of the musical hall and the physical comedy of silent cinema (see Landy 2005, and also, more recently, Brock 2016). Beyond this set of influences, Landy has also identified and explored the way *Flying Circus* mixed high and low culture, arguing that this crucial aspect of Python's comedy 'made the shows accessible to wide audiences despite the often erudite character of allusions to literature, philosophy and history' (Landy 2005: 3).

Secondly, and conversely, this strand of literature has also offered key insights on what can be seen to distinguish Python's comedy from this web of (largely British) comedic influences. Once again, of particular note here is Landy's work, which has considered, in detail, how the comedy of *Flying Circus* can be related to Mikhail Bakhtin's theories of the Carnival, through its focus on the body, violence and death and on turning 'the accepted world ... on its head', using these strategies 'to call attention to the role of institutions – medicine, psychiatry, the family, the state's administration of social life, the uses and abuses of history, and especially the disciplining of the sexual body through existing social formations' (Landy 2005: 101). Of course, another key distinguishing innovation is the employment of animation within the format of the sketch comedy, something which is explored in unprecedented depth and detail in Paul Wells' chapter within this volume. As initially acknowledged in Landy's work, Gilliam's animation was important in not only informing but instigating much of the distinctive style and structure of Python's comedy. Finally, and perhaps most crucially, this strand of scholarship has also foregrounded *Flying Circus*'s 'unrelenting critique of the television medium' (ibid.: 3) as key to its impact and distinctiveness, exploring how Python built on the innovations of *The Goon Show* (in the radio medium) and Spike Milligan (in the television medium) in order to play with, explore and parody the conventions of television, myriad television formats and the structure and flow of broadcast television as a whole. Of particular importance here is Krutnik and Neale's detailed analysis of the strategies employed to do this across one case study episode of *Flying Circus*. Here, they built on Wilmut's identification of Python's use of 'the format sketch', which involved taking 'the format of something like a television quiz programme' and then emptying 'the content out of it, replacing it with something ludicrous', as well as the 'escalation sketch' – which is when, for Wilmut, an idea is allowed to 'get wildly out of hand, so that absurdity builds on absurdity' (Wilmut 1980: 198). Through a consideration of how these strategies are employed within the chosen *Flying Circus* episode, Neale and Krutnik are able to illustrate how these approaches, in tandem with the employment of 'diegetic and functional overlap', 'interruption and intrusion' and 'repetition and variation', enabled Python to 'produce a markedly "self-reflexive" style', creating 'the sense . . . not only of a distinctive and extensive comic world, but of a world that pertains to television'. Through this, they not only exposed 'the limits of conventional television formats' but linking 'their absurd arbitrariness to institutions and representatives of institutional power' (Krutnik and Neale 1990: 202).

The key arguments and observations of this initial strand of scholarship on Monty Python primarily aimed, then, to identify the innovations and distinctiveness of their television comedy. Indeed, a return to the key insights within this scholarship serves as a useful reminder of what made Monty Python so distinctive and innovative at a time, in 2020, when they have reached new heights of accessibility and respectability, after the sell-out O2 shows and purchase of their content by Netflix.

Beyond this strand of initial Python scholarship, a second strand of work encompasses four edited volumes on Python, published between 2006 and 2017. The aims and agendas of these volumes are, in our view, distinct from our book, in both their focus and the disciplinary approaches adopted. Gary C. Hardcastle and George A. Reisch's 2006 volume, *Monty Python and Philosophy*, includes analyses from scholars of philosophy and political science of sketches or aspects of both the Python television show and films, but with the emphasis placed on how the chosen sketches and films illustrate philosophical issues or ideas rather than placing focus, through film, television and media studies frameworks, on Monty Python itself and the production practices and play with relevant modes and media that underpin Python's comedy and its cultural status. The same is the case with Joan E. Taylor's 2015 volume *Jesus and Brian*, which brings together biblical scholars to consider *Life of Brian*'s representation of the historical Jesus and his times through the disciplinary lens of religious and archaeological studies. Tomasz Dobrogoszcz's 2014 volume *Nobody Expects the Spanish Inquisition* includes a range of valuable and insightful critical essays on Python from the perspective of cultural theory and history – some of which are referenced in chapters within our book – but with a primary focus on representation, rather than this book's broader approach of assessing Python over time and context in relation to production, form, medium, fandom and consumption. Finally, the aforementioned *Python Beyond Python* is devoted to exploring the creative work of the Python team members outside of Monty Python. This is distinct from our book, which remains focused on evaluating and assessing the impact and continued resonance of the Monty Python comedic canon across time and media, including assessments of the contribution of Python team members (particularly Terry Gilliam and Terry Jones) to Python's appeal, impact and resonance.

Alongside the publication of these edited volumes, there has been a smattering of book chapters and articles published on aspects of Monty Python and their work between 2009 and 2016. Among these, two further key strands can be identified, which our volume aims to build and significantly expand upon. The first is the valuable work that has been done to address the specific innovations of Python's feature films, as distinct from Python's television output. Most prominently, Justin Smith and Neil Archer have considered the ways in which *Monty Python and the Holy Grail* and *Monty Python's Life of Brian* 'explore and address the medium in which they are working', not only in their play with cinema conventions but through their comedic interrogation of 'the illusory reality constructed through the feature film' (Archer 2016: 56), particularly with regard to the tensions between faithfully depicting past historical eras on film and a comedic awareness of 'the impossibility' of doing so (Smith 2010: 120).

The second key contemporary strand of literature is the growing body of work on representations of sexuality and gender within Python's film and television output. Challenging previous work, which has championed Python's progressive critiques of myth, convention, authority and institutions, this scholarship has identified Python's portrayal of gender and sexuality as the 'blind spot in the Pythons' comic project', with copious examples existing across their television and film work which suggest 'an investment in traditional gender roles that persists' in spite of Python's 'recognition that all other identities are constructed performances' (Aronstein 2009: 115). For Susan Aronstein and Adam Whybray, this is most evident in the two types of female characters who largely populate Python's comedic world – 'the sexualised, hyper-feminine' characters played predominantly by Carol Cleveland (Whybray 2016: 172) and the 'wide array of frumpy and clueless housewives' played in drag by the Python members. For Aronstein, they operated 'as a satire on British middle-class mores and customs even as they reified misogynist clichés' (Aronstein 2009: 118), with, in particular, the Pythons' 'Pepperpot' characters functioning as screeching versions of the staple of 'the grotesque Bad Mother' (Whybray 2016: 172). Further to this, Aronstein has also identified the ways in which, in the television programmes in particular, 'explorations of male gender-bending', in sketches such as 'Camp Square-Bashing' (episode 22, 'How to Recognise Different Parts of the Body') and 'The Lumberjack Song' (episode 9, 'The Ant, an Introduction'), illustrate ground-breaking attempts, in Python's work, to address and interrogate the performativity of male identities. However, the way 'the excessive camp of the performances' plays into 'the homophobic stereotypes of the "poof" and the "fairy"' frequently leads, for her, to the shutting down of these 'radical possibilities' (Aronstein 2009: 118).

But Aronstein's work in particular has also considered and reflected on the tensions and nuances in these representations, particularly when considering their uses and meanings within the Python feature films. With regard to *The Holy Grail*, for instance, Aronstein notes that its status as a feature film rather than a short television sketch means that the 'narrative's sustained critique of the entire British political and social system' enables all 'universal' and 'innate' categories to be questioned more consistently, including in relation to constructions of gender and sexuality (Aronstein 2009: 115). The puncturing and parodying of Sir Lancelot's hypermasculine idiom of chivalry (and its attendant qualities of violence and chaos) within the film, for instance, allows space for Prince Herbert's seemingly 'marginal' representation of alternative masculinity to be given prominence within Python's comedic world (and a moment of victory as he begins to sing as Lancelot dangles forlornly from a rope). In addition, Amy-Jill Levine (2015) has highlighted Judith Escariot's active and articulate role within the narrative of *Life of Brian*, as well as the potentially gender subversive status of the film's stoning sequence. Such nuanced readings enable scholars to, in Neil Archer's words, be 'specific about the aims and meanings of humour' in Monty Python's work, in order to consider the strengths and limits of these aims while also, importantly, positioning this work 'within its specific time and place' (Archer 2016: 55).

The central aim of our book, then, is to build on these valuable strands of recent work and insight by revisiting, reflecting on and interrogating the range of factors and elements that have been identified (in popular culture and existing scholarship) as contributing to Python's celebrated status as 'something different' – addressing Python's continuing status as a comedy touchstone associated with irreverence, anti-authoritarianism, the alternative and the unconventional, fifty years after its inception, across generations and across the globe. Consequently, the chapters in this book avoid an uncritically celebratory approach to Python's comedy by assessing its shifting cultural meanings and ambiguities.

Drawing on and significantly expanding on existing scholarly insights, this book's emphasis is therefore on *historicising Python's comedy and its impact*, tracing its meanings from a range of social, cultural, national and transnational perspectives, and focusing, in an unprecedented manner, on these questions from the perspectives not only of form, theme and representation but also production and creative practice and long-term reception and consumption. Because of our emphasis on Python as a multi-media comedy phenomenon (encompassing not only Python's audio-visual output but also, in particular, its employment of music and song across multiple media), the book is primarily an evaluation of Monty Python's impact on comedy and popular culture through the framework of film, television and media studies. However, the book draws, when relevant, on concepts and frameworks from a range of disciplines, including literary studies, art history, medieval studies, comedy studies, animal studies, cultural studies, memory studies and fan studies.

The book is therefore divided into four parts, which move the reader from a reconsideration of some of Python's key influences and pioneering approaches to comedy, to an investigation of its continued popularity, durability and presence within popular culture. Part One, 'Situating Python', addresses a range of influences and qualities popularly associated with Python (spanning literature, theatre, cinema, music and radio) but which are also frequently taken for granted and rarely interrogated in detail. Here, Rick Hudson explores the range of influences from absurdist and surrealist art, theatre and literature that, for him, have fed centrally but distinctly into *Monty Python's Flying Circus*; Gina Wisker identifies the roots of Python's comedy within not only satire but also Gothic horror, exploring the intertwining of these influences through an investigation of the treatment of death and the class system across their comedic output; and Anna Martonfi returns to a consideration of the relations between *The Goon Show* and *Flying Circus*, highlighting similarities but also, crucially, distinct differences in the two shows' representations of the Second World War. As already acknowledged, Python has consistently been aligned with absurdism, surrealism, satire, the carnivalesque and the broader British post-war comedy tradition of the 1950s and 1960s. However, as these chapters contend and illustrate, the nuances and complexities that characterise these influences – as well as the relations between them and their creative uses by the Pythons – need to be teased out and explored, in order to sharpen and revise our understandings of Python's comedy and its continued relevance and durability.

The three chapters in Part Two, 'Python's Practices, Forms and Mediums', all relate to the most celebrated aspect of Monty Python's comedy – its employment of, clever play with and self-conscious commentary on aspects of Python's chosen medium (whether television, film or other media). Through detailed focus on the relations between visual, aural/sonic, spoken, performed and written modes of expression in Monty Python's television series, films, records and live shows, this section provides original perspectives on Python's status as a form of comedy where expressivity and creativity encompasses more than clever wordplay and memorable dialogue, and which is fundamentally grounded in and conscious of medium specificity, in innumerable ways. Here, James Leggott reflects on and explores the different formal, conceptual, representational and intertextual uses and references to music across the full range of Python's comedy output; Paul Wells provides a detailed overview of

Terry Gilliam's animation work throughout the Python canon, considering the eclectic nature of his influences, his working practices and his particular thematic preoccupations and stylistic motifs; and Ewan Wilson builds significantly on existing scholarship on *Monty Python and the Holy Grail* through his consideration of the ways in which the creative practices of the film's two directors, Gilliam and Jones, can be understood and related to traditions of medieval literature and medieval art. This section's originality, then, relates, in many ways, to these chapters' rigorous and insightful charting of the working practices involved in producing Python's comedy, from the factors that informed choices of library music within the television series, to the delineation of Terry Gilliam's distinct approaches to animation practice, to the creative relations between Terry Jones and Terry Gilliam in the directing of *The Holy Grail*.

The chapters in Part Three, 'Contexts and Representations', consider key representations within Python texts, from countercultural forms, to human–animal relations, to potentially offensive representations of race, gender, sexuality and religion, using a critical and context-aware approach. The section moves from Caroline Langhorst's nuanced analysis of representations of the 1960s counterculture within key *Flying Circus* sketches, to Brett Mills' re-evaluation and insightful critique of key Python sketches through the framework of animal studies, to Kathleen J. Cassity's timely reassessment – particularly in light of recent controversial comments on this issue from both John Cleese and Terry Gilliam – of *Life of Brian* from the perspective and framework of 'political correctness'. The chapters in this section also all work, through their analysis, to place key concepts within comedy theory in historical and contemporary context, most prominently through developing and interrogating Python's association with comic incongruity.

Part Four, 'Cult, Fandom and Python', addresses another frequently invoked but underexplored element of Monty Python's enduring appeal – its cult status and following. Here, Ernest Mathijs puts forward a case for an appreciation of *Monty Python's The Meaning of Life* through an analysis of those aspects of the film that chime with the historical appreciation of cult cinema (its intertextuality, and its relations with other celebrated cult texts, as well as its transgressive qualities); Jeffrey Andrew Weinstock attempts to redress the academic neglect of Python's cult status by focusing on the cultic qualities of *The Holy Grail*, with an emphasis on quotability, comic inversion, silliness and self-reflexivity; and Kate Egan draws on findings from the audience research project *Monty Python Memories*, in order to explore the forms of cross-generational fandom, between fathers and daughters, recounted in the memories of Python's female fans. Through identifying a range of relevant cult ideologies and themes (pollution, waste, hyperbole, transgression, freakery), textual qualities (silliness, incongruity, performance styles, quotable lines and their relations to key sketches/scenes) and consumption practices (intergenerational and cross-gender fandom), this part considers these markedly under-theorised issues and, consequently, sheds important light on the global cult status of Monty Python, as an enduring touchstone of alternative British comedy.

Our book therefore aims to reconsider and reappraise its object of study from a range of new angles and perspectives, to challenge or revise received wisdom on Monty Python's meanings, status and appeal, and to reflect critically on its ongoing influence and popularity. Through its range of critical essays – which draw on new historical, analytical, theoretical and empirical research – *And Now for Something Completely Different* provides a multi-faceted assessment of Monty Python's influences, practices, forms, representations and cultural impact, from the perspective of fifty years of its existence and increasingly wide circulation in innumerable forms and guises.

Works Cited

Archer, Neil (2016) *Beyond a Joke: Parody in English Film and Television Comedy*. London: I. B. Tauris.

Aronstein, Susan (2009) '"In My Own Idiom": Social Critique, Campy Gender, and Queer Performance in *Monty Python and the Holy Grail*', in Kathleen Kelly and Tison Pugh (eds), *Queer Movie Medievalisms*. London: Ashgate, pp. 115–28.

BAFTA (n.d.) 'Outstanding British Contribution to Cinema in 1988'. <http://awards.bafta.org/award/1988/film/outstanding-british-contribution-to-cinema>

BAFTA (2009) 'BAFTA Monty Python Special Award Press Release', 19 August. <http://www.bafta.org/media-centre/press-releases/bafta-monty-python-special-award-press-release>

BBC (n.d.a) 'Monty Python at 50', *History of the BBC*. <https://www.bbc.com/historyofthebbc/anniversaries/october/python50>

BBC (n.d.b) 'The Frost Report'. <http://www.bbc.co.uk/comedy/thefrostreport/>

BBC (2014) 'Ripping Yarns', 28 October. <http://www.bbc.co.uk/comedy/rippingyarns/>

BBC (2019) 'Sir Michael Palin "Will Probably Be Only Knighted Python"', 12 June. <https://www.bbc.com/news/entertainment-arts-48613364>

Brock, Alexander (2016) 'The Struggle of Class against Class Is a What Struggle? *Monty Python's Flying Circus* and Its Politics', in Juergen Kamm and Birgit Neumann (eds), *British TV Comedies: Cultural Concepts, Contexts and Controversies*. Basingstoke: Palgrave Macmillan, pp. 51–65.

Chilton, Martin (2014) Review of 'Monty Python's The Meaning of Life', *The Telegraph*, 20 April. <https://www.telegraph.co.uk/culture/film/filmreviews/10765951/Monty-Pythons-The-Meaning-of-Life-review.html>

Chortle (2019) 'Monty Python Release a New Single', 27 November. <https://www.chortle.co.uk/news/2019/11/27/44885/monty_python_release_a_new_single>

Cleese, John (1989) 'Graham Chapman's Eulogy', *FuneralWise*. <https://www.funeralwise.com/plan/eulogy/chapman/>

Cleese, John, et al. (2003) *The Pythons Autobiography by the Pythons*. New York: Thomas Dunne Books.

Dex, R. (2013) 'Monty Python Reunion Tickets Sell out in 43 Seconds as Group Announce Four New Shows', *Independent*, 25 November. <https://www.independent.co.uk/arts-entertainment/comedy/news/monty-python-announce-four-new-shows-as-reunion-tickets-sell-out-in-43-seconds-8962301.html>

Dobrogoszcz, Tomasz (ed.) (2014) *Nobody Expects the Spanish Inquisition: Cultural Contexts in Monty Python*. Lanham, MD: Rowman & Littlefield, pp. 125–36.

Eggers, Dave (2006) 'And Now for Something Completely Difficult . . .' *The Guardian*, 12 September. <https://www.theguardian.com/stage/2006/sep/13/theatre>

Encyclopaedia Britannica (n.d.) 'Monty Python's Flying Circus'. <https://www.britannica.com/topic/Monty-Pythons-Flying-Circus>

Hardcastle, Gary C. and George A. Reisch (eds) (2006) *Monty Python and Philosophy: Nudge Nudge, Think Think*. Chicago: Open Court.

Hewison, Robert (1981) *Monty Python: The Case Against*. London: Eyre Methuen.

IMDb (n.d.) 'Monty Python Live at the Hollywood Bowl: Trivia'. <https://www.imdb.com/title/tt0084352/trivia?ref_=tt_trv_trv>

Krutnik, Frank and Steve Neale (1990) *Popular Film and Television Comedy*. London: Taylor & Francis.

Landy, Marcia (2005) *Monty Python's Flying Circus*. Detroit, MI: Wayne State University Press.

Levine, Amy-Jill (2015) 'Beards for Sale: The Uncut Version of Brian, Gender and Sexuality', in Joan E. Taylor (ed.), *Jesus and Brian: Exploring the Historical Jesus and His Times via Monty Python's Life of Brian*. London: Bloomsbury, pp. 167–84.

Lynch, John (2018) 'Netflix Has Bought the Comedy Catalog of Monty Python Including All Your Favorite Classics and Potentially New Material', *Business Insider*, 22 March. <https://www.businessinsider.com/netflix-picks-up-monty-python-comedy-catalog-2018-3?r=US&IR=T>

McCall, Douglas (2014) *Monty Python: A Chronology, 1969–2012*, 2nd edition. Jefferson, NC and London: McFarland.

Miller, Jeffrey S. (2000) *Something Completely Different: British Television and American Culture*. Minneapolis: University of Minnesota Press.

Mills, Richard (2014) 'Eric Idle and the Counterculture', in Tomasz Dobrogoszcz (ed.), *Nobody Expects the Spanish Inquisition: Cultural Contexts in Monty Python*. Lanham, MD: Rowman & Littlefield, pp. 125–36.

Morgan, David (1999) *Monty Python Speaks! The Complete Oral History of Monty Python, as Told by the Founding Members and a Few of Their Many Friends and Collaborators*. New York: Dey St.

Neale, Steve (2001) 'Sketch Comedy (*Monty Python's Flying Circus*)', in Glen Creeber (ed.), *The Television Genre Book*. London: British Film Institute, pp. 62–5.

New York Times (2005) '"Spamalot" and "Doubt" Win Tony Awards', 5 June. <https://www.nytimes.com/2005/06/05/theater/theaterspecial/spamalot-and-doubt-win-tony-awards.html>

Palin, Michael (2006) *Diaries 1969–1979: The Python Years*. New York: Thomas Dunne Books.

'Pythons, The' (n.d.) *MontyPython.com*. <http://www.montypython.com/python_The_Pythons/14>

Rainey, Sarah (2011) 'Life of Brian: Facts and Figures', *The Telegraph*, 11 October. <https://www.telegraph.co.uk/culture/8818328/Life-of-Brian-facts-and-figures.html>

Reinsch, Paul N., B. Lynn Whitfield and Robert G. Weiner (eds) (2017) *Python beyond Python: Critical Engagements with Culture*. London: Palgrave Macmillan.

Smith, Justin (2010) *Withnail and Us: Cult Films and Film Cults in British Cinema*. London: I. B. Tauris.

Taylor, Joan E. (ed.) (2015) *Jesus and Brian: Exploring the Historical Jesus and His Times via Monty Python's Life of Brian*. London: Bloomsbury.

Ventham, Maxine (2002) *Spike Milligan: His Part in Our Lives*. London: Robson Books.

Verkaik, Robert (2009) 'BBC Bosses Almost Lost Faith in "Disgusting" Monty Python', *Independent*, 1 June. <https://www.independent.co.uk/arts-entertainment/tv/news/bbc-bosses-almost-lost-faith-in-disgusting-monty-python-1693829.html>

Wagg, Stephen (1992) 'You've Never Had It So Silly: The Politics of British Satirical Comedy from *Beyond the Fringe* to *Spitting Image*', in Dominic Strinati and Stephen Wagg (eds), *Come on Down? Popular Media Culture in Post-war Britain*. London: Routledge, pp. 254–84.

Whybray, Adam (2016) '"I'm Crushing Your Binaries!" Drag in Monty Python and Kids in the Hall', *Comedy Studies* 7(2), 169–81.

Wilmut, Roger (1980) *From Fringe to Flying Circus: Celebrating a Unique Generation of Comedy 1960–1980*. London: Methuen.

PART ONE

SITUATING PYTHON

1. SIX COMICS IN SEARCH OF A . . . : MONTY PYTHON AND ABSURDIST/ SURREALIST THEATRE

Rick Hudson

It may appear self-evident, perhaps even overstated, to observe that *Monty Python's Flying Circus* was influenced by absurdist and surrealist art. Nevertheless, these terms are often applied to the TV series somewhat glibly and superficially with little or no analysis or justification. This chapter addresses this issue and assesses the degree to which Monty Python was influenced – in terms of its style, subversive content and humour – by both absurdist and surreal art and literature. Its particular focus is the influence of absurdist and surrealist theatre: specifically the plays of Harold Pinter, Samuel Beckett and Luigi Pirandello.

To enable this, this chapter will not only engage with episodes of *Monty Python's Flying Circus* and other Python products and the work of Pinter, Beckett and so on themselves, but also draw upon the work of theorists and critics who have explored comedy such as Henri Bergson, Mikhail Bakhtin and Sigmund Freud. In doing so, this chapter will demonstrate the depth and breadth of influences that fed into *Monty Python's Flying Circus* and the role played by 'serious' theatre and literature in the creation of the Pythonesque. Importantly, this chapter will not only establish the similarities between Python and the Theatre of the Absurd, but also highlight significant differences between the two.

Monty Python's Flying Circus – written by and featuring Graham Chapman, John Cleese, Terry Gilliam, Eric Idle, Terry Jones and Michael Palin – was first broadcast in October 1969 and was perceived, then as now, as a radical departure from conventional TV comedy, and as both a subversive and challenging programme. Indeed, it had been purposely created to be just this, as James Gent states in a short article on the Pythons' official website:

> The team all agreed that they wanted to overturn the conventions of traditional sketch comedy – sketches with a beginning, middle and end, punchlines, blackouts, and topical gags. Their approach to comedy would be unpredictable, aggressive and irreverent, each episode a thirty-minute stream-of-consciousness, reflecting the revolutionary times of the late '60s. (Gent 2014)

The Pythons were successful in their aim, producing a comedy series which transcended the established boundaries of TV comedy further than they had been pushed before. As Gent further notes:

> The Pythons' gleefully deconstructed the very medium of television; there were parodies of documentaries, game shows, commercials and chat-show interviews. But they also frequently subverted the very grammar of television itself – for example, the opening titles might appear halfway through an episode, or the end title crawl would unspool at the very beginning. The iconic BBC globe was regularly hijacked, with voice-over announcers heard eating or engaged in tortured personal crises in the background. Over the next few years the show received three BAFTA awards, including Best Light Entertainment Programme, and two special awards for its writing-performance, and for Gilliam's graphics. (Ibid.)

Nevertheless, *Flying Circus* did not emerge sui generis in a cultural vacuum, but was rather the net result of both cultural influence and societal environment. The show can be seen as being a fusion of the talents, tastes and writing styles of the independent members of the team, and their earlier work demonstrates nascent python-ness. We can see the satirical elements of Python at play in Chapman and Cleese's writing for and appearances on *The Frost Report* (1966–7) and *At Last the 1948 Show* (1967); the irreverent silliness and tomfoolery is evident in Palin, Jones and Idle's *Do Not Adjust Your Set* (1967–9), which also featured Terry Gilliam's animation. Similarly, *Flying Circus* was not alone in introducing surreal and unconventional content and format to British TV comedy; 1969 also saw the broadcast of Spike Milligan and Neal Shand's *Q5*, which could at times equal Python's strangeness.

Python is often perceived as a product of the 1960s, a period when British culture was transforming itself and defining itself against and critiquing the culture and society of an imperial Britain. The 1960s is often envisaged as a colourful attack on the repressed, authoritarian and – frankly – drab post-war era and its austerity (Hudson 2017a: 171–82). While it is doubtlessly true to envisage post-war Britain as a somewhat conservative and stifled environment in which the loss of empire was bemoaned and the privations of austerity were being suffered, this period is perhaps misunderstood to a large degree. While we may imagine 1950s Britain as overly restrained and cheerless, we must acknowledge that many of the cultural movements and phenomena that emerged in the 1960s had their foundations laid in the 1950s, if not earlier. American writers celebrated by the 1960s counterculture in Britain, such as Jack Kerouac, William Burroughs and Alan Ginsberg, first came to prominence in the 1950s, as did Pop artists Richard Hamilton, Eduardo Paolozzi and Andy Warhol. With the emergence of Pop Art, the 1950s also heralded the collapse of boundaries between 'high' and 'low' art that was to become so prevalent in the 1960s, and evident in *Monty Python's Flying Circus*. Of specific relevance to Python, the radio comedy programme *The Goon Show* (1951–60) was a 1950s phenomenon that also contradicts popularly held notions that 1950s culture was uniformly reactionary and sterile. *The Goon Show* has been specifically cited by all the individual members of the Python team as a seminal influence on *Flying Circus* (Landy 2005: 34). Many aspects of Python are certainly similar to elements of *The Goon Show*, not least of all the absurd and bizarre situations and characters.

Other cultural products of the 1950s had a deep and significant impact and influence on Python: specifically absurdist and surrealist theatre by playwrights such as Samuel Beckett and Harold Pinter. Terry Jones himself presented *Simply Absurd* – a documentary on Radio 4 on 10 August 2010 – in which he discussed the influence of the absurdist theatre on British comedy. Reviewing this programme for the *Daily Telegraph*, Benji Wilson comments on the impact absurdist theatre had on Python:

> 'The absurdists were trying to do something that would shock, to stir their audience up to think in a different kind of way,' [Terry Jones] says. From Ionesco's *Rhinoceros* (itself a critique of conformity in which Berenger, a central character in many of Ionesco's plays, watches his friends turn into rhinos one by one) to Winnie in Samuel Beckett's *Happy Days*, buried up to her neck for no obvious reason, the Theatre of the Absurd valued incongruity above plot or character. It is not that much of a leap to an animated foot trampling on the screen or the fish-slapping dance. (Wilson 2010)

To fully understand avant-garde British theatre of the 1950s, we have to understand both absurdism and surrealism. Although it is difficult to pinpoint a specific writer or artist as being responsible for starting a movement or style – one finds oneself merely uncovering a never-ending chain of influencers and precursors – for the sake of brevity, if nothing else, I will start this discussion of absurdist theatre with Luigi Pirandello (although Alfred Jarry and many others could be identified as the instigator of absurdist theatre with equal legitimacy). Pirandello's plays are notable for featuring many qualities we may now describe as postmodern: a self-reflexive awareness and foregrounding of the unrealness of the theatre and the fact that we are in a theatre watching a performance, not viewing a reality. This is particularly true of his most famous play *Six Characters in Search of an Author* (1921). This play opens with the actors playing actors and a director who are rehearsing for a play by Luigi Pirandello called *Mixing It Up*. The rehearsal is disrupted by the arrival of six individuals who maintain that they are not real people, but characters looking for a story to appear in. These six characters become aggrieved and an argument ensues when the director and the actors who were rehearsing start to devise and act out a play based on the six characters; the characters want to play themselves in their story. As the play continues the boundary between fact and fiction breaks down: ironically it is all fiction of course, being a play. At one point two of the cast members argue about how real drama is.

Although Pirandello's work predates the coining of the phrase 'Theatre of the Absurd' – a term originated by Martin Esslin in his book *The Theatre of the Absurd* (1961) – his plays can be identified as such. Absurdist theatre is highly influenced by existentialism, particularly the work of Albert Camus and Jean Paul Sartre, and seeks to confront a world without meaning in the absence of God. In order to do this, it jettisons any attempt to dramatically represent a meaningful reality; it favours illogical scenes and purposeless characters. Absurdist drama embraces the failure of language to convey meaning and not only emphasises the failure of art to represent reality, but questions whether there is in fact a reality to be represented. In his discussion of Pirandello, Malcolm Bradbury comments on this foregrounding of unrealness, and notes its impression on the theatre that developed in its wake, including the work of Beckett and Pinter (Bradbury 1989: 207).

Turning to Beckett and Pinter, we can see in their work similar themes and similar strategies utilised to express them. Furthermore, without even entering into any actual analysis at this point, we can see features of Pirandello's work that foreshadow what will later be termed the 'Pythonesque'. In regard to Beckett, we may not consider him to be a particularly funny writer, but a comic pulse that is a response to and an acknowledgement of absurdity beats through his work. Discussing his novel *Murphy* (1938), Peter Childs notes that humour is used as a mechanism through which the work articulates its bleak philosophical concerns (Childs 2008: 7–8). Here we can see ideas and strategies similar to those employed by Pirandello, but also tropes which would be markers of the Pythonesque. Childs also observes that this novel also employs both abrupt, comic violence and scatological humour that may seem out of place in 'high' literature:

> Murphy is eventually freed from his desires, when, while he is seated in his rocking chair, a gas leak is ignited and Murphy at last achieves the oblivion he has sought in a final 'big bang'. . . . *Murphy* is a very funny but deeply pessimistic novel, and it is entirely appropriate that Murphy's [*sic*] will ask for his burnt remains to be flushed down the toilet in the Abbey Theatre, Dublin, 'where their happiest hours have been spent'. It is appropriate to Beckett's sense of irony and futility that they will actually be scattered across the floor of a London pub in a brawl. (Ibid.: 12)

This employment of a blunt, sudden violence for comic effect, and references to toilets and the like, were to become endemic in Python. The iconic animated foot that would literally stamp out comic sequences is an exemplary illustration of this comic violence in *Flying Circus*, and the show loved nothing better than to gleefully launch into routines in which the humour derived solely from their vulgarity. This is best illustrated by a short animation sequence in episode 39 ('Grandstand'), in which a society lady politely excuses herself so that she may 'powder her nose'. The woman enters the lavatory and, from behind a closed door, we hear her loudly and violently voiding her bowels. Importantly, what we see here in Beckett and Python is a merging and juxtaposition of the 'high' and the 'low', the ribaldly comic and the philosophical, the violent and the ridiculous. However, in Beckett at least, this is not motiveless immaturity, but a means by which he sought to have an effect. This blending of contradictory styles which W. D. Howarth notes in Beckett's drama served to disturb and illuminate the audience with the express purpose of embracing its concerns: 'Into what category could one possibly put Samuel Beckett's masterpiece *En attendant Godot* (*Waiting for Godot*, 1953) – a play which, for all its comic repartee, offers the most searching reflections of the human condition?' (Howarth 1978: 121).

This blending of bleakness and the comic, George Brandt argues, is also evident in the plays of Harold Pinter which, he highlights, have been described as 'comedy of menace' (Brandt 1978: 172). Brandt observes in Pinter similarities with Beckett and other absurdists with regard to their grim use of humour:

> Pinter often makes a bleak utterance sound like a joke. Thus, in the one act play *The Dumb Waiter* (1959), the action of which has been likened to a Hitchcock story with the last reel missing, two smalltime gunmen, Ben and Gus, are waiting to perform a contract killing in the basement of a former restaurant. The situation is black enough; but theatrically the struggle for dominance between the two killers, which turns out to be a life-and-death struggle, comes over as funny. Their trivial chitchat is in a violent contrast to their lethal mission; they quarrel furiously over whether one should say 'light the gas' or 'light the kettle'. (Ibid.: 172)

So far, I believe, we have established that there are pronounced similarities between absurdist playwrights like Beckett and Pinter and *Monty Python's Flying Circus*; however, I have essentially done little more than describe how they are 'kind of like each other'. To advance this study further it is crucial to highlight that Brandt's statement above not only foregrounds the blackly comic and the sinister humour in Pinter (which is shared by Python), but also foregrounds the mundane.

Although discussions of Python often remark upon the absurdity, the strangeness and the occasional violence of the show, we must also recognise that the sketches and animated sequences frequently drew upon the familiar, the trivial and the mundane. The comedy in Python was accentuated by juxtaposing the ridiculous with the banal. The 'Marriage Guidance Councillor' sketch (episode 2, 'Sex and Violence') gains its humour not only from presenting us with a marriage guidance councillor who seduces a female client in front of her husband, but also from the fact that the husband (played by Palin) is drably dull and tiresomely mundane. 'How to Recognise Different Types of Trees from Quite a Long Way Away' (episode 3, 'How to Recognise Different Types of Trees from Quite a Long Way Away') is a sequence running through the half-hour show in which a slide photograph of a tree is repeatedly presented to viewers accompanied by John Cleese's voice emotionlessly intoning 'The larch. The larch'. It is quite difficult to explain how something so drab and ostensibly humourless could be funny, and yet this sequence has become a celebrated classic among Python fans. In this juxtaposing of the strange with the mundane, or perhaps in highlighting the strangeness of the mundane, Python demonstrates the influence not just of absurdism, but also surrealism.

Surreal is a term that has come to be accepted as a synonym for strange, bizarre or odd, so it is perhaps useful at this point to identify what surrealism actually means within art. Although surrealism shares absurdism's foregrounding of the strange and the weird, and on a superficial level 'looks' like absurdism, the ethos of surrealism is very different. Whereas absurdism grew from existentialism and was predominantly nihilistic, surrealism developed from psychoanalysis. For the surrealists, the highlighting of the strange was not intended to deny that a reality existed, but rather to confirm that a reality existed – albeit that it is subjectively constructed – and that it could not only be accessed, but revealed to be remarkable through the use of strange images and the apposition of the familiar with the unfamiliar, or placing the familiar in unfamiliar locations. In essence, the mission of the surrealists was not to celebrate the unusual for its own sake, nor to deride or deny reality, but to demonstrate that the 'real' and mundane was – if reconsidered – extraordinary (Childs 2008: 125–7). This distinction, I believe, is crucial to understanding Python as a phenomenon.

We must also acknowledge that the influence of absurdism and surrealism did not impact on Python alone. Throughout the 1960s, and well into the 1970s,

British culture was to see an ever-increasing infusion of the weird and the strange into a wide variety of cultural and media texts. It hardly needs remarking upon that many popular British TV shows were influenced and actively drew upon absurdism, surrealism and Pop Art. Popular 1960s programmes where this is perhaps most evident are those that fall within the genre that I shall refer to as 'sort-of-but-not-really-science-fiction': *The Avengers* (1961–9), *Adam Adamant Lives!* (1966–7), *Department S* (1969) and, of course, the seminal *The Prisoner* (1967–8). We can also see the impact of these movements on popular prose fiction in this period: Michael Moorcock's fantasy novels, even at their most conventional, toyed with Pop Art and surrealism, but entered an entirely new realm of the absurd and bizarre with his experimental Jerry Cornelius novels: *The Final Programme* (1969), *A Cure for Cancer* (1971), *The English Assassin* (1972) and *The Condition of Muzak* (1979). However, such elements and influences could also be witnessed in areas of culture one might think of as being less likely to embrace the weird and the avant-garde.

Poet and author Edward Upward, the 'last of the Auden Generation', had a writing career that spanned from 1938 to 2003. Despite being a friend and contemporary of the Bloomsbury group, he was to see an increased interest shown in his work in the wake of the publication of his *The Railway Accident and Other Stories* in 1969. Although a Marxist and active member of the Communist Party, Upward eschewed the social realism generally utilised by Marxist writers of his generation in favour of a dreamy, often horrific, fantastical form of prose that owed much to Lewis Carroll and H. P. Lovecraft. This dark yet whimsical surrealism is perhaps best illustrated by his series of short stories set in the fictional village of Montmere, often co-written with Christopher Isherwood. These stories frequently come to an abrupt close, or peter out after only a few pages, only hinting at or alluding to a deep lurking and unsettling conflation of the horrific and humorous which was to become – or perhaps has always been – a keystone of English humour. Indeed, in this grotesque fusion of terror and comedy we can perhaps see in Montmere an antecedent of Royston Vasey which was to feature later in the TV series *The League of Gentlemen* (1999–2002).

Scottish poet/songwriter/comedian Ivor Cutler produced work that also demonstrated absurdism and surrealism; however, Cutler's writing was to achieve its disturbing and destabilising effect by embracing a childish, nonsensical silliness rather than the horrific. Cutler was embraced by popular culture despite him being something of a fringe, avant-garde figure. Cutler had his songs broadcast by BBC radio from the late 1950s and was to perform regularly on Neil Innes' various TV programmes throughout the 1960s as well as featuring on BBC Radio 1's *The John Peel Show* from 1969. Additionally, he appeared in the Beatles' 1967 film *Magical Mystery Tour*, having won the admiration of Paul McCartney.

British culture in the 1960s also witnessed surrealism emerge in the unlikely realm of children's television due to the work of Oliver Postgate who, in collaboration with animator and puppet-maker Peter Firmin, produced short TV programmes for children that were not only hugely popular with their audiences, but steeped in surrealism and fantasy: *Noggin the Nog* (1959–65), *Ivor the Engine* (1959/1975–7), *Pogle's Wood* (1965–7), *The Clangers* (1969–72/1974) and *Bagpuss* (1974). Postgate and Firmin's animations went beyond the sort of fantasy that one is familiar with in children's fiction to produce stories and worlds that were kindly, warm, welcoming and yet sinister; conservative yet eccentric; sentimental and silly, yet melancholic; parochial yet experimental; ground-breaking yet nostalgic. Indeed, this contradiction is further emphasised by the fact that these children's TV shows were underscored by Postgate's socialist and environmental principles.

Nonetheless, even in this climate where the abnormal was being assimilated into the mainstream, Python was, and is, recognised as being distinct from these other programmes and narratives. This may possibly be due to the individual and combined talents and influences of six individual members being fused together. It may be due to these particular individuals coming together at a particular time when the conventional media was open to the challenging, new and untried. But whatever the reason, even in the revolutionary and experimental environment of the late 1960s and early 1970s, *Monty Python's Flying Circus* truly was something completely different.

Monty Python's Flying Circus did indeed share many features with absurdist theatre, and the influence of absurdism is not only demonstrated through observing similarities between episodes of *Flying Circus* and the work of absurdist playwrights, but openly acknowledged by Terry Jones himself as noted above. Nevertheless, Python is far from nihilistic: it is deeply Humanistic (and I do not use the term in a pejorative way). Like much cultural output of the 1960s and early 1970s, it was essentially satirical: critical of an establishment it saw as not only dull and staid, but unfair, unjust and reactionary. Satire attacks injustice, hypocrisy, dishonesty and corruption, and therefore – by extension – a satirist believes that there is a justice to be had and an honesty and a truth that is obscured by lies and corruption. Python – despite its often savage and violent humour and its use of absurd and surreal images, characters and situations – was deeply *human* in its outlook. Frequently the protagonist in a Python sketch will be (all too) 'human' and 'normal', but thrown into a bizarre and incomprehensible situation. We can see this in the film *Monty Python's Life of Brian* (1979). Brian – the protagonist – is very much a flawed 'ordinary bloke' who finds himself flung into absurd scenarios. These absurd situations often arise due to the pettiness, short-sightedness and irrationality of those in positions of power, or systems of power that have been corrupted by their own internal absurd rationalities.

Cruelties are often perpetrated as a consequence of naivety or incompetence, rather than malice (Hudson 2017b: 93–108).

Likewise, there is a glee in Python that is markedly absent from both Beckett and Pinter. Beckett and Pinter both utilise language and word games in order to convey meaninglessness and the inability of language to truly communicate. Bran Nicol says of Beckett:

> [H]e was concerned, from the outset, with the peculiar paradox of fiction. It was the job of literature, he thought, to reflect the meaninglessness of existence. Yet the paradox is that it must do this via language, which is endlessly (in his view) meaningful. So his writing attempts the impossible task of conveying meaninglessness through meaning, or trying to convey nothingness through something, or silence in words. (Nicol 2009: 53)

He expands upon this point as follows:

> Beckett's writing is the counterpart of abstract visual art of the painter Mark Rothko, who exemplifies Susan Sontag's new postmodern sensibility in art, and whose paintings defy any viewer to say plausibly what they are 'about' other than what the title tells us. Beckett's prose does something equivalent, though of course language cannot be as abstract as colour and his fiction still features peoples, places, and situations which can be taken as corresponding to those in the outside world. Nevertheless his prose writing is dedicated to the idea of upholding the notion that fiction is not 'about' anything, does not 'refer' to anything outside itself. (Ibid.: 53)

Python similarly utilised language and word games, but with a different intent, and with a joyful spirit absent from Pinter and Beckett. 'Eric the Half a Bee' (written by Eric Idle and John Cleese and originally released as a single in 1972 on Charisma Records) takes delight in its own silliness. The humour in the song arrives from a number of sources: the forced rhymes, the deadpan delivery of its absurdity, the contrast between the rather pompous language and the daftness of the subject matter. It is at once complete nonsense, yet has an internal logic of its own:

> Half a bee, philosophically, must *ipso facto* half not be. But half the bee has got to bee, *vis-à-vis* its entity – d'you see? But can a bee be said to be or not to be an entire bee when half the bee is not a bee, due to some ancient injury?

And yet, while it is about nothing, it has meaning: it is a send-up of popular song, and satirises that song format.

Similarly, language games and wordplay are evidenced in Python sketches such as in 'Argument Skit' (episode 29, 'The Money Programme'); this routine cheerily engages in wordplay with a focus on pedantry and literalism, centring on an argument over the meaning of argument. Although this sketch derives its humour from the vagaries and frailties of language, it in no way indicates or implies that language or existence itself are meaningless. Far from it, this sketch is a comic view of frustrations we encounter in our day-to-day lives: not just problems with language, but frustrations with civil servants and individuals providing commercial services. It may not be a particularly revolutionary satire, but a satire it remains: it is 'about' and 'refers' to the reality the audience mutually experience, albeit it uses the mechanism of absurdity to do so.

It is a mistake to suggest that just because Python is lighter in tone than Pinter and Beckett, it is lighter in substance. If we return to the comparison earlier in this chapter between the section of Beckett's *Murphy* and the *Flying Circus* animation about the society woman – both of which involve toilets – we may be led to think that Beckett's reference to lavatories carries more intellectual 'clout'. Murphy's failure even to see the flushing of his ashes down the toilet is emblematic of futility and meaninglessness, whereas the *Flying Circus* animation is just – surely – an exercise in crude humour in the extreme.

However, we may interpret this differently in the light of the 'laughing truth' of the Menippean satire as explored by Mikhail Bakhtin. For Bakhtin there is a truth and even a poetry in the vulgar and the scatological (Bakhtin 1984b: 112–19). Art may, such as in the writing of Rabelais, celebrate the 'base' elements of life and culture as a means of comically undermining authority and its oppressive and dictatorial norms (Stam 1989: 158). If we view this animation sequence with Bakhtin's ideas in mind, we can re-evaluate it not just as vulgar lavatorial humour, but as subversive critique of the societal norms of Britain. To do so we have to acknowledge that the animation is funny because the subject is not only a woman, but an upper-class society woman at that. Our culture tells us that *women do not go to the toilet*, they are too busy pressing flowers and writing wistfully in their occasional diaries, and posh women certainly don't go to the toilet, and most definitely do not experience loud and explosive bowel movements. By presenting us with a scenario in which a woman, and a posh woman at that, goes to the toilet and loudly defecates, this sequence undermines our cultural values in two ways. Firstly, it bursts the bubble of a particular cultural illusion that women are (or should be) somewhat purer in body and mind than men and confronts us with the truth that women do in fact go to the toilet. Secondly, it acknowledges that we know and have always known that women – even posh ones – go to the toilet, and that we know and have always known that a particular reactionary vision of 'femininity' is a construct and a lie. If we accept this Bakhtinian interpretation, then we can see that Python – even at its silliest and crudest – has a more radical and challenging quality than we may hitherto have suspected.

Monty Python's Flying Circus was and is famed for its lampooning of TV shows and TV itself. It regularly satirised established TV formats and genres, such as the gameshow in 'Blackmail' (episode 18, 'Live from the Grill-O-Mat'); however, it also questioned and deconstructed the phenomenon of TV itself on a number of occasions, and did so as effectively as Pinter and Beckett challenged the fabric of the play. In 'Psychiatrist Milkman' (episode 16, 'Déjà Vu'), the sketch is caught in a repeating loop and collapses in on itself. 'Flying Fox of the Yard' (episode 29, 'The Money Programme') is a very brief sequence which – nevertheless – manages to deconstruct itself, the sketch that preceded it, television comedy, comedy as a whole and *Monty Python's Flying Circus*.

The cultural and intellectual impact of comedy is often underrated; even William Shakespeare's comedies are considered – by consensus – to be lesser than his tragedies and his histories. However, it has been the subject of a considerable body of academic study which has interrogated both its social purpose and its operational procedures. In *Jokes and Their Relation to the Unconscious* (1905 [1976]), Sigmund Freud subjected jokes and humour to a psychoanalytic study and observed that 'jokes are used as an envelope for thoughts of the greatest substance' (Freud 1905 [1976]: 135). Many scholars have since enquired into how comedy is utilised as a means of critique and attack on a society, individuals or groups within society. Alison Ross particularly looks at how comedy can be put to either reactionary or subversive use depending upon whether the humour is targeted by those in power against the vulnerable, or whether the humour is aimed at the higher power strata in society by the general population, or those who speak for them (see Ross 1998). Mikhail Bakhtin's work on François Rabelais maintains that laughter itself is a subversive act against tyranny and oppression (see Bakhtin 1984a). However, it is perhaps Henri Bergson (1859–1941) whose work is most crucial for understanding the role of humour in both Beckett and Pinter as well as Monty Python. Crucially, however, it is perhaps also Bergson who can help us understand the key *differences* between Python and these absurdists.

Bergson's position on comedy – given in *Laughter* (1899) – is that 'we laugh at human nature when it behaves with machine-like rigidity' (Howarth 1978: 16). This is perhaps best illustrated by his discussion on Molière which W. D. Howarth outlines as follows:

> [C]haracters are comic because of the rigidity of their outlook on life, the mechanical inflexibility of their behavioural responses. Monsieur Jourdan, the 'would-be nobleman', who is quite happy to wear a new coat, made with its pattern upside-down, once his tailor has persuaded him that this is the latest fashion amongst the gentry, is an . . . excellent

example of this comic rigidity: everything he says or does is determined by the way he thinks the nobility behave. Another example is Argan, the hypochondriac hero *Le Malade imaginaire*, who carries his obsession with ill-health and medicaments to such lengths that he anxiously asks how many grains of salt he should take with his boiled egg. These are caricatural portraits, it is true, and sufficient imagination has gone into their creation to make them ready targets for our laughter; but the reality they caricature is never so remote that they become mere creatures of fantasy. (Ibid.: 106–7)

We can claim that the humour of the absurdists and Python functions in accordance with this mechanical analogy; nevertheless, there is a profound difference in how this 'machine-like rigidity' manifests itself and is exploited for humorous effect. In Pinter and Beckett, life itself is a futile machine and the characters in their plays are mere faulty, or even superfluous, components in its meaningless grinding operation. By contrast, in Python the humour lies in the mechanical rigidity of particular individuals and organisations that inveigle reasonable citizens into their ridiculous mechanisms and procedures. Like the (not particularly funny) work of Franz Kafka, in which the ordinary, even anonymous, citizen is trapped on a downward spiral track of irrational systemisation, Python frequently pitted a hapless individual against illogical authority figures and organisations, as in, for example, 'New Cooker Sketch' (episode 14, 'Face the Press'). The similarities between the work of Kafka and Python are considerably marked; indeed, both Kafkaesque and Pythonesque have entered the popular lexicon as adjectives that are freely used to indicate the strange, irrational and bizarre. Looking at the 'New Cooker Sketch' as an illustrative example, the sketch begins in one situation which is both absurd and mundane and then accelerates through increasing levels of weirdness as it progresses. A woman has bought a new gas cooker and wishes it to be fitted; however, the gas board employees who come to fit the appliance give a relatively mundane reason why they can't complete the task. These gas fitters call upon colleagues, who also are unable to fit the cooker for other reasons. From this point more and more gas board employees are called, each of whom gives an increasingly absurd bureaucratic reason why they can't fit the gas cooker and why another colleague needs to be called in to fit the cooker, leading to the suggestion that the woman should gas herself to speed up the process. The sketch ends – or rather, morphs into another – with the sight of an endless line of gas board employees extending down the street. This sketch has similarities to the writing of Kafka not only in that it highlights how the individual may be caught in a ludicrously officious bureaucratic process, but also by the fact that in the scenario of this sketch and much of Kafka's fiction, the citizen becomes a victim in an irrational trap from which they cannot escape.

The scenario also escalates in absurdity and claustrophobic hysteria at an alarming rate. The sketch/piece of fiction frequently opens with a scene in which an unwitting character, thinking that they are in quite a mundane situation, finds this mundane situation take on an odd slant. Nevertheless, despite the oddness of this situation, usually the scenario is still within the realms of the plausible, if unlikely. However, in both Python and Kafka, the protagonist's situation becomes rapidly more bizarre in incremental steps. Very quickly, the character has found themselves whisked along speedily from the mundane, to the odd, to the absurd. Both Python and Kafka utilise this strategy both as a means of highlighting how absurd the mundane actually is, and also to demonstrate how vulnerable we are to the absurd and irrational once it begins to intrude on our lives, how helpless we are once this irrationality has us in its grip, and how impossible it is to escape this absurdity.

Although some characters in Python are comic because they are set up in opposition to stereotypes, such as 'Hell's Grannies' (episode 8, 'Full Frontal Nudity') and 'The Bishop' (episode 17, 'The Buzz Aldrin Show'), Monty Python is riddled with caricatures that would sit well with Molière's gallery of fools. These characters are trapped by a machine-like absurd over-logic, in love with and imprisoned by the delusions of their position and supposed rank. Python routines are habitually populated by pompous and self-righteous civil servants, judges, clergymen and army officers, officious shopkeepers, sleazy gameshow hosts and pedantic bureaucrats. As such, the Pythons are *with* their audience, they share a common foe: Python sketches – despite their absurdity – are very much 'about' and 'refer to' the audience's world, rather than maintain that their world is a fiction.

For Beckett and Pinter, the mundane is not only meaningless, but mocked. It is to be mocked and derided for its futility. For them, the triviality of having a gas cooker fitted is a terrible and soul-corroding affirmation of the essential nihilism that underscores existence and evidences the meaninglessness of humanity and the universe. The Pythons, however, one feels, do not position themselves above such things. They too use and need gas cookers. For the Pythons, the need for a gas cooker is not the issue, and it is certainly not taken as an emblematic device to represent the yawning void of nothingness at the heart of being. The Pythons – like us – need a working gas cooker. The Pythons – like us – are frustrated by the fact that something seemingly as simple and mundane as having a gas cooker fitted becomes hugely complex and time-consuming when a government department (as was the case at the time of *Flying Circus*'s broadcast) has to be called in to oversee its installation. At the heart of *Python* there is a very real link with the reality of the audience's lives rather than a distancing from it.

In using humour to attack the institutions and practices predominant in British society, Python was recognised as being part of a wider move towards satirical comedy that was becoming more prevalent in the 1960s and 1970s on British TV as its practitioners and its audience recognised the value of comedy as a means of attack on the powerful – a means of attack that carried greater weight than more 'serious' cultural forms. As Friedrich Dürrenmatt noted in 1966:

> Man's freedom manifests itself in laughter, his necessity in crying; today we have to demonstrate freedom. The tyrants of this planet are not moved by works of poets, they yawn at their lamentations, they consider their heroic lays silly nursery tales, they fall asleep over their religious poetry, there is only one thing they fear: their mockery. So parody has crept into all genres, into drama, into lyrical poetry. (Dürrenmatt 1966: 128)

Yet despite there being so many examples of satiric and parodic work produced in this period, *Monty Python's Flying Circus* retains its status as a subversive, ground-breaking, anarchic, boundary-defying and (let's not forget) funny text, and the programme's appeal has far outlived its initial 1969–74 run. Pythonesque remains our best available adjective for the absurd and nonsensical, whether we are talking about fiction or reality. While the post-Python output of the individual team members may ostensibly seem tamer and more conventional, they continue to challenge the viewer and familiar media format. John Cleese's *Fawlty Towers* (1975–9) revitalised the stale format of the sitcom and gave it greater bite; Terry Jones's history programmes, such as *Crusades* (1995), brought revisionist history to popular television; Eric Idle has subverted the affected and anodyne world of musical theatre with *Spamalot* (2005); Michael Palin's genial travel programmes – for example, *Around the World in Eighty Days* (1989) – have quietly challenged the format of the travel programme by making the production of the show overt; and Terry Gilliam's film work – exemplified by *Brazil* (1985) – blended the Pythonesque with the Kafkaesque and Orwellian to blatantly satirise contemporary society.

The Pythons have demonstrated – both in *Monty Python's Flying Circus* and beyond – an influence and debt to the Theatre of the Absurd, yet their output has extended beyond its parameters by both embracing a more humanist ethos and engaging a vast audience by utilising the avant-garde within the popular domain. Few of us have cause to return dead parrots to pet shops, fear the Spanish Inquisition or take our mother's corpses to undertakers in sacks, but fifty years after its original transmission, *Monty Python's Flying Circus* remains one of the most relevant, most subversive and challenging television programmes in TV history.

Works Cited

Bakhtin, Mikhail (1984a) *Rabelais and His World*. Bloomington: Indiana University Press.
Bakhtin, Mikhail (1984b) *Problems of Dostoevsky's Poetics*. Minneapolis: University of Minnesota Press.
Bradbury, Malcolm (1989) *The Modern World: Ten Great Writers*. London: Penguin.
Brandt, George (1978) 'Twentieth-century Comedy', in W. D. Howarth (ed.), *Comic Drama: The European Heritage*. London: Methuen, pp. 165–87.
Childs, Peter (2008) *Modernism*, 2nd edn. London and New York: Routledge.
Dürrenmatt, Friedrich (1966) *Theater-Schriften und Reden*. Zürich: Arche.
Esslin, Martin (1961) *The Theatre of the Absurd*. Garden City, NJ: Doubleday.
Freud, Sigmund ([1905] 1976) *Jokes and Their Relation to the Unconscious*. London: Penguin.
Gent, James (2014) 'Monty Python'. <http://www.montypython.com/python_the_pythons/14> (last accessed 20 December 2016).
Howarth, W. D. (1978) *Comic Drama: The European Heritage*. London: Methuen & Co.
Hudson, Rick (2017a) 'Thrilling Adventures in Post-colonial Culture: From Empire to Commonwealth in *Ripping Yarns* and British Popular Culture', in Paul N. Reinsch, B. Lynn Whitfield and Robert G. Weiner (eds), *Python beyond Python: Critical Engagements with Culture*. New York: Palgrave Macmillan, pp. 171–82.
Hudson, Rick (2017b) 'Grotesque Unrealism: Terry Gilliam's *Jabberwocky*', in Paul N. Reinsch, B. Lynn Whitfield and Robert G. Weiner (eds), *Python beyond Python: Critical Engagements with Culture*. New York: Palgrave Macmillan, pp. 93–108.
Landy, Marcia (2005) *Monty Python's Flying Circus: TV Milestones Series*. Detroit, MI: Wayne State University.
Nicol, Bran (2009) *The Cambridge Introduction to Postmodern Fiction*. Cambridge: Cambridge University Press.
Ross, Alison (1998) *The Language of Humour*. London: Routledge.
Stam, Robert (1989) *Subversive Pleasures: Bakhtin, Cultural Criticism and Film*. Baltimore, MD and London: Johns Hopkins University Press.
Wilson, Benji (2010) 'How Monty Python Was Formed', *The Telegraph*, 4 August. <https://www.telegraph.co.uk/culture/tvandradio/7927128/How-Monty-Python-was-formed.html> (last accessed 20 December 2016).

2. 'NONE SHALL PASS' AND 'THE SKULL BENEATH THE SKIN': MONTY PYTHON, THE BRITISH CLASS SYSTEM AND DEATH

Gina Wisker

Social hierarchy and death are two intransigents blocking us all. In Britain, the class system permeates every assessment of other people, every exchange. For elsewhere, perhaps, substitute or add other constructs in which people invest and by which we are controlled, i.e. money, politics, religion or a grasping after eternal youth. Man-made constructions of governance and religion, illegitimate power and torture enabled by tyrants and their followers, are an everyday reality; they're human constructions dominating the physical and the imaginary. So, also, death dominates life. The energy and drive of the Monty Python troupe is all about debunking dominant absurdities and seizing the day – *carpe diem* made comic, with clever clarity. What links the class system and death, two intransigents which will not let anyone pass, it seems, blocking the way forward, physically, psychologically, spiritually, like a Black Knight in a clearing (*Monty Python and the Holy Grail*, 1975), is the issue of levelling. Death is a great leveller. No one escapes death. The class system and all forms of complex structuring of hierarchy based on rock-solid but transient principles are an absurd investment in a scaffold fashioned from a set of rules invented somewhere by someone or other. It is a construct. It only has substance because we invest in it and apply it. Death is similarly skirted round with repertoires of belief but, unlike the class system, it is in the end unavoidable.

These two ever-present and taboo topics, death and the class system, and our contradictory responses to both, run throughout British humour drawn from the broad British satirical tradition and also from a wide range of international and local influences that have been less recognised as affecting that tradition. Like much British satire, the work of the Monty Python troupe is a mixture of slapstick, farce and political incisiveness that operates through ridicule, irreverence, a sharp cutting through pretentiousness and performance, through artifice and arrogance, puncturing the pomposity and the lies of dominant systems and the social everyday. Their origins are middle and upper middle class, their politics left-wing but not extreme, against narrow-mindedness in all its forms and origins, and ready to satirise the stupidities, excesses and divisiveness of political parties. Reflecting on their recent live shows in 2014, Taylor Parkes comments:

> Politically, they were your standard-issue *Guardian*-reading media types. In the run-up to the general election of 1970, all of them bar Idle appeared in a Cleese-penned instructional film for Labour Party canvassers; no one who's ever seen *Life of Brian* could possibly be in any doubt as to their opinion of the revolutionary Left. (Parkes 2014)

Extremes are butts of their satire whatever way you voted.

Many of the reviews which preceded the 2014 stage revival seem provoked by a challenge to the reviewers' own nostalgia. Parkes, however, captures the engaged critique of 'bullshit' at the heart of their absurdist comedy in an avant-garde age where there was for many years the opportunity for satire, a healthy response to conservatism and contradictory political behaviours:

> *Python* evolved out of British satire in much the same way psychedelia evolved from the protest movement, or Situationism from left-Libertarianism: disillusionment with straightforward political solutions, a belief in the transformative power of the imagination, a desire to open minds by force. Not that the Pythons ever actually thought of their work in those terms – they'd tell you they were just trying to make people laugh, that the weirdness was only the influence of Milligan and Peter Cook (or in Gilliam's case, Walerian Borowczyk or Harry Everett Smith). (Parkes 2014)

The rich comic mix of the Monty Python troupe punctures the complaisance and unthinking arrogance of wealth, class and power, consistently reminding us of the skull beneath the skin in ways which might (or might not) transfer outside of Britain.

This chapter, accordingly, concentrates on two themes, death and social hierarchy, particularly the British class system, briefly considering Monty Python in the context of a range of international comedic and philosophical influences from Juvenal to carnival, with an underpinning of existentialism, through to the ongoing twentieth- and twenty-first-century British satirical tradition.

Nobody Expects

In itself, if we rely on historical accounts, the Spanish Inquisition cannot be said to be at all a subject for comedy. But as a historical record, reality, cultural construct and the butt of the energetic satire of the Monty Python troupe, it is blackly comic, farcical, absurd and, ultimately, more manageable, at least in the imagination. Irreverence for seemingly unquestionable power over life and death informs the delight of the comedy we share with Monty Python. As the Spanish Inquisition (Cardinal Ximinez played by Palin, Cardinal Fang by Gilliam and Cardinal Biggles by Jones) burst in on ordinary middle-class homes and force ordinary people to endure torture with soft cushions, so the terrifying, warped power maintained over life and death by the hierarchy of the Catholic Church in the Renaissance period is both there on the screen in all the flamboyant brutality it evokes, and also, with the alternative power of satire, utterly nonsensical and undermined. It is a very British home, and these overdressed wielders of religious and political power are undercut, met by a double refusal of their power: the lack of understanding of the basis for their right to terrorise, and the homely everydayness of the middle-class woman who is their intended (rather random) victim. Monty Python, the mainly Oxbridge-educated, surrealist-influenced comedy troupe, use visual and verbal satire to capture the terrors and the forces, real and imagined, that govern us. Then, enriched by centuries of satirical tradition and a few dashes of pantomime, carnival, farce and existentialism, they puncture these forces.

Each seeming intransigent, the class system and death tantalisingly offer scope for their own undermining and do so by way of comedy through the questioning of taboos, boundaries and blockages. The absolute nature of death can be queried with belief in ghosts and the afterlife, religious or not, and the class system, that system of social inequality based on birth, is troubled by other systems of power based on money, meritocracy, bullying and random Othering. It is into these liminal clearings of querying, queering and questioning that the surreal satirical comedy of the Monty Python troupe enters. Their acute sense of the class system is based on their position within it, their irreverence founded in an existential and satirical vision that is international in influence and also very British, an irreverence for the range of puny, invested constructs that straitjacket people – law, religion, polities, hierarchy. These constructs and death, the ultimate leveller, are managed by wit and by farce: a large cartoon foot flattening anyone and anything, particularly if they are being pompous or excessive.

The Monty Python troupe started with the Cambridge Footlights and the Oxford Revue, recognised as public school in origin. Michael Henderson (2013) argues: 'The most extraordinary aspect of Python's international success is the Britishness of the humour. More specifically it is the humour ("Who threw that slipper?") of the British public school . . . They had all grown up in a small-c conservative world.' Oddly, he thinks their work is only of interest to the middle classes: 'Python was a middle-class thing, rooted in college quad and JCR . . . you will find very few working-class people who get it.' The criticism that they only appeal to the small class group whom they satirise is intriguing given the massive popularity of Monty Python throughout the 'baby boom' universities in 1969 when they first aired (in the UK, working-class and lower-middle-class students arrived then in new or expanding universities and polytechnics in large numbers). They had a very broad appeal, crossing age and class. It might have been useful to have heard of Proust and Sartre and found them confusing, but you could also laugh if you ever had to wait for the gasman and then several came at once but were unable to fix the leak, or you'd bought a budgie in a corner shop from a man in a brown mac. It is very British and their treatment of class is thoroughly satirical.

Their immediate preceding British origins and influences are several, each clever, funny, satirical, political and social. These include the radio programme *Round the Horne* (1965–8), the absurdism of Peter Sellers and *The Goon Show* (1951–60) and the intellectually based satirical comedy of *Beyond the Fringe* (1960), with Jonathan Miller, Alan Bennett, Peter Cook and Dudley Moore (the latter in the 1970s as Derek and Clive with their upper-class duffer Sir Arthur Streeb-Greebling, precursor of the Pythons' upper-class twits). Their subversion is also based on the performances of Gilbert and Sullivan: 'It isn't such a big step from I Am the Ruler of the Queen's Navee to the Upper Class Twit of the Year Race' (Henderson 2013).

Donald Hoffman draws attention to the plummeting sheep, dead parrot and the existential references in Monty Python sketches, arguing that 'no tradition remains intact in the presence of the Pythons' quest for silliness' (Hoffman 2002: 141). Some Python roots are in pantomime, the class- and sex-oriented bawdy of Sid James, Hattie Jacques, the Ealing comedies, *Carry On* films (1958–92) and Dick Emery (1963–81). All undercut and poke cruel, hilarious fun at the pretentiousness and hypocrisy of the class system and, in *Carry On up the Khyber* (1968) (with its veiled sexual reference), the arrogance of British imperialism based on constructions of racialised social hierarchies. Since Python, both *Little Britain* (2003–5) and Harry Enfield (1990–2, 1994–9) took on their satirical, political juxtaposition of the ridiculous and unlikely with the everyday targeting of hypocritical approaches to gender and sexuality, social class and disability with some outrageous sketches, their roots in the bawdy humour of British seaside towns. Class and power are satirised in *The Harry Enfield Television Show* (1990–2) and *Harry Enfield and Chums* (1994–9) with a long-running skit ('The Self-Righteous Brothers'), in which two blokes in a pub (resembling Derek and Clive) become insistent about controlling situations where celebrities and royalty might want their advice or company, undercutting the class system with a peculiarly British form of self-aggrandisement and anger. Monty Python, however, is more surreal.

Social Satire and Existentialism: Puncturing the Pompous and Pretentious; Juvenal, Pope and Sartre

Chief among the roots and influences of Monty Python are social satire and existentialism. The great classical satirist of the powerful and the ordinary, Juvenal (55/60–127 CE), exposed human vanity (Juvenal [2 CE] 1998) in ancient Rome, while Alexander Pope (1688–1744), drawing from Juvenal, took exquisite delight in puncturing the pomposity and artifice of those around him in aristocratic and society circles. He was deliberately nasty and cuttingly accurate in revealing the ridiculous celebration of the trivial and artificial among the rich in, for example, 'The Rape of the Lock' (1712), where the loss of a small piece of hair is treated as a cataclysmic event in the eyes of a socialite. Everywhere in satire the grinning skull beneath the painted skin is a target for exposure and wit which expose hubris, pomposity and a self-deluding belief in one's own success, loveliness and time-defying modes of behaviour. The cry of *carpe diem*, seize the day and live it to the full, is always ironic, because death is just around the corner. Referencing Ernest Becker's arguments that man seeks infinity but ultimately is 'a worm and food for worms' (Becker 1974: 26), Katarzyna Małecka sees in the Pythons' work 'man's existential paradox' (2014: 4).

Mortal vulnerability unforgettably opens the first show. A giant foot stamps on a man's head, which sprouts flowers; the head of a cabaret-dressed woman explodes; a falling angel squashes Cardinal Richelieu. The grey-suited announcer is in league with the mayhem of dead pigs and we are invited to consider the comedic drama of famous deaths, including that of Genghis Khan. This is dark comedy mixed with slapstick, carnival and cartoon.

Satirical comedy from the farcical to the cuttingly mean has its partner in Gothic horror, which also punctures artifice, deliberately undercutting complacency, comfort based on maintaining pretence, holding off the terrible end just on the edge of the precipice. Horror also represents people as objects, as does comedy. Each has its taboos: death, the decaying body, religion. Each treats complacencies as revelations of insecurities. What they also have in common is a reduction of human vitality to the objectification of the manipulated. Dehumanisation accompanies defamiliarisation. Things and people are not just rendered strange, weird, unfamiliar; they are exposed as mindless objects.

The vanity of human wishes, the skull beneath the skin, are inevitabilities. Everything is just a construct, in decay, and every attempt at fancy clothing, grandeur, is a show. Self-delusion is dangerously blinkered, unutterably silly and hilarious to the acute eye of the satirist and their audience. This kind of social satire has its excessive, exploding hilarity in pantomime, in carnival, in switching gender codes and dress, social roles, exposing artifice while demonstrating excess in dressing up, painting, self-display. For the Monty Python troupe, the satirical tradition of Juvenal and Pope, which critiqued the vanity of human wishes, is tempered with a healthy dose of existentialism, of the sort found in Jean Paul Sartre's *La Nausée* (1938) (and we must not forget that Mrs Jean Paul Sartre is a regular character in Python sketches). To bowdlerise this somewhat, one of the tenets of *La Nausée* is that we agree to labels and names, to values and rules, they are not intrinsically part of things. Everything is labelled – this is not what something or someone 'is' (if there were such a definable essence), but instead we construct meanings and values round the labels which we agree and share. There is only immediacy and appearances: 'Now I knew: things are entirely what they appear to be – and behind them . . . there is nothing' (Sartre 1938). In his introduction to *La Nausée*, Hayden Carruth (1963) notes of Sartre's development as an existentialist that

> [l]ater in his philosophical development the idea of freedom became Sartre's main theme. Man, beginning in the loathsome emptiness of his existence, creates his essence – his self, his being – through the choices that he freely makes. Hence his being is never fixed. He is always becoming, and if it were not for the contingency of death he would never end. Nor would his philosophy.

There is free choice over labels, meanings invested in words, hierarchies and political commitments or acts, hence a political refusal to collude with illegitimate enforced power (such as Nazism, in Sartre's case).

Based on superficiality and tenuousness, so also social hierarchy, the class system is exposed as a construct that only really has power if people invest that power in it. Social hierarchy and, in Britain, its concrete embedding in the class system, has led to enormous abuse, particularly with the upper classes, who believe they are one step down from divinity and have a right to certain power and quality of life. Criticism of the Pythons for their public or grammar school then Oxbridge origins underestimates their brilliantly comic irreverence for politics, power, hierarchies and class. Emphasising the surreal weirdness of the Pythons' humour, and their very broad appeal, Parkes notes:

> Very rarely was Python political, but it was a protest all right – a protest against bullshit and bullying, sloppy thinking and humbug, a gleeful assault on philistinism and pseudery. What's more, it was weird. Not 'wacky', not 'delightfully loopy' – *really, really weird*. At its best, Python could be a disturbing experience, disquieting, disordered, disruptive . . . something close to Dada. It was not just absurd, but absurdist: cosmic satire, a mockery of meaning. (Parkes 2014)

The work of Monty Python might be truly weird but it is also rooted in the mundane, in the often bizarre details of the everyday and the unavoidability of life, and death. We cannot escape the inevitability and the contingency of death, but it is possible to refuse its psychological stranglehold on life and, unlike death, the social class system is not inevitable. The class system and forms of social hierarchy are no more than embedded human constructions, as are all forms of differentiation, including gendered, religious and racial Othering, systems in which the Other once constructed can be abjected, persecuted, destroyed (Kristeva 1988). Dehumanisation is fostered in a view of life as composed of hierarchies of worth and human rights (or their lack). There is then, I would argue, in this undermining and exposure, an underlying value of free choice, of equality and social justice running through the work of Monty Python, as well as manic humour and a lot of old-fashioned bawdiness.

These are the (historically originated and existential) bases of Monty Python's satire, but it is also a particular form of British irreverence to anything established and unable to see its own temporary nature, its instability and its self-aggrandising folly. The Pythons can poke fun at the odd responses of working-class gasmen in identical brown coats, queuing down a working-class street, unable to fix a gas cooker ('New Cooker' sketch, 1970), at unionised labourers in overalls, and mothers (Pythons in drag) having tea parties – any role and level. However, they reserve their cruellest and most absurd satire for the upper classes, universally seen as (sometimes dangerous) inbred twits. These arrogant, entitled twits are defused, shown as having no right to any more rights than anyone else. Human constructed symbols are also exposed as just that – symbols, proxies and replicas of an undiscoverable real. Upsetting and debunking an artificial order is the job of carnival, and its very British sister, pantomime.

Carnival and Bakhtin

At the roots of Monty Python's work lie multiple expressions of unease: satire, black comedy through to farce, and Gothic horror. Some influences on the Pythons' humour derive from a long-standing tradition of farce and slapstick, common in popular culture, and a version of carnivalesque (Bakhtin, 1895–1975), which Bakhtin developed in *Rabelais and His World* (1965). Carnivalesque defined moments of temporarily licensed behaviours challenging capital and power, mocking and overturning authority. In the space of carnival, as in *Twelfth Night* (Shakespeare, 1623) and traditional Trinidadian carnival times (Earl Lovelace's *The Dragon Can't Dance*, 1979), it is possible to expose the pomposities and control of the ruling classes, bureaucracies, belief systems and hierarchies of power, as they affect everything and everyone. A major butt of carnival is social hierarchy, birthright, inheritance, entitlement and social position. Social and ontological freedom explodes, liberating behaviour and puncturing myths and narratives concerning birth, money, power, gender, ethnicity; overturned are symbols of status, and the beliefs and structures which follow them and limit worldviews. The hypocrisy of the pompous and the powerful is undercut, exposing hubris and the vanity of human wishes, and revealing that wet blanket, mortality, the skull beneath the skin. Carnival, the rebellion and table-turning of the proletariat, might be temporary, after which the toys are put back in the box and everything returns to order, but these explosive critical moments of radical energy destabilise carefully maintained rules and belief systems. It can and will happen again. Monty Python's surreal comedy, often expressed in Terry Gilliam's active artwork, is destabilising and will not let any of us remain complacent, conservative, foolishly reassured that the structures of behaviour, belief, right and wholeness of self, family, religion, civil society, the divine right of kings, are solid. They are exposed as rather tentative, delicate, foolish human constructs subject to dissolution. Monty Python causes laughter and unease. The more unease, the more unsettled the audience; the more laughter, the more release. Mortality, death, is also the last laugh.

Pantomime and Angela Carter

Pantomime, a grand old British carnival tradition of class and gender reversals, is another key influence on Monty Python. Angela Carter, whose family lived a middle-class family life in South London, was brought up on Hollywood films and the carnival excess and performance of British pantomime, embedded in the class system. She writes of pantomime, 'in pantoland, everything is grand. Well let's not exaggerate – grandish. Not like what it used to be but, then what isn't, even so, it is brightly coloured – garish in fact' (Carter 1991: 1); 'everything is excessive, sexualised, phallic or else demonically aggressively female' (ibid.). There is an emphasis on procreation as comic and 'nostalgia for naval heroes, the rise of the poor, for instance Dick Whittington and his cat are set against "Baron Hardup of Hardup Hall", father of Cinderella, stepfather of the ugly sisters' (ibid.: 2). Music, 'illusion and transformation' (ibid.: 1) predominate, mixing the real (horses on stage) and the cartoon illusory (pantomime horses on stage). Pantomime's power is to undermine and query power: 'in pantoland, which is the carnival of the unacknowledged and the fiesta of the repressed, everything is excessive and gender is variable' (ibid.: 4). It is based, as is *Twelfth Night*, on the mid-winter carnival of the Feast of Fools, and 'the orgiastic non-time of the Solstice, which once upon a time, was also the time of the Saturnalia, the topsy-turvy time . . . when a master swapped places with a slave and anything could happen' (ibid.). Carter's well-researched exploration of that very British tradition of panto delves back historically and out internationally for roots. She does not talk of her contemporaries, Monty Python (Terry Jones interviewed her in 1981), but these are also the roots of their very British social satire: rebellion against social hierarchy, heritage, wealth. The dressing up and bizarre rituals of the rich are rendered first foolish, then challenged and overturned by the riotous poor in brief Saturnalian carnivalesque moments, puncturing the class system's constructions at Twelfth Night, at carnival, in panto, and in the tradition of British satire of which the Pythons are the great twentieth-century champions.

Like Carter, the Pythons range far and wide through history, myth and religious systems to undermine the seeming solidity of the constructions of class and the many ritualistic, spiritual and physical issues around death. Like panto, they cross-dress, use cartoon excess (not Dick Whittington's Cat but killer kitty), bawdy musical interludes and prat falls. Their satire reveals the elision of the untouchable belief systems of worth through birth and of the finality (or not) of death. Breeding, inheritance, heredity, the 'solid' base on which class systems are based, and the belief systems around death, a highly elaborate constructedness of ritual, medical, cosmetic, religious and spiritual, which attempts to defy and deny death, set against its terror, physical corruption and decay, are equally sent up. The running sores beneath the skin, the taboos and terrors of death and the afterlife, are exposed symbolically, debunked, flouted. Fundamentally class and belief systems are undercut by both the accident of birth and the inevitability of death.

Pantomime, carnival, satire and Monty Python revel in each of these. And they do so in a very British way.

'Upper Class Twit of the Year'

The first series established a delightful lack of reverence and decorum for the British ruling classes in the 'Upper Class Twit of the Year' sketch, which parodied both the endless competitive drive and the utter incompetence, physical and mental, of these future rulers of the nation. It opens on a sporting pitch with some kind of race about to take place. Everyone and everything is dysfunctional. Identical with bowler hats and receding chins, Gervaise, Vivian, Oliver, Simon, Nigel (their names are upper class; they haven't a clue) can't respond to starter's orders because they can't cope with directions, or a sense of direction. The hurdles are puny, like matchboxes, yet these public school, bowler-hatted, incompetent twits have no idea how to tackle them. The suggestion is that inbreeding among the upper classes is so complete that there is no brain left, although each is a stockbroker or similar with a powerful influential job probably through nepotism, so these clearly physical and mental incompetents blindly succeed due to their inherited wealth and entitlement. Prestige and influence substitute for intelligence and worth. Their runs are versions of the Ministry of Silly Walks. They are totally unable to connect brain and body, and run at the high jump wooden frames, which they are meant to go under.

Lacking direction and any skills, they tackle taking the bras off the dummies, which end up broken. Oliver runs himself over. In the end they determine who wins according to who has shot themselves, so the podium has only coffins on it. They're so totally stupid, destroying themselves so sportingly. A range of 'chinless wonders' and upper-class twits with double-barrelled names limp and lisp through the Monty Python series, sending up any notion of class superiority.

The Parrot in the Room

Death, the threat of death, its inevitability; the power over life and death operated by religious men in power; sorcery and physical decay; the whole querying of the liminality between life and death: these are very big issues that draw in politics, religion, law, psychology, social hierarchies, justice and inevitability. Death is the 'elephant in the room', rarely spoken of except in tones of reverence and sadness, despair and apprehension. It might be a great leveller, but it also offers many opportunities for black comedy and irreverence.

In the 'Dead Parrot' sketch, a pet is returned to a pet shop. The parrot was obviously passed off as alive and well when sold, and has now passed on. Whatever collusion took place between the salesman and new owner at that point is unknown, but the ontological state of the returned parrot is, it would seem, indisputable, as it is clearly not moving and looks stuffed. We suspend disbelief watching drama. A stuffed parrot could pass as live on stage with our agreement, but this scene highlights the artifice and the collusion of comedy sketches as drama, while itself being a mixture of the earthy and the surreal. It is an everyday annoyance, returning shoddy goods and having sales people insist that you are in the wrong rather than that the purchase is flawed or their marketing policies are flawed. The 'Dead Parrot' sketch combines issues of death and social hierarchies, a clash between pet shop owner (an expert) and an irate customer (a man with the money and the rights). This is an argument based on power and knowledge. This parrot was indeed a shoddy purchase; it is actually dead. The sketch also exemplifies the relative experience of death, set against its finality: disputed but also proven. The shuffling of the truth, the pretence, the sly little jibes selected from the repertoire of bawdy and erudition, and a linguistic range which moves between low-level cunning and intellectual referencing of French art, philosophy and political traditions makes this and so many other Python scenes hilarious on a whole range of levels. The Python team were able to insert the ridiculous into the everyday, facetiously showing off their own knowledge while bringing in sardonic, satirical wit to puncture pretentiousness. Everyday exchanges in the street between people take on a resonance of absurdity, so that after Python it is not possible to take anything as given: the class system, myths and behavioural systems, even our approaches to death.

There is nothing dignified about death in these sketches or films either. The Black Knight in can-like armour refusing passage (recalling Spenser's *Faerie Queene*, 1590), while his torso cannot stop fighting and recognise that it must be actually a dead torso, plummeting sheep, exploding people, or a dead parrot and a customer demanding their money back, are equally absurdly amusing.

Monty Python and the Holy Grail (1975)

The British class system, that very tight, historically established gridlock, has roots in structures based on wealth and birth, and grows from the belief in the divine right of kings (the concept that the right to rule derives from God and that kings are answerable for their actions to God alone). Structures of social hierarchy, therefore, have some foundations, a certain kind of enforced legitimacy, in views of God and the universe. Irreverence for hierarchy and social class, divinely legitimated or not, runs throughout *Monty Python and the Holy Grail*. Grand visions behind the recognition of Arthur as King of the Britons are punctured when the Lady of the Lake, dressed in purest white, raises the sword Excalibur from the lake and gives it to Arthur, thus confirming his divine right (something spiritual and magical), and also opening the whole event to ridicule. The divine right of kings is only so much hierarchical mystical nonsense to Dennis the peasant, who deflates and demystifies the event with his common-sense view that 'strange women lying about in ponds distributing swords is no basis for a system of governance', followed by calling the Lady of the Lake a 'watery tart'. In *The Holy Grail*, the king goes around telling people he's the king. Dennis's peasant companion responds with 'well I didn't vote for you', which challenges his status, and when Arthur explains that you don't vote for the king, Dennis, the more intelligent, politicised peasant, points out that the ruler should be voted in by the people's democratic vote.

Hoffman argues that both the medieval issues and practice of power – divine kingship and government – are satirised, particularly with the idea that: 'the king is easily recognisable because he is the only one not covered in shit' (Hoffman 2002: 138). Death, a commonplace, is also satirised. 'Not dead yet' is a constant refrain with, for example, the refusal of the Black Knight to recognise that he has lost the battle, even though all his limbs have been hacked off – a reference to Robert Bresson's film *Lancelot du Lac* (1974), with its almost farcical, excessive hacking off of limbs and spouting of blood from huge wounds. This 'reduces the notion of chivalric heroism to the very bottom line of absurdity' (Hoffman 2002: 138). Myth, death, hierarchy and the combination of religion and kingship link them all, as well as the reverence regarding the historical versions we have of medieval times, so that the 'absurdity at the heart of both chivalry and anarchy is made visible and, consequently, made ridiculous' (ibid.).

There are many cartoon deaths and death threats in *The Holy Grail*, highlighting the constructedness of filmic and TV cartoon scenario representations, sending itself up. Arthur's seriousness is tried by the silliness of the knights who dance the cancan on the round table and sing of eating Spam a lot. This is pantomime, farce and, as Day suggests, a clear product of the 'post-Vietnam political and social cynicism of the 1970s' (Day 2002: 133). If we move away from the secular constructions of class and death, funeral costs, and into the philosophical, metaphysical and spiritual, we see that this film, alongside much of Monty Python and much good satire, destabilises the bases in which people invest, whether secular – hierarchy of birth, wealth and its outer accoutrements – or spiritual – the miracle of birth and the terror of dissolution.

Death is also made silly partly in the engagement with Python-originated mythical beasts, and Hoffman, while acknowledging that there were no recorded fights with dragons in the Arthurian era, discusses the Python creations based on a variety of mythical creatures (including killer kitty) with which Arthur and the knights were thought to have engaged in the UK and Europe. These include 'the Killer Rabbit of Caerbanog', building on the 'Trojan Rabbit', which appears earlier in the film, but much more deadly (and very Welsh-sounding), who 'returns us to the times of gore and corpses' (Hoffman 2002: 144). There is also the 'Legendary Black Beast of Aaaaarrrrrggghhh!', so named because the cartoonist dies as he draws him and scribbles 'aargh', but he has much to do with mythical creatures such as Cerberus and Hydra in classical mythology. Death is here comic and mysterious. It leaves indecipherable traces and mistakes upon which whole sets of belief and behaviours are built.

Beginning with the brilliant social analysis of Dennis the peasant, it is entirely possible to be very silly and very Marxist simultaneously. Indeed, if the condition of man under capitalism is essentially alienated and absurd, silliness becomes the most appropriate and accurate response. The Pythons, then, are true Brechtians and true Marxists:

> not in spite of their silliness, but because of it even if the object of their demystification is trivial (such as the cinematic intermission), it provides the basis for the questioning of systems and media that are too often assumed to be eternal and unchanging. (Hoffman 2002: 145)

Humour combines with social criticism, and absurdity undermines all systems, beliefs and communication. In a post-existential and Marxist moment, the Pythons expose the silliness of systems, using satire, slapstick, farce and pantomime to emphasise their horror and threat, managed through comic forms. Like carnival, perhaps, this is only a brief release before the systems reimpose themselves and the toys go back in the box. Their power, however, is permanently queried.

Monty Python's Life of Brian (1979): Social Hierarchy and Death

In *The Secret Life of Brian*, a 2007 TV documentary reflecting on an earlier TV debate (1979) with Malcolm Muggeridge and the Bishop of Southwark, systems of control based on belief came under scrutiny when the Pythons discussed a range of theoretical versions of religious moments in *The Life of Brian* (1979). They argued how, in reading this film as blasphemous, some viewers in some cultures, including the UK and US, missed the point. Their desire was to show the life and death of an ordinary bloke, an everyman, Brian, alongside Christ. They focus in this film, and across their work, on socially constructed hierarchies, constraining belief systems, and on mortality and death. This comic treatment is part of dealing with taboo subjects through normalising them. It is also part of a tradition of black humour and irreverent satire that, in the Monty Python troupe, mixes, in an unusual, idiosyncratic manner, with surrealism, the fantastic spliced with the realistic. Focusing on both British and international contexts and examples, Monty Python are known for debunking grand beliefs, myths, oppression and historical grand narratives in equal measure, often through replaying those myths and narratives.

According to Laura Basu (2014), Terry Jones in an interview in 2011 stated he would not make a movie like *The Life of Brian* now as it would be too risky in the climate of religious resurgence. It did, however, produce what Giselinde Kuipers (2011: 177) calls a 'humour scandal', which surprised the Pythons. Terry Jones commented to the *Radio Times* that, at that time, religion 'seemed to be on the back burner and it felt like kicking a dead donkey' (Jones 2011). However, there was a backlash against the film (e.g. see Hewison 1981). Basu marvels at how little storm *Four Lions* (Morris 2010), about a set of London jihadis, caused and how much *The Life of Brian* caused, considering issues of free speech.

The Life of Brian tells the story of Brian (Graham Chapman), an ordinary everyday Jewish boy born at the same place and time as Jesus, who gets mistaken for him. Brian, whose mother is called Mandy (Terry Jones), discovers his father might have been a Roman soldier, joins a Jewish resistance group and a protest, and ends up on a cross, encouraged by a fellow sufferer to sing 'Always look on the bright side of life'. Another line, 'Always look on the bright side of death/Just before you draw your terminal breath', is even more blackly humorous, since the group on the crosses are facing crucifixion.

The Pythons were somewhat bemused at the extremist religious backlash to the film. When Jesus appears he is always played straight as baby Jesus with a halo, or as an adult, for example at the sermon on the mount, while the comedy is directed not at the Christian religion but 'towards the blind following of leaders and doctrines, and its disastrous consequences' (Basu 2014: 180). At the time, Eric Idle said 'it became clear early on that we couldn't make fun of the Christ since what he said is very fine (and Buddhist), but the people around him were hilarious and still are!' (Morgan 1999: 174). Philip Davies's theological research explores and exposes the careful work done here (Davies 1998: 400). Rather than an attack on the Bible, the film is a well-researched satirical tool particularly aimed at 'a universal picture of human absurdity', as Basu (2014: 181) notes. In one scene a Roman centurion, played by John Cleese, discovers Brian writing 'Romans go home', and in a very public-school teacher manner insists he write it as lines, as a punishment. This anti-Roman graffiti therefore gets replicated hundreds of times on the palace wall, so 'Britain's deeply entrenched class system and its stuffy establishment figures thereby become objects of fun' (ibid.).

The Life of Brian was the subject of scholarly lectures in Auckland (2016) following a London conference (and book) (Taylor 2015) uncovering how the film and Brian himself are carefully based on scholarship about the historical Jewish Jesus.

> That was very much key stuff in the 1970s. But the main point is that Brian is not Jesus – he is mistaken for a Messiah when he is an ordinary guy. The real Messiah exists but people misunderstand him and complain about him. (Taylor 2016)

Essentially the normalising of Brian undercuts hierarchies – religious and social. While emphasising the often-problematic ways in which people act in concert to perpetuate evils against each other, some social, some leading to persecution and death, Brian is a voice for sensible equality rather than religious or mythically inspired views of who has power and rights.

> **Brian**: Look you've got it all wrong. You don't need to follow me. You don't need to follow anybody! You've got to think for yourselves, you're all individuals!
> **Crowd** (in perfect unison): Yes, we're all individuals.
> **Brian**: You're all different!
> **Crowd**: Yes, we're all different,
> **Homogeneous man**: I'm not.
> **Crowd**: [multiple silencing sounds]
> **Brian**: You've all got to work it out for yourselves!
> **Crowd**: Yes, we've got to work it out for ourselves!
> **Brian**: Exactly!
> **Crowd**: Tell us more!

Death, social hierarchies and the class system lie at the heart of the film. While the Pythons are very British (apart from Gilliam) in location, dress and history, revelling in self-mockery of self-aggrandisement, which itself is also very British, their references are also continentally European, Middle Eastern, their influences international.

DEATH COMES TO DINNER: *MONTY PYTHON'S THE MEANING OF LIFE* (1983)

Nobody expects the Spanish Inquisition, but perhaps if they have (or even if they have not) read Edgar Allan Poe's 'The Masque of the Red Death' (1842) they would recognise an uninvited dinner guest who will devastate their rich complacency and remind them sharply of mortality. Social class and death come together in *The Meaning of Life*, Part 7 (1983). The Grim Reaper, Death himself, with hood and scythe, desolate location and blasted tree, heads towards a lone building and knocks at a door. A man in a suit answers, dealing with this arrival like any other visitor and introducing him to the twee little middle-class candle-lit dinner party with 'Mr Death's come about the reaping, I don't think we need anything'. They're polite of course, they're middle class, so they invite him in for a drink and some post-prandial conversation but Death does not know the norms of genteel behaviour (and he is rather repetitive and boring). They try to bring him into the conversation about a death which they've just been talking about but he keeps saying 'I am the grim reaper', rejects red wine and insists he's not of this world. None of this interaction works well for either party. This is not enough dinner conversation for the little gathering, and his ultimate power and grandeur are undermined by their prosaic expectations.

CONCLUSION

As Parkes notes of Monty Python in general:

> Like all popular avant-garde art, its appeal was beautifully basic. This was comedy stripped to its root: two incompatible ideas colliding, noisily and painfully. Comedy returned to its primary purpose: to inform the powerful, the headstrong and the vainglorious that everything is bullshit – life is a joke, your finery is meaningless and worms will be feasting on you sooner than you think. (Parkes 2014)

The Pythons go beyond 'the vanity of human wishes' and '*carpe diem*', however. Theirs is Gothic horror-inspired satirical comedy. Insights and a puncturing of complacency accompany the hysterical laughter injecting horror into social class-based comedy, in which death and the end of the world as we know it are eagerly awaited.

To return to the Spanish Inquisition: it was real, it was legitimated by the power of religion and government. Perhaps Monty Python selected it as an example of non-British deadly nonsense, but by making it ridiculously British they utterly undermined its stranglehold on the imagination. The British class system, snobbishness and elitism are prime Python targets, as is the cosiness and complacency to take such instances and behaviours seriously. There is a constant edge to the everyday, so that the surreal and exposure of the contradictions and stupidities make it all more or less tolerable, giving us power to criticise and to do something else than be trapped in the mundane. The power of hierarchy (in Britain, social class) and the power over life and death which such hierarchies wield are real. Death is the ultimate reality and leveller of all systems. Monty Python, and particularly the films *Monty Python and the Holy Grail* and *The Life of Brian*, expose the dangerous, potentially deadly, damaging investment in belief systems, and the hierarchies, structures, constraints and attendant punishments for infringements. They reveal the imperatives and the rituals (on the left, one cross each; none shall pass) as based, at worst, on embedded whimsy. A group of costumed manic comics in a suburban living room have other powers, however: the freedom and irreverence of carnival's radical querying, undermining and rejection of all hierarchies, physical and psychological. The work of *Monty Python* enacts a healthy, existentially informed irreverence for the imposition and straitjacketing of all regulations, rules and dominant beliefs that constrain us. Laughter helps us all face up to the very worst, the inevitable, to death, and so undermine its domineering terrorising of life. This is the achievement of irreverent successful satire – it punctures the power and gives the imaginative energies of life the last laugh.

However, Eric idle should perhaps have the last laugh. Sopan Deb in a 2018 interview asks Idle: 'Nothing is more identified with you than the song "Always Look on the Bright Side of Life", which is, of course, the title of your memoir. Will you have it played at your funeral?' He replies: 'I don't know. I won't be there.'

Works Cited

Bakhtin, Mikhail ([1965] 1968) *Rabelais and His World*, Helene Iswolsky (trans). Cambridge, MA: MIT Press.
Basu, Laura (2014) 'Who Can Take a Joke?: *Life of Brian, Four Lions* and Religious "Humour Scandals"', *Relegere: Studies in Religion and Reception* 4(2), 177–206.
Becker, Ernest (1974) *The Denial of Death*. New York: Macmillan USA.
Carruth, Hayden (1963) 'Introduction', in *Nausea*. Cambridge, MA: New Directions. <http://users.telenet.be/sterf/texts/phil/Sartre-Nausea.pdf> (last accessed 26 August 2019)
Carter, Angela ([1991] 1993) 'In Pantoland', in *American Ghosts and Old World Wonders*. London: Chatto & Windus.
Davies, Philip R. (1998) '*Life of Brian* Research', in Stephen D. Moore and J. Cheryl Exum (eds), *Biblical Studies/Cultural Studies: The Third Sheffield Colloquia*. Sheffield: Sheffield Academic Press, pp. 400–14.

Day, David D. (2002) '*Monty Python and the Holy Grail*: Madness with a Definite Method', in Kevin J. Harty (ed.), *Cinema Arthuriana: Essays on Arthurian Film*. New York: Garland, pp. 127–35.

Deb, Sopan (2018) 'Eric Idle Interview: "Monty Python entered the BBC through a backdoor and refused to leave"', *The Independent*, 6 October. <https://www.independent.co.uk/arts-entertainment/tv/features/eric-idle-interview-monty-python-bbc-biography-always-look-on-the-bright-side-of-life-a8570116.html> (last accessed 26 August 2019)

Henderson, Michael (2013) 'Don't Flog a Dead Parrot: Leave Monty Python in the Past', *Spectator*, 30 November. <http://www.spectator.co.uk/2013/11/flogging-a-dead-parrot/> (last accessed 26 August 2019)

Hewison, Robert (1981) *Monty Python, the Case Against: Irreverence, Scurrility, Profanity, Vilification and Licentiousness Abuse*. London: Methuen.

Hoffman, Donald L. (2002) 'Not Dead Yet: *Monty Python and the Holy Grail* in the Twenty-First Century', in Kevin J. Harty (ed.), *Cinema Arthuriana: Essays on Arthurian Film*. New York: Garland, pp. 136–48.

Jones, Terry (2011) 'Terry Jones: Monty Python Wouldn't Do a Film about Muslims', interview, *Radio Times*, 11 October. <https://www.radiotimes.com/news/2011-10-10/terry-jones-monty-python-wouldnt-do-a-film-about-muslims/> (last accessed 26 March 2020)

Juvenal ([2 CE] 1998) *The Sixteen Satires*, Peter Green (trans.). London: Penguin Books.

Kristeva, Julia (1988) *Strangers to Ourselves*. New York: Columbia University Press.

Kuipers, Giselinde (2011) 'The Politics of Humour in the Public Sphere: Cartoons, Power and Modernity in the First Transnational Humour Scandal', *European Journal of Cultural Studies* 14(1), 63–80.

Lovelace, Earl (1979) *The Dragon Can't Dance*. London: André Deutsch.

McCabe, Bob (1999) *Dark Knights and Holy Fools: The Art and Films of Terry Gilliam*. New York: Universe Publishing.

Malamud, Randy (2010) Monty Python conference, 28–29 October, Lodz, Poland. <https://sites.google.com/site/montypythonconference/programme>

Małecka, Katarzyna (2014) 'Death and the Denial of Death in the Works of Monty Python', in Tomasz Dobrogoszcz (ed.), *Nobody Expects the Spanish Inquisition: Cultural Contexts in Monty Python*. London: Rowman & Littlefield, pp. 3–22.

Morgan, David (1999) *Monty Python Speaks*. London: Ted Smart.

Parkes, Taylor (2014) 'A Revolution in the Head: The Other Side of Monty Python', *The Quietus*, 1 July. <http://thequietus.com/articles/15649-monty-python> (last accessed 26 August 2019)

Poe, Edgar Allan (1842) 'The Masque of the Red Death', *Graham's Magazine*.

Pope, Alexander ([1712] 2007) *The Rape of the Lock*. London: Vintage Classics.

Sartre, Jean Paul (1938) *La Nausée*. Paris: Editions Gallimard.

The Secret Life of Brian (2007) Channel Four.

Shakespeare, William ([1623] 2015) *Twelfth Night*, Michael Dobson (ed.). London: Penguin.

Spenser, Edmund ([1590] 2003) *The Faerie Queene*, Thomas P. Roche Jr and C. Patrick O'Donnell Jr (eds). London: Penguin.

Taylor, Joan E. (ed.) (2015) *Jesus and Brian: Exploring the Historical Jesus and His Times via Monty Python's Life of Brian*. London: T&T Clark.

Taylor, Joan E. (2016) 'Lecture on Monty Python's *Life of Brian* and Jesus', University of Auckland, 27 April. <http://livenews.co.nz/2016/04/18/lecture-on-monty-pythons-life-of-brian-and-jesus/> (last accessed 26 August 2019)

3. DER VER ZWEI PEANUTS: DEPICTIONS OF A DISTANT WAR IN *MONTY PYTHON'S FLYING CIRCUS*

Anna Martonfi

INTRODUCTION

In this chapter, I examine the portrayal of the Second World War in *Monty Python's Flying Circus* by contextualising it within post-war sketch comedy programmes characterised by absurd or surreal humour. The key argument of the chapter concerns the Second World War depicted as an event in the past in *Monty Python's Flying Circus*, rather than as a paradigm of a perpetual present as in some sketch comedy shows preceding the Pythons, most notably the radio programme *The Goon Show*. The two programmes arguably share similarities in comedic style: they both operate with a set of unlikely, extraordinary characters; repeatedly place themselves outside the framework of traditional comedy programming by disregarding the structure of jokes and placing numerous highly self-referential elements; and in both shows the comic absurdity is achieved by setting the opening scene in an ordinary situation which, in turn, is transformed into something unexpected and bizarre (Brock 2015: 55; Landy 2005: 34). Yet in their approaches to the Second World War, the two comedy shows arguably differ radically. *The Goon Show*, which ran from 1951 to 1960, was created by comedians who had experienced the war first hand, while *Monty Python's Flying Circus*, which was broadcast between 1969 and 1974, was the collaborative effort of six baby boomers. Apart from the difference in personal experiences, another crucial factor to take into account is the larger connotations and implications of the generational shift between the two shows and their creators, the Pythons belonging to and flourishing in a 1960s and early 1970s 'countercultural moment' (Landy 2005: 15–16). Perhaps consequently, the former show utilises the subject of the Second World War as its constant point of reference, using its tropes even in the episodes explicitly set in different eras; whereas by contextualising its war sketches within contemporary settings, *Monty Python's Flying Circus* reframes the war as an event in the past, not, as in *The Goon Show*, as an event in the present.

In order to successfully interrogate the perception in these two programmes of the Second World War, I rely heavily on looking at the primary texts of the two shows themselves, and the most significant material supporting the above claim are the sketches and episodes themselves related to the war in *Monty Python's Flying Circus* and *The Goon Show*. That said, I imply here that one of the crucial reasons why the war is depicted in different ways in the two shows stems from the creators' personal experiences – namely that the Goons were in active service during the war while the Pythons were not. Therefore, to a certain extent this chapter adopts an auteurist approach, and operates within the framework of performing textual analysis on the war sketches, but with emphasis on contextualising them both within the social, historical and economic circumstances of post-war Britain, and reflecting on some relevant aspects of the creative personnel responsible for the programmes. Thus, the discourses this chapter taps into – and relies on – consist partly of material on world history, British social and cultural history, the specific history of the British Army and that of the Second World War, and partly of autobiographical and biographical works on the creators of the two shows, and – where available – academic literature on the programmes themselves.

The Goon Show

> The Goons of course were my favourite. It was the surreality of the imagery and the speed of the comedy that I loved – the way they broke up the conventions of radio and played with the very nature of the medium. (Chapman *et al.* 2003: 73)

Perhaps no lengthy introductory paragraphs are needed to *Monty Python's Flying Circus* for the benefit of the readers of this volume; I would, however, like to briefly introduce *The Goon Show* before unpacking some of its characteristic aspects below. *The Goon Show* was a radio comedy programme that ran on the BBC Home Service throughout most of the 1950s. Its original cast members were Spike Milligan, Peter Sellers, Harry Secombe and Michael Bentine. After the first two seasons, during which the show was called *Crazy People*, Bentine left the programme and the three remaining actors gradually created the name and format of the show that would become extremely popular especially among ex-servicemen of the Second World War.[1] From the mid-1950s onwards, *The Goon Show* established itself with episodes about the most unlikely plots and plans, with a set of recurring characters of various army ranks, and adventures taking place in or around battlefields.

What *The Goon Show* also achieved during its ten seasons, apart from being a highly popular and 'subversive' programme set in a surreal fantasy world, was revolutionising the use of radio techniques (Wagg 1992: 256). By the beginning of the 1950s, the Drama Department of the BBC had developed the use of realistic sound effects, something that was more or less alien to the comedy programmes of the time, where the sound effects were 'a knock on the door and tramps on gravel' (Wilmut 1978: 47). It was producer Peter Eton, who came to the show with significant drama experience, who opened the way for the Goons' radical use of radio techniques, most significantly the sound effects of explosions, shots, shell whooshes and bombardments. In the same way the Pythons changed television comedy in the late 1960s, so did the Goons with regard to radio comedy – a dying genre – in the 1950s.

In the analysis below, I will look at some of the more iconic war episodes from *The Goon Show*, such as 'The Dreaded Batter Pudding Hurler (of Bexhill-on-Sea)' from the fifth series and 'Tales of Men's Shirts' from the ninth. However, it is by examining some other episodes and sketches that take place in explicitly different settings, either in terms of space or time, or both, that *The Goon Show*'s characteristic take on the Second World War is clarified. The evidence for this argument is twofold: both the sound effects emulating sounds of battles, and the complex relationships between the programme's set of characters, point towards *The Goon Show* using the war as its dominant setting.

'The Dreaded Batter Pudding Hurler (of Bexhill-on-Sea)' is set in 1941 in the small coastal town of Bexhill-on-Sea where, incidentally, Spike Milligan was posted for about eighteen months during the Second World War as a soldier (Milligan 1972: 33). The narrative concerns a mysterious criminal who, using the darkness of the blackout in Bexhill, attacks the elderly gentlefolk of the town with freshly baked batter puddings. It displays the characteristic structure of *The Goon Show* episodes, with the show's varied set of buffoons and idiots taking centre stage. The relations between these characters is far from consistent: those who aid the central goon, Neddie Seagoon (Harry Secombe) in one episode, might want to hamper his efforts in another.

In 'The Dreaded Batter Pudding Hurler', Neddie is called in to investigate the case, and is helped in his endeavours by most of the cast of buffoons and idiots: Henry Crun (Peter Sellers) and Minnie Bannister (Spike Milligan), the original victims of the pudding hurler; Major Bloodnok (Sellers), an army-type buffoon; and finally Eccles (Milligan) and Bluebottle (Sellers), two archetypal goons. Whereas these power games and relations vary from episode to episode, it is usually Grytpype Thynne (Sellers) and Moriarty (Milligan) who are cast as the villains. In 'The Dreaded Batter Pudding Hurler', they are unmasked as the criminal masterminds behind the pudding attacks in circumstances that position the narrative within a highly self-referential framework: after drifting for many weeks on a lifeboat, Neddie and Major Bloodnok find Moriarty in a gas stove in the opposite corner of the boat. Not having eaten for several days, however, they are facing the dreadful dilemma of arresting the criminal genius and go on starving or eating the tempting batter pudding and returning with no evidence on the basis of which they could arrest Moriarty. The episode's conclusion takes the narrative out of its diegetic context:

> **Bill:** We invite listeners to submit what they think should be the classic ending. Should Seagoon eat the Batter Pudding and live or leave it and in the cause of justice – die? Meantime, for those of you cretins who would like a happy ending – here it is.
> **Grams:** Sweet background music, very, very soft
> **Harry:** Darling – darling, will you marry me?
> **Bloodnok:** Of course I will – darling.
> **Bill:** Thank you – good night. (Milligan 1973)

When juxtaposing this *The Goon Show* episode with episode 7 of the first series of *Monty Python's Flying Circus*, revolving around a blancmange invasion of planet Earth, a significant generic shift is apparent. The theme of the two programmes is essentially the same: an attack involving puddings; the generic positioning of the two, however, highlights some of the differences explored further below. Whereas the Goons chose a Second World War setting, the Python team did their version of pudding throwing as a science fiction spoof: the Python pudding story lampoons contemporary science fiction and fantasy programmes, such as *Doctor Who* or *The Twilight Zone*; there are not even subtle references to the Second World War.

When *The Goon Show* episodes are set in different time-frames, as in the case of 'The Phantom Head Shaver', 'The Affair of the Lone Banana', 'Napoleon's Piano' or 'The Mighty Wurlitzer', the characters still move within the same paradigm of the war: Major Bloodnok is a cowardly and greedy army officer, Eccles is still the prototype of the dumb soldier, and Neddie occupies a dubious position of authority. Furthermore, the non-Second World War episodes also operate with army humour and army references, which can take the form of sound effects that imitate gunshots and explosions – these latter occur in the vast majority of *The Goon Show* episodes.

'The Affair of the Lone Banana' starts and ends with huge explosions, since the plot, as in the case of 'Foiled by President Fred', takes place in South America during a revolution. This proves to be fertile ground for including pistol shots, explosions, bombs and other sounds of warfare. In 'Foiled by

President Fred', one of the weapons used is a double-action hydraulic-recoil eighteen-inch Howitzer – the type of weapon used by Milligan during the Second World War (Milligan 1976). 'Napoleon's Piano', just like 'The Affair of the Lone Banana', ends with an enormous explosion – this time on the English Channel. 'The Phantom Head Shaver' includes a military cordon around the town of Brighton and a court scene with battle-like sound effects, besides the usual pistol shots and explosions.

Further exploiting the theme of shells and explosions, most of *The Goon Show* episodes culminate in one of the characters, usually Neddie Seagoon, Eccles, Bluebottle or Bloodnok, having to take considerable risks, such as delivering sticks of TNT or other explosive devices, or dismantling one to hamper Grytpype-Thynne's and Moriarty's plans. The significance of this is firstly that, unlike in the war, within a 1950s British context such sequences of events are highly unlikely, placing *The Goon Show* episodes once again within a surreal context and the paradigm of the Second World War. Secondly, the behaviour of *The Goon Show* characters in these situations, particularly when the events take place outside of a Second World War setting, still operates within army modes and hierarchies.

Apart from the explosions, however, in 'The Phantom Head Shaver', which is said to take place in 1898, there is another significant allusion to the war, as referred to by Neddie Seagoon:

> I have on me several documents of identification – including a letter of personal trust from the Commander of the British Army; a memo of recommendation from Mr Anthony Eden, the Foreign Secretary; a special pass signed by Mr Clement Atlee [sic], the leader of the Opposition; and last but not least, a permit to go where I please, signed by the Prime Minister the Right Honourable Sir Winston Spencer Churchill. (Milligan 1973)

These politicians were at the time of the transmission (October 1954) indeed in the offices attributed to them by Neddie; they were also, however, occupying the same positions in parliament after Churchill became prime minister in May 1940, aside from Attlee being deputy prime minister instead of leader of the Opposition. It is also interesting to note that Neddie not only includes the Commander of the British Army in his list of protectors, but starts with him, emphasising the connotations of the war. Churchill, voiced by Peter Sellers, is evoked in other episodes as well, for instance in 'The Canal' and indeed in 'The Dreaded Batter Pudding Hurler', further contextualising the programme within a Second World War framework.

Another frequently used panel in *The Goon Show* is travelling, more precisely sea travel, something that is featured in 'The Dreaded Batter Pudding Hurler' as well as in 'Tales of Men's Shirts'. In 'The Affair of the Lone Banana' and 'Foiled by President Fred', the two shows that include South American revolutions, there arises naturally the issue of reaching the faraway continent; these episodes thus present opportunities not only for gunshots and explosions, but a chance for a sea voyage. In 'Napoleon's Piano', the narrative concerns a journey through the Channel on top of a piano. Sea voyages serve a double purpose in this context: they highlight the distance between the reality of post-war Britain and a faraway Gooniverse, and create an evocation of the journeys army personnel took in order to serve in the war, by juxtaposing the sea journeys with the sound effects of explosions.

In 'Tales of Men's Shirts' from the tenth series, the Second World War is even more in the forefront than in 'The Dreaded Batter Pudding Hurler (of Bexhill-on-Sea)'. The programme draws on the trope of the Nazi wonder weapon within a familiar *The Goon Show* framework of a surreal plot conceived by Grytpype-Thynne and Moriarty, which needs to be solved by Neddie Seagoon. The setting is, significantly, moved to Nazi Germany from the home front, and the episode features a whole array of Second World War references: army jokes, special effects of explosions, the heavy use of a German accent, military cowardice and sea travel.

The Nazi master weapon in question is a colourless and odourless material that, if applied to a British soldier's shirt-tail, explodes upon sitting down. Following the usual pattern of *The Goon Show* plots, Neddie is sent to Germany to investigate; he travels by sea on Grytpype-Thynne and Moriarty's ship, and finds the two of them to be the criminal masterminds behind the scheme. The structure of the narrative, the relations between the characters, the panels used in the shows or the self-reflexive nature of the humour remain largely unchanged. What is significant in this episode, however, is its position within the timeline of the programme: it was one of the last *The Goon Show* episodes to be transmitted in 1960 in its original run, and was reprised eight years later as a one-off television broadcast, the penultimate performance of *The Goon Show*, with John Cleese taking the position of compere, providing a further link between the two programmes.

Contextualising this episode, both its original broadcast and the television reprise, within British comedy traditions serves to highlight that it was not necessarily simply the passing of time that allowed the Pythons to take a different approach to the war than the Goons did. In 1960, and especially 1968, with a significant shift towards satire, the multitude of Second World War references in 'Tales of Men's Shirts' evoke another set of connotations than they might have in the early or mid-1950s, and certainly other than those of contemporary comedy culture. Notably, 1968 was also the year when, with *Dad's Army*, 'war . . . became a respectable topic for sitcoms' (Lenz 2015: 37). The emphasis on *became* signals a change not only within the context of sketch comedy programmes, but also within the wider framework of British comedy traditions.

These eight years saw the emergence of another generation of comedians spearheading the satire boom, like Peter Cook, Dudley Moore, Jonathan Miller and Alan Bennett of *Beyond the Fringe* fame; and David Frost, for whom all British Pythons worked at some point in their pre-Python careers (Chapman et al. 2003: 155–6). It also saw the 'Swinging London' phenomenon gain popularity (Landy 2005: 18), epitomised by the Beatles, whose fame, accents and their disruption of existing social and cultural structures, as well as some stylistic and thematic choices in their films, were precursors to much of Python itself. The Beatles can also be seen to function as a link between the Goons and the Pythons, between one generation of comedians and the next. Not only did both the members of the Beatles and of the Oxbridge Mafia listen to *The Goon Show* (Wilmut 1982: xvii), but there are also tangible links in the form of friendships and professional relationships forged in comedy. The Beatles' acceptance of a collaboration first with George Martin, their producer, and then with Richard Lester, director of two of their feature films, hinged on the two men having previously worked with the Goons, Martin producing their comedy record output and Lester directing the Goons' short film, *The Running Jumping and Standing Still Film*, as well as episodes of *A Show Called Fred*, a televisual incarnation of *The Goon Show* (Rawlings 2017: 183). Then, continuing the cycle, in 1979 it was George Harrison who, after EMI pulled out, put up the money for the Pythons' *Life of Brian* (Chapman et al. 2003: 366–7). While emphasising the influence of the Goons on the coming generation of comedians, Roger Wilmut also speaks of a 'real watershed' that came as *The Goon Show* was airing its last episodes in 1960, and *Beyond the Fringe* first appeared at the Edinburgh Festival the same year (Wilmut 1982: xvii–xviii). One of the key aspects of this watershed could be seen to centre on the representation of the war in the two generations' comedy output.

Python and the War

When looking at two Monty Python sketches that are explicitly set in the Second World War, the 'Lethal Joke' sketch from the first episode of *Monty Python's Flying Circus* and the 'Mr Hilter' sketch from the twelfth, a paradigm shift from the Goons' approach to the war becomes apparent. As seen in the brief juxtaposition of the pudding-attack trope in the two programmes, Python uses contemporary audio-visual, particularly televisual, modes to contextualise its sketches – especially when it comes to reframing historical events (Brock 2015: 54). This is precisely the premise of *The Complete and Utter History of Britain*, the pre-Python programme written by Michael Palin and Terry Jones; and, as seen below, in both of the two Python war sketches the Second World War gets recontextualised this way within contemporary televisual and/or societal modes, shifting the temporal settings for comedic purposes. Landy calls these the 'explosions and physical mutilation that expand in meaning to include dismemberment of cultural forms' (Landy 2005: 44); her choice of words gains extratextual relevance when thinking about the implications of explosions in a Second World War context.

The first case study from *Monty Python's Flying Circus* appears in the very first episode of the series. The episode entitled 'Whither Canada?' uses and lampoons a number of television formats such as quiz shows in the 'Famous Deaths' sketch, television interviews in the 'Sir Edward Ross' sequence, art programmes in the 'Arthur "Two-Sheds" Jackson' and the 'Picasso Cycling Tour' sketches and television documentaries in the 'Lethal Joke' sketch. This context already signals the aforementioned shift, positioning the sketch within a contemporary framework. The plot exploits the Nazi super-weapon theme of 'Tales of Men's Shirts', but turns it around, into a British super-weapon that won us the war: a joke that is so funny, it kills whoever hears it. After a few casualties during the invention and the testing of the joke, it is translated, strictly word by word, to German and is deployed in action, killing masses of German soldiers. The enemy attempts, without success, to invent their own master weapon, and after the war is over the joke is buried forever, never to be told again. The sketch itself could, seemingly, easily be part of a *The Goon Show* plot; there are a few crucial points both in the narrative and more importantly in the format of the sketch that indicate significant differences. On the one hand, the 'Lethal Joke' sketch unambiguously positions the British as victorious; on the other hand, it frames the events as a documentary spoof, referencing them as the past, positioning the war as distant, as something to remember.

By unpacking the sketch, we notice both the several formal and stylistic elements that indicate its generic position as documentary spoof, and also the initial ambiguity of the timelines in the sketch. There is jaunty background music, an omniscient voice-over (Eric Idle) who announces that '[i]n a few moments [Ernest Scribbler] will have written the funniest joke in the world' (Chapman *et al.* 1990: 10), and a contemporary news reporter (Terry Jones), who reports on the events from Ernest Scribbler's front garden. The presence of both the omniscient narrator and the reporter, however, blurs the line between past and present, as the presence of the reporter seems to signal that what we see is happening that very moment, while the voice-over clearly references it as the past. The ambiguity prevails: as the police arrive at the scene and start their investigation, the voice-over stops, and it seems that even if the invention of the lethal joke happened in the past, it must have been the recent past, since no elements in the *mise-en-scène* indicate a temporal shift.

It is not until the voice-over returns that the temporal setting of the sketch is clarified, and is indicated to be the Second World War. The voice-over and the images converge in depicting how the military top brass became interested in the joke and began to utilise it to improve Britain's chance against the Nazis in the war. Gradually the sketch turns into a BBC dramatised documentary-spoof with sequences such as the testing of the joke on Salisbury Plain, the Joke Brigade in action, and a scene in a Nazi interrogation room. All these shots are in colour, indicating that it is the dramatised version of the historical events that we see. There are no attempts to present the events in black-and-white, for instance, which would tap into our sense of realism and create the impression that we see real footage of the war. What further accentuates the documentary form is the character of the Colonel (Graham Chapman), featured in the sketch as a military expert outlining the development of the joke as an efficient weapon in actual battle.

As in *The Goon Show* episodes, the 'Lethal Joke' sketch is also full of explosions; in the case of the Python sketch, however, nobody is hurt, not even symbolically, by the bombs and shells. In the case of the 'Lethal Joke' sketch it is not physical weapons, but humour and intelligence that have a devastating effect on people. This way the Pythons subvert the very essence of the Goons' contextualisation of the war: in *The Goon Show*, even in the sketches that were set in the present the characters fell victims to Second World War weaponry. In contrast, in *Monty Python's Flying Circus* even in the Second World War it was not rifles and grenades that were doing the killing but humour.

Furthermore, in *The Goon Show* the Second World War episodes depict events from an insider perspective with Grytpype and Moriarty being the criminal minds behind even Nazi Germany's hideous acts, while the Pythons shift the focus and report on the killing joke as outsiders. The sketch uses the form of a dramatised historical documentary-spoof, with two-dimensional characters who function merely to illustrate the events; there are no main characters involved, creating a distance that signals that even when somebody dies as a result of hearing the joke, it is inconsequential. In this sketch, just like in the *Goon Show* episodes examined above, the narrative evokes the war on a large scale: the military apparatus is involved, so are the Nazi Germans, Prime Minister Chamberlain, and even Hitler. In the 'Lethal Joke' sketch, however, the lack of main characters and the fact that the sketch serves to outline the events inform its positioning as distant and external.

In the sketch, its creators use the techniques offered by television not only for lampooning television genres but also for creating comedy by visual effects, just as *The Goon Show* used radio techniques to their advantage. The Pythons effectively satirise pre-war politics of appeasement, and by juxtaposing a well-known joke with the well-known and menacing image of Hitler at a Nazi rally, they also subvert his threat for comedic purposes. When the voice-over starts describing the devastating effect of the joke, he says that it was '[o]ver sixty thousand times as powerful as Britain's great pre-war joke'.

At this moment there is a cut to the archive footage of Neville Chamberlain brandishing the 'Peace in our time' piece of paper. The voice-over goes on, 'and one which Hitler just couldn't match'. Cut to archive footage, this time of Hitler, presumably from a propaganda piece, where we see him in a close-up, and the superimposed subtitles read: 'My dog's got no nose.' Cut to a young soldier who replies to Hitler, and the subtitles are: 'How does he smell?' Back to Hitler speaking, the subtitles read: 'Awful' (Chapman *et al*. 1990: 12).

Another element that links the 'Lethal Joke' sketch to *The Goon Show* is the use of a German accent that apparently the Pythons enjoyed just as much as the Goons did. The joke itself, which can be heard throughout the entire sketch only in German – to spare the viewers from an untimely death perhaps – is in fact merely German-sounding gibberish. The scene in the Nazi interrogation room also provides a splendid opportunity to speak English with a German accent.

> *Cut to Nazi interrogation room. An officer from the joke brigade has a light shining in his face. A Gestapo officer is interrogating him; another (clearly labelled 'A Gestapo Officer') stands behind him.*
> **Nazi** (John) Vott is the big joke?
> **Officer** (Michael) I can only give you name, rank, and why did the chicken cross the road?
> **Nazi** That's not funny! *(slaps him)* I vant to know the joke.
> **Officer** All right. How do you make a Nazi cross?
> **Nazi** *(momentarily fooled)* I don't know . . . how do you make a Nazi cross?
> **Officer** Tread on his corns. *(does so; the Nazi hops in pain)*
> **Nazi** Gott in Himmel! That's not funny. (Chapman *et al*. 1990: 13)

After these dramatised scenes – the Gestapo office, the German joke laboratories and their own V-joke 'Der ver zwei peanuts, valking down der strasse, and von vas . . . assaulted! Peanut. Ho-ho-ho-ho' (ibid.: 13) – the camera cuts to a modern BBC2 interview, where the voice-over/reporter (Eric Idle) can be seen in a woodland glade. He closes the sketch with an appropriately solemn and majestic speech about the Second World War and joke warfare that was 'banned at a special session of the Geneva Convention' (ibid.: 13–14). As he walks away an inscription becomes visible: 'To the unknown Joke'. Using Eric Idle's character as the omniscient voice-over/reporter, the sketch effectively frames joke warfare, and the wider context of the war, as an event in the past, playing with televisual modes to emphasise the distance between the then and the now, positioning the war as something to remember. As Landy suggests, the use of the German accent itself, and I would argue the success of the British joke as opposed to the failure of the German one, taps into tropes and 'myths about the superiority and culturally sustaining nature of British humor' as well (Landy 2005: 81).

The other Second World War sketch unpacked in this chapter is the 'Mr Hilter/Minehead By-election' sketch in episode 12, framed by another television genre spoof, a fast-paced report programme on current affairs entitled *Spectrum*, which returns to the screen right after the 'Minehead by-election' sequence finishes. The sketch itself begins with an ordinary British couple, Mr and Mrs Johnson (Eric Idle, Maureen Flanagan), arriving at a boarding house in Minehead, Somerset. The Johnsons discuss their journey at length with the landlady (Terry Jones), who then turns to introduce them to the residents of the boarding house. Among them are Adolf Hitler (John Cleese), Heinrich Himmler (Michael Palin) and Joachim Von Ribbentrop (Graham Chapman), who are poring over a map, allegedly planning a hike to Bideford. Hitler, wearing full Nazi uniform, is introduced to the Johnsons as Mr Hilter, Himmler is in evening dress with an Iron Cross on, presented as Mr Bimmler, and Von Ribbentrop is in uniform as well, introduced by the landlady as Ron Vibbentrop. The Nazi leaders even receive a phone call from a 'Mr McGoering', after which the landlady tells the Johnsons about Mr Hilter's plans to stand as National Bocialist candidate at the North Minehead by-elections.

Alexander Brock evokes the incongruity theory of humour in connection with *Monty Python's Flying Circus*, contextualising the programme as a series of 'potential point[s] of attack for incongruities' (Brock 2015: 55). This seems particularly apt when interrogating the 'Mr Hilter' sketch, especially when placing it within the context of the Second World War. The core of the sketch is that the Pythons took Hitler just as he was: his looks (although taller, Cleese gave quite an impressive impersonation of Hitler), his accessories, uniform, anger, the scene of yelling from balconies, Italian mates, cheering and Sieg Heils – though only from a gramophone – and his companions, Von Ribbentrop and Himmler, and transferred him to Britain, late 1960s. They seem not to change a thing: Hitler's beliefs, methods and aims are the same in the sketch as what one knows from history books. He still is a National Socialist preaching loudly to the masses, promising them things that 'historically belong to them' (Chapman *et al.* 1990: 153) and he still wishes to invade Poland.

> **Landlady:** Oh it's the North Minehead by-election. Mr Hilter's standing as a National Bocialist candidate. He's got wonderful plans for Minehead.
> **Johnson:** Like what?
> **Landlady:** Well for a start he wants to annex Poland.
> [. . .]
> **Hitler:** I am not a racialist, but, and this is a big but, we in the National Bocialist Party believe das Überleben muss gestammen sein mit der schneaky Armstrong-Jones. Historische Taunton ist Volkermeining von Minehead.
> **Himmler:** Mr Hitler, *Hilter*, he says that historically Taunton is part of Minehead already. (Ibid.: 152–3)

The Pythons effectively use the clash of these notions: Hitler and his world taken without changes from 1930s–1940s Nazi Germany and mixed into British small-town consumer society of the late 1960s, a milieu characterised by a 'presumption of affluence' (Landy 2005: 16), for comedic purposes. This way Python, once more, does the opposite of what the Goons did in *The Goon Show*: instead of extending the paradigm of the Second World War to the whole world and every time-frame, they take a slice of the Second World War and extinguish its sharpness in the mild milieu of post-war, post-austerity Britain. The Nazi ideals that were quite popular and at one point dangerously accepted in British politics seem ridiculous in the little Somerset boarding house.

The sketch also offers the Pythons an excellent opportunity to use the incongruous juxtaposition of the two worlds for comedic purposes, and play with the bad English and the German accent of the war criminals.

> **Landlady**: Ooh planning a little excursion are we Mr Hilter?
> **Hitler**: Ja! Ja! We make a little . . . *(to others)* Was ist rückweise bewegen?
> **Von Ribbentrop** *(Graham)*: Hike.
> [. . .]
> **Landlady**: Oh I'm sorry I didn't introduce you this is Ron . . . Ron Vibbentrop.
> **Johnson**: Oh not Von Ribbentrop, eh? Ha, ha, ha.
> **Von Ribbentrop** *(leaping two feet in fear, then realizing)*: Nein! Nein! Nein!! Oh!! Ha, ha, ha. No different other chap. No I in Somerset am being born Von Ribbentrop is born in Gotterammstrasse 46, Düsseldorf, West Eight. So they say! (Chapman *et al.* 1990: 151)

In *The Goon Show*, explosions, shell whooshes and violent deaths were abundant even in peacetime, and even when there were no Nazis around characters spoke with German accents and Howitzer guns were used; in contrast, the Python sketches on the Second World War seem to lose their violent nature because the war-mongers are forced into suburbia. Not even Hitler himself and his most faithful Nazi comrades can do harm to suburban Britons, let alone Grytpype or Moriarty.

That said, the Nazi leaders' attempts to conceal their identity are only for show as they are as aggressive in their ambitions as ever; they, however, meet either complete ignorance or slight repulsion from the British. The landlady of the boarding house treats Hitler and his companions as she treats every other guest, relating to their ambitions as though they were practising an eccentric hobby. The first yokel and few children who are the only people present, apart from Himmler and Von Ribbentrop, when Hitler makes a speech from the balcony are left blank after the rant, showing only signs of slight disbelief. Even when the sketch turns into a vox pops-type sequence of interviews, aiming to assess precisely the response to Hitler and his National

Bocialist Party, the reaction of the British to the Nazi threat is lukewarm and largely indifferent.

> **Yokel [#2]:** I don't like the sound of these 'ere boncentration bamps.
> **Pepperpot:** Well I gave him my baby to kiss and he bit it on the head.
> **Stockbroker:** Well I think he'd do a lot of good for the Stock Exchange.
> (Chapman *et al.* 1990: 153)

The fact that the 'Mr Hilter/Minehead By-election' sketch does not aim specifically at using the trope of the war or the Nazis as a source of comedy, but rather the comedic clash of the two worlds, seems to suggest that the present and contemporary connotations inform heavily the Pythons' treatment of Second World War subjects. The sketch is as much a critique of British societal norms of the late 1960s as of the figures of Nazi German leaders. Furthermore, while the latter are definitely ridiculed in the sketch, the former are heavily satirised for their ignorance and complacency: even if they register that something is amiss with the strange men from the boarding house, they simply fail to care. Unless there is direct involvement, as in the case of the stockbroker who embraces the Nazi agenda because he believes it to be beneficial for the stock exchange, the characters remain largely indifferent to Hitler's threat – which, again, works to discredit his political ambitions and notions.

Apart from looking at specific sketches in *Monty Python's Flying Circus* that relate directly to the war, I'd also like to note one of the few recurring characters of the show: the aforementioned Colonel, who appears for the first time briefly in the 'Lethal Joke' sketch, and then returns in the eighth episode to provide a running gag, continuously disrupting the diegetic framework of the programme. This eighth episode, entitled 'Full Frontal Nudity', includes one of the most iconic Python sketches, the 'Parrot Sketch', and serves to position the character of the Colonel as an ultimate authority figure, exerting his influence on the programming structure of the entire show. The Colonel is emphatically 'old school', a representative of the other side of the counterculture movements and 'generational tensions' (Landy 2005: 15); crucially, he has no sense of humour and claims 'most people like a good laugh more than [he does]' (Chapman *et al.* 1990: 102). On several occasions, for instance in the famous 'Parrot Sketch', when he deems a sequence to be silly he simply stops it by breaking the fourth wall and giving instructions to the crew on how to proceed with the programming. This informs, on the one hand, the self-reflexive nature of the show: instead of remaining within the framework of a sketch comedy programme with fictitious sketches, it highlights production and programming practices, normally not at our disposal, and taps into our sense of realism. If the sketches we see are fictitious, as it is explicitly stated by him, then surely the Colonel and his complaints must be genuine. On the other hand, his interruptions disrupt the structure of comic sketches as we know them, as the Colonel stops them allegedly before the punchline; therefore, the source of comedy becomes twofold: it is no longer the particular joke or punchline we are meant to laugh at, but instead at the shift from diegetic to supposedly non-diegetic content, as well as at his actual dialogue, and, crucially, at the characteristic traits of the Colonel himself – his squareness, humourlessness and rigidity, which serve to mark him as generationally other.

When comparing the Colonel to the military personnel and authority figures in *The Goon Show*, his traits gain significance in highlighting the different approaches to the war, and particularly the military apparatus in the two programmes, as well as the generational differences and the connotations of these. In *The Goon Show*, those related to the armed forces, namely Major Bloodnok, in most episodes Neddie and Eccles, or even Bluebottle, are depicted as irrational, usually cowardly, surreal and often unbearably unintelligent, though generally likeable characters. As opposed to this, the Pythons' Colonel is a painfully dull character from an older generation, whose only function is to keep law and order, everything proper and straight. In his other sketches, such as the 'It's a Man's Life in the Army' (episode 4), in which he protests against the usage of the army's slogan in the programme for other purposes, or the brief 'Mary Recruiting Office sketch' (episode 30), where it is the anagram of the word 'army' that is posted outside the office and he has to send a number of nuns away, the Colonel remains a solid, strict and tedious figure of authority, a protector of morals and values.

Conclusion

Having unpacked some war sketches in both *Monty Python's Flying Circus* and *The Goon Show*, the two programmes arguably have different takes on the Second World War, and on military authority in general. It is not only that the frequent explosions, sea voyages, plotting and cowardice of the characters suggest that the Second World War is the temporal setting and general framework in which *The Goon Show* operates, but also that the Goons' assessment of the war involves a much more personal dimension than the Pythons'. Operating with recurring characters who often die in each show but then are resurrected in the next, within familiar settings such as Bexhill, and using familiar weaponry, *The Goon Show* uses tropes of the war to process its trauma, and arguably extend its paradigm to the whole series. As opposed to the Goons' intimate relationship to the war, the Pythons use various means to negotiate it as something external that belongs to the realm of memory and to another generation. Emphasising contemporary settings, frameworks and self-referential, televisual contexts, as well as nominating a character like the Colonel as representative of the war and of the military, the Pythons effectively reframe the Second World War as a distant event, belonging to another generation.

Note

1. A chronology of *The Goon Show* is accessible here: <http://www.thegoonshow.net/history.asp>

Works Cited

Brock, Alexander (2015) '"The Struggle of Class against Class Is a What Struggle?" Monty Python's Flying Circus and Its Politics', in Juergen Kamm and Brigit Neumann (eds), *British TV Comedies: Cultural Concepts, Contexts and Controversies*. London: Palgrave Macmillan, pp. 51–65.

Chapman, Graham, *et al.* (1990) *Monty Python's Flying Circus: Just the Words*, vols 1–2. London: Methuen/Mandarin.

Chapman, Graham, *et al.* (2003) *The Pythons Autobiography by the Pythons*. London: Orion.

Landy, Marcia (2005) *Monty Python's Flying Circus*. Detroit, MI: Wayne State University Press.

Lenz, Bernard (2015) '"Your Little Game": Myth and War in *Dad's Army*', in Juergen Kamm and Brigit Neumann (eds), *British TV Comedies: Cultural Concepts, Contexts and Controversies*. London: Palgrave Macmillan, pp. 36–50.

Milligan, Spike (1972) *Adolf Hitler: My Part in His Downfall*. Harmondsworth: Penguin.

Milligan, Spike (1973) *The Goon Show Scripts*. London: Sphere Books [edition without page numbers].

Milligan, Spike (1976) *'Rommel?' 'Gunner Who?'*. Harmondsworth: Penguin.

Rawlings, Roger (2017) *Ripping England! Postwar British Satire from Ealing to the Goons*. Albany, NY: State University of New York.

Wagg, Stephen (1992) 'You've Never Had It So Silly: The Politics of British Satirical Comedy from "Beyond the Fringe" to "Spitting Image"', in Dominic Strinati and Stephen Wagg (eds), *Come on Down? Popular Media Culture in Post-War Britain*, London and New York: Routledge, pp. 254–84.

Wilmut, Roger and Jimmy Grafton (1978) *The Goon Show Companion*. London: Sphere Books.

Wilmut, Roger (1982) *From Fringe to Flying Circus: Celebrating a Unique Generation of Comedy 1960–1980*. London: Methuen.

PART TWO

PYTHON'S PRACTICES, FORMS AND MEDIUMS

4. THE ROYAL PHILHARMONIC GOES TO THE BATHROOM: THE MUSIC OF MONTY PYTHON

James Leggott

In 2005, a CD was released entitled *De Wolfe Music Presents: Monty Python's Flying Circus*, its front cover advertising '30 musical masterpieces' from the 'infamous television programme 1969–1974'. The casual or unwary comedy fan may well have been disappointed to discover that, rather than containing songs and ditties such as the 'The Lumberjack Song', 'Spam' or 'Dennis Moore', the album merely featured full-length versions of the incidental music heard occasionally, albeit often effectively, on the TV series. Although the release of the De Wolfe compilation, drawing from the holdings of one of the earliest and most significant 'libraries' of tracks for film and television production, is just one demonstration of the increasing collector and scholarly interest in historical stock music, it surely also confirms the strong association in the popular imagination between Python and music.

The 'musicality' of Python can be evidenced in various ways: the reach and popularity of songs such as 'Always Look on the Bright Side of Life', the production of a song book and musical compilation albums (*Monty Python Sings*, first released in 1989 and later expanded), the liberal sprinkling of songs across the albums and live shows, and the widespread connotations today of a Sousa march with absurdist imagery and flatulence rather than the Liberty Bell of its actual title. But beyond that, as an act with an irreverent, countercultural reputation, Python has also been received and interpreted in ways analogous with contemporaneous music and musicians. In addition to the *Sgt. Pepper*-evoking name, the reception as a cult act (particularly in the United States following the enthusiasm of radio DJs) and the patronage by pop musicians (not least George Harrison, and the Beatles by extension), Python also offers a narrative of artistic tension, break-up and reformation familiar to many rock bands. Furthermore, the team's cult status, particularly in the United States, came in part via the promotion of their albums via FM radio, hence the importance, for some fans, of Python's sonic qualities – including musical numbers – above their visual signatures.

It is unsurprising, then, that Python music has been the arena for (sometimes heated) debate about the group's creativity and legacy. A review of the De Wolfe incidental music collection on the left-field music and pop culture website *The Quietus*, for example, registered how the odd collision between signifiers of stiff Britishness (such as militaristic or regal, Elgar-type compositions) and of flamboyant international exotica alerted the listener to the 'inherent contrast in the Pythons' cultural landmarks' (Ross 2009), as well as capturing something of the mood of early 1970s Britain: the reviewer concludes that 'those behind the *Flying Circus* soundtrack were possessed of highly developed musical minds' (ibid.). In other words, this unofficially curated assortment of musical items, mostly heard only fleetingly in the television show, where they would have been chosen for a range of reasons and some (in all likelihood) purely for their availability, nevertheless offers another legitimate tool for the analysis of an already well-excavated cultural phenomenon. Another article in *The Quietus*, this time by Taylor Parkes, used the occasion of the 2014 'reunion' performances to critique what he considered popular misperception of Python as providers of mere 'silliness', and the role played by music in this process. The culprit, he argued, echoing grumbles heard elsewhere among fans, was Eric Idle – generally considered the 'musical' Python (Wright 2017: 20) and described by Terry Jones as the 'musical authority' of the group (Morgan 1999: 72) – and his 'silent takeover of Python' since the success of his *Spamalot* musical (which opened in 2005), which had 'set the tone ... in terms of diluting the comedy with musical interludes and choreography' (Parkes 2014). In a similar vein to other 'jukebox' musicals of recent years repurposing and narrativising pop material associated with a particular artist or time period, *Spamalot* weaves disparate Python songs and ditties (some barely sketches in their original form) from the TV show, films and albums into an expanded adaptation of *The Holy Grail* (1975). This move was anticipated by the *Eric Idle Sings Monty Python* live recording of 1999, which begins with the conceit that 'Monty Python' is one of the great unrecognised composers, existing in an alternative universe where its version of 'Anything Goes' is preferred to that of Cole Porter; this is a reminder of episode 42, 'The Light Entertainment War', where Porter's ode to licentious behaviour is supplanted by a literal, corporeal alternative: 'Anything goes in/Anything goes out/ Mutton, beef and trout', etc. A similar approach would be taken in the fan-serving *Monty Python Live (Mostly)* reunion shows of 2014, to all intents and purposes a 'greatest hits' compilation reflecting and reinforcing the canonisation of particular sketches and songs. As evidenced by the two overtures to each act introducing key musical motifs, the choreographed musical numbers in the show are not merely functional (i.e. covering scene changes or compensating for the performers' physical shortcomings), but often provide bridging strategies between sections, sometimes combining elements in new ways: for example, the 'Nudge Nudge' and 'Blackmail' sketches are divided by a 'rap' song incorporating elements of both.

One might argue that the use of music in *Spamalot* or the *Live (Mostly)* shows for purposes of structural coherence and audience gratification/nostalgia is alien to the spirit of the original *Flying Circus* (*MPFC*) programme, where music and songs are arrayed disruptively, flippantly and abrasively as part of a critique of television formats and clichés. According to this train of thought, the official Python 'sheet music book', *The Fairly Incomplete and Rather Badly Illustrated Monty Python Song Book* (1994), is closer to the 'authentic' Python attitude, in at times offering impediments to actually being functional for the musician/performer: for example, the melody of 'I'm So Worried' is given in an appropriately 'shaky' font, 'Never Be Rude to an Arab' ends with a visual equivalent of a bomb explosion, 'Eric the Half a Bee' is (oddly) given in spherical form and the 'Summarising Proust' song is mostly illegible.

It is not the intention of this chapter to arbitrate between the differing assessments of the role of music in either enriching or 'diluting' an enjoyment of Python comedy, but to consider some of the occasions and means by which Python conveys an attitude towards music – by which I mean musicians and performers, as well as live and recorded music and song.

Approaching Python Music

Before doing so, however, it is necessary to acknowledge the scale and complexity of the task of mining Python music for meaning and coherence. Moreover, as many of my forthcoming examples will suggest, Python's defamiliarising approach to music is in many respects equivalent to and demonstrative of their broader comedic strategies, chiefly the 'dismemberment of cultural forms' (Landy 2005: 45), the 'inversion of conventional social images' (ibid.: 37) and the confusion of generic codes. With respect to the Python attitude to music, it is common to observe the blurring of 'high and low': that is, the collapsing together of the classical/elitist/intellectual and the popular/quotidian/demotic. As Marcia Landy summarises, 'sketches drew heavily on canonical works of drama, literature and film [to which we might add music and composers] . . . but emptied them of their revered mode of presentation and interpretation, often turning them into nonsense' (ibid.: 83). Hence, classical composers and music are reimagined in humdrum contexts (Mozart presenting a tawdry TV show, for example), while politicians and philosophers concern themselves with the Eurovision Song Contest, and a disease can be turned into a musical. Another rather self-evident observation is that, for the Pythons, music is but one tool for deconstruction of the medium of television and the 'rules' of light entertainment. In his diary, Michael Palin cites the decision to include 'two city gents dancing to balalaika music' in the background of the 'cheese shop' sketch (episode 33, 'Salad Days') of the third series as evidence of the evolution of the team's style of humour away from the 'revue' or satirical origins of their previous work (on the *Frost Report* [1966–7] and such), towards the 'illogical and confusing' (Palin 2006: 77). There is certainly incongruity to the prospect of a cheese emporium 'licensed for public dancing' (as a flash-picture of the exterior informs us before the television sketch starts), and the incessant live bouzouki accompaniment may well be a means to complicate the *mise-en-scène* of what Palin himself describes as a potentially formulaic 'parrot shop type of sketch', with John Cleese reprising the role of an increasingly frustrated customer. Although the sketch, here and in its various iterations (recorded album and live versions) reaches its end via Cleese casually shooting the shopkeeper, his mania reaches its peak about a minute earlier with his instruction of the musician to 'shut up'; this moment is particularly dramatic in the *Secret Policeman's Ball* (1979) rendition, where Cleese – who frequently comes near to 'breaking' character in the sketch – takes particular relish (as does the audience) in his banishment of the (non-Python) dancers and musician off stage. In some ways, then, the sketch works as a loose metaphor for Python's attitude to music in its evocation of a three-way antagonism between shopkeeper, customer and musical source; there is also a parallel with the shooting (rather gorily in the *Live [Mostly]* version) of Terry Gilliam as he sings his unsophisticated 'I've Got Two Legs' ditty.

As might be expected, as well as having characters bursting randomly into song, or sketches disrupted by singers, *MPFC* often plays with the conventions of non-diegetic music. In episode 7, 'You're No Fun Anymore', an alarmed character is reassured that 'it's only the incidental music'. There's a meta-textual spin on this joke in episode 9, 'The Ant, an Introduction', when an unwanted house-guest interrupts a courting couple and demands to change the romantic music (which the viewer may have assumed to have been non-diegetic) on the record-player to something far more strident: the fact that he aggressively replaces a record identified by Larsen (2008: 124) as Dudley Moore's group playing 'I Love You Samantha' with Sousa's 'Washington Post' invites explanation as an 'in-joke' expression of Python's own confidence in its assault on the contemporary comedic landscape. Another variant on this gag drives the 'Psychiatrist' sketch (episode 13, 'Intermission'), where Notlob suffers from grim 'auditory hallucinations' of 'folk' songs and inoffensive pop numbers such as Peter, Paul and Mary's 'We're All Going to the Zoo Tomorrow'. The surgeon given the task of operating upon Notlob conveys his authority mid-speech by playing a record of the *Dr. Kildare* (1961–6) theme tune. As with the offhand allusion (episode 35, 'The Nude Organist') to Shirley Bassey presenting 'mortuary programmes', the jokes here hinge to some extent upon a recognition of the potency and potential misapplications of outwardly 'easy' listening. There is similar formal playfulness in *The Holy Grail* and *The Life of Brian* (1979). The former incorporates a brief interrupting spoof of the musical *Camelot* (first seen on Broadway in 1960, released as a film in 1967), while the latter opens and closes with generically 'inappropriate' songs for a biblical-type epic: a grandiose, James Bond theme-style song (delivered in the fashion of Shirley Bassey) celebrating the mundane childhood and adolescence of the mistaken messiah ('his face became spotty'), and then 'Always Look on the Bright Side of Life', a cheery ode to stoicism, whose lead singer (Idle) makes direct comments to the audience as the final credits appear.

Interestingly, *MPFC* distinguished itself from its immediate comedic predecessors (and also successors) by only rarely incorporating a bounded, sustained 'musical number' of the kind regularly found, for example, in the recognised Python precursors *I'm Sorry I'll Read That Again* (1964–73) and *Do Not Adjust Your Set* (1967–9), or in the later Eric Idle/Neil Innes collaboration *Rutland Weekend Television* (1975–6). Instead, and presumably against the prevailing expectations of the time, performed songs tend to appear only briefly and incongruously; consider, for instance, the singing policeman (episode 3, 'How to Recognise Different Types of Trees from Quite a Long Way Away'), Eric Idle casually strumming snatches from Parry's 'Jerusalem' (episode 4, 'Owl Stretching Time'; the song also appears elsewhere), the 'theme tune' of Lemming of the BDA (episode 4, 'Owl Stretching Time'), the 'Spam Song' (episode 25, 'Spam'), the Spaniards singing about llamas (episode 9, 'The Ant, an Introduction'), the archaeologist Sir Robert Eversley singing 'Today I hear the robin sing' (episode 17, 'The Buzz Aldrin Show') in a 'Western'-style musical as he unearths a 'Sumerian drinking vessel of the fourth dynasty', Sergeant Duckie's Eurovision song (episode 22, 'How to Recognise Different Parts of the Body'), and the presenter of 'The Money Show' (episode 35, 'The Nude Organist') leading a chorus into song, and so forth. The 'Lumberjack Song' (episode 9, 'The Ant, an Introduction'), despite its fame, is a rare exception of a properly constructed number, with a verse/chorus structure and logical progression, if an unexpectedly 'unfinished' conclusion. There is a self-contained logic to the song, with its gradual revelation of the Mountie's cross-dressing proclivity, and the disjuncture between the 'lilting quality of the musical sounds' (Landy 2005: 73), reminiscent of 'mountain musicals' (Larsen 2008: 125), and the lyrics' invocation of complicated masculinity; its 'standalone' quality allowed it to be positioned in later live shows as the conclusion to a range of other sketches.

In interviews, members of the Python team have tended to emphasise their 'tone-deafness', and the pragmatics of incorporating music into the writing or delivery of a sketch that has otherwise 'run its course' (Python cited in the documentary *From Spam to Sperm*, broadcast on BBC1 as part of 'Python Night', 9 October 1999); a typical example can be found in episode 9 ('The Ant, an Introduction'), where the 'barber' sketch segues into the 'Lumberjack Song', whose singers return at the end of the concluding 'Visitors' sketch, now dressed as Welsh miners, singing 'Ding Dong Merrily on High' as a part of a suitably chaotic denouement to a narrative of an increasingly unpleasant house invasion scenario. And indeed, some might argue for a correlation between the increasing reliance on musical elements in later Python projects (particularly *The Meaning of Life* [1983] and the *Contractual Obligation Album* [1980]) and a degree of creative exhaustion.

The songs that are exclusive to the Python albums and live shows (i.e. they do not appear in the television shows or films) almost constitute an alternative canon, at times connecting with their other work, at others seeming disconnected, throwaway and more indicative of the individual personae of the team; the *Contractual Obligation Album* in particular has been received as the equivalent of their *White Album*, in that much of the material – predominantly musical – was conceived and recorded individually. Most album songs are predicated upon a disjunction between their concept, musical backing and vocal delivery, and the distinctly 'non-polished' singing talents of most of the Pythons (Eric Idle being an honourable exception) often adds another layer of incongruity. Thus, 'We Love the Yangtze' imagines Britain's 'top goalies' chanting, in the demotic 'football song' style, about the Yangtze river; 'Medical Love Song' gives a jaunty tune to a list of grim ailments, sung by Graham Chapman in mock-serious fashion; 'Eric the Half a Bee' has a simplistic melody and arrangement that belies its existential conundrums; and the 'Philosophers' Song', building upon the premise of a previous TV sketch, is a rumbustious number about the drinking habits of intellectuals. There are also self-consciously problematic songs: 'Never Be Rude to an Arab' sets offensive racial epithets to a slow lilting waltz; 'Sit on My Face' sails close to the wind by configuring the patriotic Gracie Fields song 'Sing as We Go' as a litany of sexual positions; the banned 'Farewell to John Denver' (removed from some releases) appears to describe the death of the artist; and 'I Bet You They Won't Play This Song on the Radio' is an anodyne-sounding contemporary pop song with self-reflexive references to its own deleted expletives. There are also deliberately 'bad' numbers that challenge the patience of the listener, such as 'Here Comes Another One' and 'I Like Traffic Lights', wherein Terry Jones monotonously plods his way through an a cappella song of childish straightforwardness before apparently losing the will to continue.

In comparison with the 'throwaway' – or indeed 'filler' – ambience of many of these songs, the musical material of *The Meaning of Life* is some of the most deliberate and detailed of the entire Python oeuvre: the sea-shanty of the opening 'Crimson Permanent Assurance' short film anticipates the melody of the 'Galaxy Song', an existential song designed (in the story) to persuade a woman to surrender her liver. 'Every Sperm Is Sacred' – an expansive (and relatively expensive) Lionel Bart-type song-and-dance number that moves seamlessly from music-hall recitative through hymn to musical-theatre chorus – is followed by a pastiche of a school hymn, and finds a correlation in the concluding 'Christmas in Heaven' number, an equivalently 'excessive' performance (including bare-breasted angels and jiving Magi), this time about the afterlife, rather than conception. The 'Penis Song', which imagines Noel Coward incongruously taking delight in school-yard slang for male genitalia, is a highly unusual Python number in being a pastiche of a specific composer/performer.

On a broader level, a handful of individual television episodes use music as a conceptual bedrock. For example, episode 31 ('The All-England Summarise Proust Competition') bears analysis as a contrapuntally designed consideration of music 'out of place', with – to pursue the musical analogy – interlocking motifs relating to the unexpected endeavours of choral groups (summarising Proust, or climbing mountains), animals revived through the power of classical music, an office-bound performance of Sandy Wilson's *The Devils* (a loaded gag reliant upon audience familiarity both with an English revue/musical composer of rather innocuous reputation, and with Ken Russell's controversial 1971 film of the same name), and characters meta-textually complaining about other characters breaking into song. One might speculate here whether the considerable use made in this particular programme of Fred Tomlinson, the 'in-house' musical arranger, and his group of singers, was the original intention, or simply a pragmatic way to capitalise on his involvement (and cost, one would assume). In a similar way, the later episode 'Light Entertainment War' (episode 42), as its ascribed title suggests, is particularly dense in its bricolage of spoken and sung allusions and library music pertaining both to musical theatre and to patriotic, war-associated orchestral/popular music, all built upon a ground of variations upon the Neil Innes song 'When Does a Dream Begin'. First heard (its chordal progression only identifiable retrospectively) via a texturally accurate pastiche of the *Steptoe and Son* (1962–74) theme music, it is briefly heard in the background of other sketches, before being performed directly by Innes at denouement of the episode in its 'full' iteration, in the style of a 1930s popular song. The use of the song, and its place within the episode, certainly raises a few questions about the convergent points between Python and its associated canon. By the time of this episode, Innes was arguably the 'secret' Python, performing his own numbers in their live shows and contributing the most modish musical pastiches to their albums (such as the glam-rock pop used to illustrate academic discussion in 'Background to History' on *Matching Tie and Handkerchief* [1973]). Although conforming to the Python technique of 'ending with a song', and vaguely chiming with scripted discussions about the importance of sentimentality, the subversive aspect of the 'When Does a Dream Begin' sequence – within the Python body of work so far – is that it is essentially played 'straight'; Innes sings to camera in a piece of black-and-white footage deliberately 'distressed' so as to appear like war-time film footage. Such well-observed pastiche of this level of sophistication and deliberation would be a hallmark of Innes and Idle's *Rutland Weekend Television* but arguably feels out of place thus far in Python material, which in comparison is characterised by a more haphazard and 'amateurish' attitude to music.

Musical Choices and Inscrutability

To a certain degree it is difficult to ascertain which musical decisions in *MPFC* were circumstantial and arbitrary – background music, for example, determined by questions of access and cost – as opposed to strategic; Larsen (2008: 400) notes that many of the requested musical cues on file at the BBC archive were rejected in favour of inexpensive British light music by composers such as Trevor Duncan and Reg Wale, thus providing a practical explanation for the surfeit of a particular type of 'pleasant' middle-brow orchestral music. But what to make, for example, of a brief comment in Michael Palin's published diary, on the occasion of a meeting at the BBC with the director Ian MacNaughton, Terry Gilliam and Terry Jones involving the selection of a brass-band performance of a Sousa march for the programme's theme tune? Palin observes that brass-band music carries both 'patrician' and working-class associations, and that this particular choice is not 'calculated or satirical or "fashionable"' (Palin 2006: 6). A casual remark, perhaps, but one to support a possible thesis about the deliberately opaque deployment of music in Python, and the avoidance of the modish and contemporaneous. Palin's diaries contain various anecdotes about encounters with rock-star fans and would-be collaborators (from George Harrison to Pink Floyd and Led Zeppelin), yet also convey an antipathy to chasing musical fashion; there is mention of the Pythons refusing to appear on the pop show *Top of the Pops* (1964–2006) to support the release of a Harrison-produced version of 'The Lumberjack Song' (Palin 2006: 286), and a withering assessment of a slick *Top of the Pops*-style pop performance by fellow comedians The Goodies in a fundraising live show for Amnesty International (ibid.: 335). Although accounts by the Python team of their creative and production decisions tend, where music is discussed, to focus upon the use of songs, there are sufficient discussions to convey how some choices were not taken lightly. For instance, there is detailed conversation in *Monty Python Speaks* (Morgan 1999: 134–6) covering the problems with the original sound design of *The Holy Grail*, which led to Neil Innes' original score of realistic 'semi-religious chant' – perhaps initially deemed an appropriate sonic correspondence to the film's visual palette – being replaced with 'mock heroic' library music, of the kind often used for tonal short-hand or code confusion in the TV series.

Palin's aforementioned reference to 'fashion', or the avoidance of it, in the context of musical selections, is telling in another way. A rare countercultural evocation in *MPFC* is perhaps the 'Hell's Grannies' sketch (episode 8, 'Full Frontal Nudity'), although its power was mostly circumstantial; according to Larsen (2008: 114), its broadcast the day after the infamous events of the Altamont musical festival apparently caused some anxiety at the BBC. Larsen also identifies a couple of brief but overtly camp appearances by Terry Gilliam (in episodes 9, 'The Ant, an Introduction', and 33, 'Salad Days') in flamboyant clothes (in one case, a cape over pink underwear) as insinuations of the gender-bending attire of glam-rock performers (ibid.: 430). But generally speaking one of the remarkable aspects of Python's entire output is its very limited engagement with the 'progressive' edge of pop/rock music. Nestled among the abundant visual, scripted or aural references to classical music, musical theatre and light entertainment (singers such as Petula Clark, Cliff Richard, Lulu, The Ronnettes, Frankie Laine) are only a handful of nods to the kind of performers or cultural developments with whom Python might be said to share a kinship. Richard Mills has argued that, where countercultural evocations appear in Python, they are most likely in connection with Eric Idle as performer (and likely writer): for instance he plays a hippie emerging from a man's stomach (episode 13, 'Intermission'), and appears briefly as John Lennon (episode 24, 'How Not to Be Seen') talking about 'starting a war for peace'. Mills emphasises such influences upon Idle as the Bonzo Dog Doo-Dah Band, the Beatles and Peter Cook, who all 'exemplify surrealism or Dadaism in a popular or low-cultural framework' (Mills 2014: 127), and hence inspired the Pythons' surrealist address to a broad audience. Aside from the aforementioned 'Background to History' sequence on *Matching Tie and Handkerchief* incorporating brief Neil Innes parodies of faddish music, Eric Idle's 'Rock Notes' news sketch – on the *Contractual Obligation Album* – broadly satirises the absurdity of rock-band names ('Toad the Wet Sprocket', etc.) and their sagas of break-ups and reformations. In its acknowledgement of a rock-literate audience, it is nearer in spirit to Idle's *Rutland Weekend Television*, which in a 1975 episode (episode 4, 'Rutland Weekend Whistle Test') had included a lengthy and closely observed spoof of the BBC's *Old Grey Whistle Test* (1971–88) and its espousing of 'serious' rock performance (and incorporated a mention of Toad the Wet Sprocket); *Rutland Weekend Television* also included cameos from George Harrison, a parody of Ken Russell's *Tommy* (1975), and also famously begat The Rutles, the Beatles parody expanded from a *Rutland Weekend Television* sketch into a dedicated mockumentary (1978), and ultimately a real recording and touring outfit led by Innes.

Even the more youth-oriented developments in pop music of the era, surely ripe for mockery, undergo little observance; exceptions being a parody of the inanities of BBC Radio 1 DJs (episode 35, 'The Nude Organist') and a *Top of the Pops*-style spoof of studio pop performances (episode 24, How Not to Be Seen'), where 'Jackie Charlton and the Tonettes' – actually, a collection of static packing crates connected to microphones – 'perform' Ohio Express's 1968 pop song 'Yummy, Yummy, Yummy'. As satire, this works fairly obviously as critique of formulaic, bubble-gum pop and the clichés – cameras tracking the stage and zooming modishly into lights – of pop television. This antagonism to the blandness of modern pop music (a fairly minor yet emblematic Python strand) arguably reaches its apotheosis in the 'Christmas in Heaven' sequence in *The Meaning of Life*, which begins in the vein of musical theatre before moving towards 'disco' embellishments as comparably 'tasteless' as the song's sentiment, delivery and visualisation. Such moments aside, the general Python disinclination to engage textually with pop/rock culture or with cutting-edge or cult musicians is rather curious, although given that the group were not shy in conveying, for example, their familiarity with avant-garde cinema (through parodies and scripted mentions), it may simply be that here they had no particular interest, knowledge or desire to ingratiate themselves with their youthful audience through vogue-ish citation.

Allusive Density and Inscrutability

Paradoxically, given that some key examples of Python music have had a historical reach to a constituency beyond their audiences and fans, it would seem that Python scholars have been somewhat overwhelmed by its allusive density and inscrutability. Even a rare example of sustained analysis of musical instances by Liz Guiffre and Demetrius Romeo, in a chapter in a collection on music and comedy television, limits its view to the first series, and reaches only a tentative conclusion about how original and library music was used to 'play with audience expectations and ultimately subvert these for comedic effect' (Guiffre and Romeo 2017: 39). While Guiffre and Romeo pay close attention to examples such as the selection of Sousa's 'Liberty Bell' as theme tune, the deconstructive use of Parry's 'Jerusalem' and the importance of the 'Lumberjack Song' as a confident reach to a broad audience base, they steer clear of any speculation upon the satirical or self-referential connotations of references, particularly in relation to the programme's various intimations of the contemporary or near-recent televisual landscape (for example, by way of television theme tunes).

The Python fan or scholar might assume that the various musical allusions and in-jokes of the TV show have already been well excavated. There is certainly useful spadework in Darl Larsen's massive, episode-by-episode encyclopaedia, including cross-referencing between the very vague musical 'suggestions' given in the *Just the Words* transcription books (edited by Roger Wilmut from the 'original scripts and video tapes' [Chapman *et al.* 1990: 'Acknowledgements']), the 'request lists' for musical elements held in the BBC's Written Archives and the extant versions of the programmes in circulation. To take but one example of how Larsen unpicks a dense set of connective tissues, we might note the prominent role of the singer Eartha Kitt in the world of 'The Cycling Tour' (episode 34, 'The Cycling Tour'), as part of a surrealist plot that resists easy paraphrase but seems to involve its hero swivelling between identities as a light entertainment singer (Clodagh Rogers and Eartha Kitt) and various political figures (Trotsky, Edward Heath), while a briefly seen poster for the climactic 'Saturday Night at the Moscow Praesidium' mentions not just Kitt but the spies Burgess and Maclean, and fellow satirists Dudley Moore and Peter Cook. This is merely one example of the show's many conflations of 'light entertainment' and 'serious' political/historical/academic allusions, to which we might add Cardinal Richelieu's impersonation of Petula Clark (episode 13, 'Intermission'), the 'Election Night' candidate whose name includes renditions of songs such as 'Don't Sleep in the Subway' (episode 19, 'It's a Living'), 'The Ronettes' (not the real ones) singing a ditty about King George III (episode 40, 'The Golden Age of Ballooning') and so forth. In relation to 'The Cycling Tour', Larsen observes that Eartha Kitt was not only known at the time for being politically engaged (via public anti-war statements), but had appeared recently in the British comedy *Up the Chastity Belt* (1971), directed by the writer/producer/satirist Ned Sherrin, very much part of the Python 'orbit' of television and arts personalities. But the question remains as to the impact of such contextualisation – i.e. Kitt as potentially a strategically chosen figure, rather than merely a whimsical allusion – upon our reading of the show.

In other words, while the analysis of the use of music in Python may bring enlightenment, it is also yet another rabbit-hole for the unwary fan/scholar. Furthermore, pursuing some of the connecting webs draws attention to the lack of a definitive Python resource, as well as the instability of the TV show as trustworthy archive. The *Just the Words* script-books tend to offer only vague descriptions of background music ('stirring military music' [Chapman *et al.* 1990: 8] and so on), but Larsen and others have noted occasional contradictions between the script-books, the scripts held by the BBC's Written Archive Centre and the copies of the show in circulation, which themselves were subject to edits and censorship, sometimes in relation to musical elements; the fan/scholar has recourse to the wisdom accrued on websites such as the (now defunct) *Some of the Corpses Are Amusing*, which carries information and speculation on excised material (such as the removal of legally challenged pieces of music).

It's Wolfgang Amadeus Mozart

Having introduced some of the general functions of music in Monty Python and noted the significance of 'light entertainment' allusions, I want to turn to a specific case study of the Python musical attitude: their handling of classical music, that is, 'serious' music in the concert tradition. Again, as with the Pythons' disinclination to acknowledge 'progressive' rock music, there is barely any mention (to my knowledge) of twentieth-century or 'avant-garde' classical composers in the vein of Britten, Schoenberg or Stockhausen; we get no suggestion of what Arthur 'Two Sheds' Jackson's work might sound like, although Arthur Ewing's 'musical mice' act is vaguely reminiscent of the 'prepared piano' experimentations by the likes of John Cage. Notably, the programme's very first episode ('Whither Canada?') begins with such a reference, in the form of the 'It's Wolfgang Amadeus Mozart' show, in which the composer (John Cleese) incongruously introduces a studio competition for 'famous deaths'. This is but the first of a thread of recurring sketches or incidental references across the series that involve 'high art' in collision with the populist, the sensational, the domestic or the banal. Other examples include: the interview wherein the contemporary composer Arthur 'Two Sheds' Jackson is humiliated through repeated mention of his hobby and his sportsman-like moniker; the repeated motif of a naked Terry Jones playing an organ; the self-explanatory and scatological 'The Royal Philharmonic Orchestra Goes to the Bathroom' sketch; the exploding Blue Danube; Ludwig van Beethoven struggling to complete his Fifth Symphony due to domestic interruptions and a visit from the rat-catcher Colin Mozart (son of Wolfgang); Mrs Little and her son Mervyn trying and failing to keep their hamster alive by playing Mozart concertos to it ('There's nothing we could do, Mervyn. If we'd have had the whole Philharmonic Orchestra in there, he'd still have gone'). The 'It's the Arts' sketch (episode 6, 'It's the Arts') about an unremembered Baroque composer with a ridiculously long name conforms to Landy's (2005: 83) observation of serious art and artistry degenerated to 'nonsense'. Aside from the vague idea that Baroque music is exemplified by its florid and sometimes formalistic properties, and perhaps its demands for listener patience, the sketch does not particularly demand a familiarity with the periodisation of European classical music; rather, it pokes fun at the idea of a 'great name' being anything but, and is prefaced by deliberately 'schoolboy' humour, in the form of the presenter's Freudian slip when listing important composers: 'Beethoven, Mozart, Chopin, Brahms, Panties – I'm sorry'. The Pythons' iconoclastic position in relation to 'great names' is illustrated most boldly via the sleeve of *Another Monty Python Record* (1971), which purports to be a vandalised cover of a legitimate recording of Beethoven's Second Symphony. The album itself, however, purports at times to be, as the result of a production error, a collection of Norwegian folk songs. Python has fun elsewhere with folk traditions (the 'fish slapping dance', for instance), but the conflation of traditional indigenous musical culture and the 'art' tradition here seems to point to their comparable 'humourlessness', at least in their presentation and categorisation.

Placing these sketches and conceits together, one notes a persistent emphasis upon the vulnerable or endangered body of the performer, composer or audience – and in the case of Mr Ewing's sadistic 'mouse organ' act (a pun on 'mouth organ'), the instrument itself: the mice struck by his mallet so as to replicate 'The Bells of St Mary' (episode 2, 'Sex and Violence'). These violent evocations are commensurate with the general Python preoccupation with the 'dead or dying body' (Landy 2005: 67); a process that culminates in the 'Decomposing Composers' song (on the *Contractual Obligation Album*) describing the bodily decay of various composers (and is of course visually formalised in the famous title sequence ending of a massive slamming foot coinciding with an unexpected 'raspberry' instead of the final note of Sousa's 'Liberty Bell' melody). These, and other instances, are but one element of Python's recurrent juxtaposition of the 'high' – the rarefied and the intellectual – with the 'low' – the everyday and the corporeal – seen elsewhere via equivalent allusions to art, literature, philosophy, art cinema and so forth. One might be given pause, however, by the 'Farming Club' special on the life of Tchaikovsky (episode 28, 'Mr. and Mrs. Brian Morris' Ford Popular'), an archetypal 'genre-mixing' sketch predicated upon the composer's homosexuality and involving 'experts' using Polari-style descriptions of his work ('sammy super symphonies', etc.), before showing a (pretend) Sviatoslav Richter playing a piano concerto while escaping from a 'sack'. Perhaps problematic within a contemporary context, a sympathetic reading of the sketch might see its target as Ken Russell's sensationalist treatment of the material in *The Music Lovers* (1971), and the BBC's own salaciousness in its reporting of it. It is open to question, then, whether all these classical musical references constitute an ingratiating appeal to an acculturated audience, speak from an anti-intellectual position (as epitomised by the irrationally anti-snob instructor in 'Flying Lessons' [episode 16, 'Déjà Vu'] who considers the word 'aeroplane', nonsensically, to be as pompous as 'I'm off to play the grand piano'), offer a satirical comment on the appropriation of 'canonical cultural texts for mass cultural consumption' (Landy 2005: 83), or are just inscrutably deconstructive or whimsical.

In this regard, the 'Beethoven's Mynah Bird' sketch (episode 21, 'Archaeology Today') makes a fruitful case study, in its complex combination of a rather regressive premise (the universality of the nagging housewife) with the assumption of some knowledge of the composer's life and times (Beethoven's encroaching deafness, and his influence upon Felix Mendelssohn) but also a meta-textual address to audiences familiar with previous British comedy. Firstly, there are distinct echoes, whether intentional or not, of Dudley Moore's 'Ludvig' character from *Not Only But Also* (1964–70) and elsewhere. But secondly, as John Cleese, in the Beethoven role, makes a fumbling attempt at the opening motif of the Fifth Symphony on the piano, he plays a phrase suggestive of Sousa's 'Washington Post'. That same march had been the basis for John Cleese's 'Rhubarb Tart' song, recorded as a single in 1967, following airings on both the *At Last the 1948 Show* (1967) on television and *I'm Sorry I'll Read That Again* on the radio. Given that tune's authorial kinship with Monty Python's own theme tune, it is tempting to read Cleese's artless conflation of Beethoven and Sousa motifs as emblematic of the programme's own confusion of musical registers and codes. The sketch also weaves in passing references to Richard ('Dickie') Wagner and 'Mr and Mrs P. Anka' (presumably the singer Paul Anka), visually named as fellow residents, alongside a possibly random collection of philosophers and journalists; the first allusion has a modicum of rationality given the references elsewhere to a continuum of key Austro-Germanic composers from Mozart (here represented by his son Colin) to Wagner, but the presence of the others defies easy understanding. Not for the first time in Python, a song is used to draw the strands of the sketch into a resolution. Here, Beethoven's creative rescue is signalled by way of a brief excerpt of Jimmy Durante's comedic but incongruously gruff and low-brow 'I'm the Guy Who Found the Lost Chord', first heard in his 1947 film *This Time for Keeps* and later released as a single.

Conclusion

In his book on parody in British film and television, Neil Archer confronts directly the problem of trying to '"explain" something as intractable and frequently abstract as humour, especially in the case of Python's absurdist style' (Archer 2016: 55). At the beginning of his chapter on Python films, Archer admits to his concern about the 'silly' being deemed 'somehow out of analytical bounds' (ibid.), and advocates for 'digging a bit further' in relation to the 'often complex or allusive nature' of Python comedy (ibid.). This has been my goal in this chapter, but I would acknowledge that any single-minded analytical pathway through Python is doomed to find complication and contradiction as much as enlightenment. On the one hand, it is possible to see and hear Python music and musical references as indicative of the team's broader strategies and preoccupations. On the other, Python music raises unique interpretative challenges, in that its most famous examples in the programmes, films and albums have had an afterlife far beyond the expectation of their originators. If 'Always Look on the Bright Side of Life' was quickly taken up, according to the account in *Monty Python Speaks*, by the military – apparently, those aboard the *HMS Sheffield* during the 1983 Falklands conflict sang it when the boat had been struck by an Exocet missile, as did RAF pilots in the Gulf War (Morgan 1999: 195) – does this limit or enhance its subversive take on a certain strand of patriotic, stoical British music often belittled elsewhere? How does this make a fit with 'Sit on My Face', the repeated damage done to 'Jerusalem' or the mockery of national anthems like the Marseillaise, seen performed by a man operating a tape recorder hidden in his nose (episode 9, 'The Ant, an Introduction')? Either way, the complex and persistent recontextualising of Python music – songs and motifs transferred from one medium to another, placed in different narrative positions, or woven into new shapes and forms – poses questions about the stability and parameters of the canon: for instance, pre- and post-Python musical endeavours have been included in retrospectives and compilations, and Neil Innes (for a while) performed his own material when touring with the group. And a final contradiction stems from the proof, upon closer inspection of Python texts and author reflections, that the team were simultaneously flippant, particular, deliberate and obfuscating in their choice of musical subjects and referents. To paraphrase the title of their first musical compilation album, Monty Python *sings*, but it also listens carefully, and demands its audience and scholars do the same.

WORKS CITED

Archer, Neil (2016) *Beyond a Joke*. London: I. B. Tauris.
Chapman, Graham, *et al.* (1990) *Monty Python's Flying Circus: Just the Words*, vols 1–2. London: Methuen.
Chapman, Graham, *et al.* (1994) *The Fairly Incomplete and Rather Badly Illustrated Monty Python Song Book*. London: Methuen.
Guiffre, Liz and Demetrius Romeo (2017) 'And Now for Something Completely Different (Sounding): Monty Python's Musical Circus', in Liz Guiffre and Philip Hayward (eds), *Music in Comedy Television: Note on Laughs*. Abingdon and New York: Routledge, pp. 31–42.
Landy, Marcia (2005) *Monty Python's Flying Circus*. Detroit, MI: Wayne State University Press.
Larsen, Darl (2008) *Monty Python's Flying Circus: An Utterly Complete, Thoroughly Unillustrated, Absolutely Unauthorized Guide to Possibly All the References*. Lanham, MD, Toronto and Plymouth: Scarecrow Press.
Mills, Richard (2014) 'Eric Idle and the Counterculture', in Tomasz Dobrowoszez (ed.), *Nobody Expects the Spanish Inquisition: Cultural Contexts in Monty Python*. Lanham, MD: Rowman & Littlefield, pp. 125–36.
Morgan, David (1999) *Monty Python Speaks!* New York: Avon Books.
Palin, Michael (2006) *Diaries 1969–79: The Python Years*. London: Weidenfeld & Nicholson.
Parkes, Taylor (2014) 'A Revolution in the Head: The Other Side of Monty Python', *The Quietus*, 1 July. <http://thequietus.com/articles/15649-monty-python> (last accessed 1 February 2018)
Ross, Daniel (2009) 'Monty Python's Flying Circus: 30 Musical Masterpieces', *The Quietus*, 23 June. <http://thequietus.com/articles/01925-various-artists-monty-python-s-flying-circus-30-musical-masterpieces-album-review> (last accessed 1 February 2018)

Some of the Corpses Are Amusing [online]. <http://sotcaa.org/history/ukonline/python_frame.html?/history/ukonline/python/python_tv_01.html> (last accessed 1 February 2018)

Wright, Rebecca (2017) 'How Eric Idle Found His Grail: The Journey of *Monty Python*'s *Spamalot* from Film to Broadway', in P. N. Reinsch *et al.* (eds), *Python beyond Python: Critical Engagements with Culture*. London: Palgrave Macmillan, pp. 17–36.

5. THE DISRUPTIVE METAMORPHOSES OF AN IMPISH GOD: GILLIAM'S SATIRIC ANIMATION

Paul Wells

> 'I was a rather important part of the writing, even though that meant pictures.'
>
> – Terry Gilliam (The Pythons 2003: 178)

In one of the *Monty Python's Personal Best* compilations (Python (Monty) Pictures 2005), Terry Gilliam playfully claims that the group's TV series was once not a satiric ensemble sketch show, but one long cartoon, anticipating *South Park* by many years, and only changed by the manipulations of the BBC eager to employ Oxbridge alumni. A ruse, of course, but a playful assertion of the significance of animation in helping to define, cohere and challenge in the Monty Python oeuvre. Gilliam's role as 'the American' in the group, and his special status as 'the animator' as well as a writer and performer, gave him the requisite distance to offer 'something completely different' to the ensemble, especially in the variegation of the visual and aesthetic dynamics of the sketches and continuity of narratives. Central to this, of course, is the place of animation per se, and how Gilliam's particular distinctiveness in using 2D cut-out collages drew upon the compositional strategies of fine art and the modernist idioms of pop culture surrealism in redefining both the place and presence of animation on television, and as a ready vehicle for satire.

Gilliam extended the intellectual framing of the Monty Python 'text' by playing with commercial idioms, challenging the Oxford and Cambridge University 'class consciousness' in the group and embracing American counterculture values. In bringing the critical and anarchic outlook of *Mad* magazine from his own cartoon work in Harvey Kurtzman's *Help!* publication (1960–5), he helped advance the modern underground *adult* sensibilities that were later associated with such figures as Robert Crumb. Gilliam enhanced the British anti-establishment model of his colleagues by making the physical comedy of Hogarth more abrasive and the social comment of Gilray more direct but, most importantly, by rendering all high-status and revered institutions diminished by the absurdity and plain silliness of their representation in his animation. As Gilliam was to later remark, '[t]hat's the thing I like about Python – it goes from incredibly intelligent to incredibly infantile' (McCabe 1999: 36). This discussion, then, looks at the work of Gilliam within the context of Monty Python, addressing the influence of Bob Godfrey, his approach to animation practice, his engagement with fine art (from Botticelli to Bronzino), his specific models of critique and his particular preoccupations as a social commentator.

Gilliam created photo comic strips (known as Fumetti) when working at *Help!* and, having seen John Cleese in the *Cambridge Circus* on Broadway, invited him to appear in one, entitled 'Christopher's Punctured Romance', the title drawn from a Chaplin short, *Tilly's Punctured Romance* (1914). Aware of the emergence of a new post-war comedy in Britain, as the gentle class-conscious Ealing comedies gave way to the anarchic surrealism of *The Goon Show* (1951–60), as well as the rise of politically charged satire like *The Frost Report* (1966–7), Gilliam ultimately moved to England, where Cleese introduced him to producer Humphrey Barclay. Influenced by the American surrealist comic Ernie Kovacs, the rising anti-war fervour against America's presence in Vietnam, his own developing skills in illustration (he published *The Cocktail People* with writer, Joe Siegel) and his emergent practice of 'low-rent' table-top animation, Gilliam believed he had the qualities to embrace opportunities in the more progressive conditions for production in London in the late 1960s. At the British independent television franchise holder for London, Associated-Rediffusion, Barclay bought sketches from Gilliam for the cult children's series, *Do Not Adjust Your Set* (1967–9), and engaged him on *We Have Ways of Making You Laugh* (1968), first as a live caricaturist of the show's guests and, later, in his first attempts at madcap 2D cut-out animation, featuring the popular Radio 2 DJ, Jimmy Young.

Gilliam had seen Bob Godfrey's influential short cartoon, *Do It Yourself Cartoon Kit* (1961), featuring the voice of Goon, Michael Bentine, and thereafter often worked at Godfrey's Biographic studio. Here he began to perfect his own 2D cut-out technique, using photographs from magazines and fine art prints, and, particularly, the use of watercolour and the airbrush in 'rounding out' two-dimensional images to give them a sense of depth, texture and volume. *Do It Yourself Cartoon Kit* was a basic deconstruction of the 2D stop-motion technique, using simple materials to illustrate the basic process of frame-by-frame animation and to exemplify certain rules – 'always have somebody chasing somebody else', for example, mocking the dominance and predictability of the American chase cartoon. More importantly, though, the film was a brief compendium of the British sense of humour, characterised by absurdity, innuendo and self-conscious irony. Gilliam embraced these characteristics but exaggerated them further in the light of the success of *Beyond the Fringe* (1960) and the satire shows that followed, which lampooned the sacred cows of the British establishment and spoke to a changing zeitgeist that the Monty Python team were to later reflect in their outlook and approach.

The Satiric Context

Gilliam suggested the music for the opening titles – John Philip Sousa's 'Liberty Bell' – so that he could animate to its march tempo. Cut-out animation does not possess the 'smoothness' of frame-by-frame drawn animation, and works best either in fast sudden motion, very slow motion or motion that foregrounds its own 'jerkiness'. Gilliam largely used the fast/slow timings in his visual gags, and deliberately used the off-set artifice of the medium to extend the surrealism of the imagery. His techniques, processes and themes will be addressed later in this chapter, but it is important to stress here that animation at this time was primarily understood as a children's entertainment medium and as a feature of commercials and credits, but rarely featured on television otherwise. The very presence of animation in a prime-time satirical show was, therefore, in itself subversive and, somewhat ironically, effectively established the style and flow of the programme, challenging the orthodoxies of the conventional sketch show, both in form and content. Crucially, this spoke to a youth audience actively seeking the 'shock of the new' – where else could they see a cancerous spot with a life of its own, 'a nasty five-frog curse on the M4' and 'a resurgence of cheap jokes about poo-poo'? By pushing the envelope in representing death, violence and bodily taboo in animation – supposedly an 'innocent' medium – this merely encouraged and influenced the rest of the team to write more challenging material. Further, the use of animation helped to extend and develop satire as an approach, enabling what the Monty Python group were to dub a 'stream of consciousness' style of comedy that liberated itself from the need for conventional punchlines (The Pythons 2003: 134–6).

Dustin Griffin, writing predominantly about literary satire, summarises what was the theoretical consensus about the form in the 1960s:

> Satire is a highly rhetorical and moral art. A work of satire is designed to attack vice or folly. To this end it uses wit or ridicule. Like polemical rhetoric it seeks to persuade an audience that someone or something is reprehensible or ridiculous; unlike pure rhetoric, it engages in exaggeration and

some sort of fiction. But satire does not forsake the 'real world' entirely. Its victims come from that world, and it is this fact (together with a darker or sharper tone) that separates satire from pure comedy. Finally, satire usually proceeds by means of clear reference to some moral standards or purposes. (Griffin 1994: 1)

I have suggested in all of my work on animation as a form that it is inherently rhetorical and enunciative. Animation is *always* rhetorical on the basis that it is both an interpretation and an intervention in the representation of material and perceived reality. Its status as an illusionist, artificially constructed and self-figurative form (where the animator is always implied and present) lends it also an enunciative quality, in which it literally announces its difference from other forms of expression. In the context of Monty Python, it offers 'bookends' to live-action and performed sketches or, alternatively, works as signifying signposts pointing backward and forward narratively and thematically. Gilliam uses animation's rhetorical quality highly self-consciously both aesthetically and conceptually, making 'vice' and 'folly' highly relative, and rendering the 'moral standards' of the programme in flux.

Griffin argues that satire has changed significantly subject to its historical context and purpose, and, beyond its more didactic moral and social agenda, it is actually a vehicle for inquiry and exploration. The satire that emerged in the 1960s could no longer distinguish sharp differences between vice and virtue given that the sexual revolution and political mobilisation had collapsed any kind of certainty about 'what man *is* and what he *ought* to be' (Griffin 1994: 36). Indeed, the whole notion of 'difference' and the early signs of an emergence of identity politics were promoting a greater relativity of 'truth' and challenging established ideas and practices. The rhetorical and enunciative status of animation was, therefore, an entirely pertinent vehicle by which to express contested issues through fresh modes of expression to challenge and discredit conventional orthodoxies. When a long-extended hand seeks to pull away the fig leaf from Michelangelo's *David* (1501–4) and is slapped by the figure's beautifully formed hand in one of Gilliam's most famous animated vignettes, there resides a coded message about maintaining decency and decorum, a respect for art, culture and social norms. When the fig leaf is finally removed though, it reveals the face of film censor, John Trevelyan, in place of where David's genitals would be, which in turn is 'censored' with a rubber stamp by the hand of the animator, Gilliam himself. Gilliam turns the moral tables, banning the banner, implicitly promoting the new order of liberal openness. As Gilliam insists,

> you get to be an impish god. You get to reform the world. You get to take the piss out of it. You turn it inside out, upside down. You bug out eyes. You put moustaches on Mona Lisas. You change the world, and for a brief moment have control over it. (Sterritt and Rhodes 2004: 128)

This speaks to Griffin's view that

> the notion of a rhetoric of inquiry and provocation assumes that satirists – though they may not have answers to all their questions – exercise an overall control over the process of exploration, leading us to raise questions we must then ponder. (Griffin 1994: 64)

Gilliam, then, becomes part of Monty Python's overall project in being less concerned with any kind of moral or political certainty. Rather, his work was much more about playing out a different kind of 'knowing', using a different kind of 'photomontage' than that used by John Heartfield, Georges Grosz and the Berlin Club Dadaists during the First World War to express the suppressed and repressed feelings of British social and cultural life. Gilliam is both personally amusing himself and speaking to the 'real world' in mocking the conventions of the media forms that increasingly define and determine it, and in poking fun at establishment thinking, which seemed no longer in tune with lived experience in Britain. This becomes especially pertinent when taking into account Gilliam's 'American-ness' in that he could simultaneously draw upon the more radical and political sensibilities of the American underground as it reacted to social change, as well as parody the more formal class-oriented critiques of British culture. Significantly, this not merely spoke to the freedoms of expression available in animation, but also recalls the more transgressive, obscene or carnivalesque aspects of satire sometimes removed by the focus upon cleverness, wit and deliberate stylisation in many satiric forms (see Thompson 1982). Gilliam's surreality and absurdity moves Python away from the dangers of a potentially patronising sense of superiority or, indeed, any specific targets, to secure a more open perspective implicitly championing broader ideas about challenging authority and mocking established patterns and expectation. This long anticipates *South Park* in its propensity for equal opportunity offence – nothing is beyond consideration for sending up or undermining in some way. Gilliam is clear on this – nothing is so important that it cannot be joked about, nor should anything be so important that it cannot recognise that it might, and indeed should, be joked about, and may actually benefit from withstanding comic interrogation (see Sterritt and Rhodes 2004: 126). In these respects, rather than targeted and polemical satire, Gilliam's cartoons become playful 'checks and balances' by which everyone from policemen to philosophers to advertisers to grannies are maintained in the public discourse.

This sense of 'discourse' recalls early satirist John Dryden, of course, whose theoretical work essentially situated satire – previously a matter of public exchange and potential legal intervention, even in its emergent literary forms – into the context of creating 'art' (Griffin 1994: 14–24). Though in the modern era this seems an obvious context in which satire would flourish, Dryden's intervention was important because it prevented all satire being directed to didactic purposes, and permitted more freedoms of creative and critical expression rather than purposive political intervention. One of the most interesting images in Gilliam's work, then – perhaps referencing Beckett's *Not I* (1972) – is a man's mouth that detaches itself from the banality of the presenter speaking through it; on its own, it articulates consciously and intelligently beyond the rhetorics of performance. It is a subtle metaphor for a number of pertinent ideas – the necessity for a more honest voice, the proper articulation of consciousness rather than clichéd small talk, the need to express differently, to be funny in a fresh way, to say something new. Gilliam's use of animation succeeds in all of these ways. I now wish to more formally address how this was achieved.

Animated Comedy

It is pertinent to further situate Gilliam's work within a broader engagement with comedy in animation. Animation, of course, borrows from all comic idioms – vaudeville performance, silent film comedy, TV sitcom, genre parodies, etc. – but, equally, it offers its own distinctive possibilities as a visual medium (see Wells 1998: 127–86, 2013: 497–520; Goldmark and Keil 2011; Buchan 2013: 521–44). Inevitably, it also draws from a wider range of pictorial traditions – children's illustration, the political cartoon, the comic book, fine art – but it takes on its own conditions by being rendered in animated form. Frank Thomas and Ollie Johnston, two of Disney's 'Nine Old Men', the original animators who in essence first created and theorised the twelve principles of classical drawn animation, claimed that '[i]n animation the sight gag is a series of drawings depicting a funny bit of action that can induce a laugh as much from the way the situation is drawn as from the content of the joke' (Thomas and Johnston 1987: 15). Gilliam, of course, is not working in drawn animation, but it is still clear that his *curation* of the still cut-out image and his manipulation of the image with scissors and paint invests it with situational narratives and possibilities. These are then made amusing as much from their composition (normally an *incongruity* from a repositioning of figures and objects in terms of context and expectation) as from the ways in which they are then made to move. Much of this manipulation in the service of the sight gag is often also resonant with symbolic or metaphoric meaning – in *The Holy Grail* (Terry Gilliam and Terry Jones, 1975), for example, Gilliam uses a vintage image of the long-bearded cricketer, W. G. Grace, as the face of God, a visual pun on the iconic bearded representation of God in many paintings, but also a play on the sportsman's name and its pertinence to God-like qualities.

These *associative relations* (see Wells 1998: 93–6) are at the heart of Gilliam's representational approach to creating sight gags, and rarely rely on the kind of personality-based humour Disney was to specialise in. Rather, they are accumulating but related improvisations of visual incongruity that emerge from the suggestiveness of the image itself – for example, the top half of a man's face is positioned as if it were part of a terrace of houses, his glasses reminiscent of the windows in a house. His glasses are then smashed in an act of vandalism, and his eyes plucked out as if they were objects stolen by a burglar. The associative quality here is seeing the man's face as a house front because his glasses resemble windows and, as both glasses and windows can be broken, this is thereafter seen as the consequence of a break-in; as such, the things behind the windows – objects to steal – become the eyes once more that are actually behind the spectacles. In many senses, the narrative here takes longer to describe than actually perceive. Gilliam relies on a *visual literacy* in his audience that sees the signifying resemblances and affordances in the images that permit visual puns and metaphors. Gilliam loved early Disney films, and embraced the joke forms theorised and defined by the studio's animators, i.e. the spot gag, the running gag, the action gag, 'the funny drawing', etc., but his main preoccupations became developments in what Thomas and Johnston called the 'tableau gag' and the 'gag-that-builds' (Thomas and Johnston 1987: 25–32).

Thomas and Johnston note that

> the tableau gag is a held picture at the end of an action, in which the character is left with a ridiculous appearance due to some foreign substance, or object having been placed on, around, over, or in the face or figure. (Thomas and Johnston 1987: 30)

The humour here essentially emerges from the stoic acceptance of humiliation of the character involved, especially if what the character has experienced has been the consequence of the excesses cartoon-animation can play out on a character. Crucially, in this instance, the *image* of the character is violated by the very plasticity of representing the body in cartoon animation, but the *character* itself is inviolate. Donald Duck can be crushed, pulled to extremes and battered with objects, but he remains 'Donald Duck'. Whatever has occurred has happened to a known figure, and the 'slapstick' that has taken place results in the audience laughing at the character *in* the situation and the character's reaction *to* the situation. Gilliam treats the tableau *as* a situation, and does not create characters in the conventional sense as visual ciphers that predominantly function in four ways: as a violation of the body or environment by *breaking it*, *entering* it, *consuming it*, or *altering it* – things Gilliam had done in his drawing, even as a child (The Pythons 2003: 58–9). Gilliam later suggests,

> All I could do was crude, and crude things ended up being violent, somehow. Right from the beginning, the foot coming down and Wham! – you create something beautiful and then you crush it. A lot of them are about

that. I was in that phase where I was smashing things and it was funny. That kind of violence always seemed very funny to me. It was also at a time when the world was very anti-violence because the war was on. (McCabe 1999: 35)

This 'violent' expression, though, has some correspondence with Warner's four modes of metamorphosis – mutating, hatching, splitting and doubling (see Warner 2002) – which are all predicated on the protean condition of animation in representing the body, object or environment that Gilliam readily exploits. At best, 'character' for Gilliam is either a figure deliberately used for their symbolic or social identity (i.e. Trevelyan or Grace, noted above), or an iconic image from a mediated visual source (i.e. people from Victorian photographs or fine art masterpieces). Fundamentally, then, if the tableau gag in Disney 2D animation is in some way an *organic metamorphosis* – a consequence of character mutability in an extreme situation (see Wells 1998: 69–75) – then the tableau gag for Gilliam is a consequence of a *disruptive metamorphosis* that creates and extends an extreme situation.

Gilliam's interest in tableau starts specifically in improvising visual jokes using old Edwardian and Victorian photographs. The overtly 'posed' nature of figures and the sense that 'stillness' has been imposed upon them makes their postures all the more awkward and static. As such, Gilliam's interventions speak to the lack of 'life' in the figures, and begin to permit the breaking, entering, consuming and altering that are the stock of his visual interventions. A standing woman chastises a sitting man to 'sit up', punching and cajoling him until his whole figure spins out of the chair ('Breaking'). In another image, figures seem to fight under the crinolines of a woman's dress ('Breaking'), her head disappearing down into her body to investigate ('Entering'). As a small girl approaches, those in dispute insist they stay quiet, before a man's head appears replacing the woman's ('Entering'). In yet another, a portrait of a soldier is presented and figures appear in his mouth and form under his medals, crying out that they are trapped and want to escape ('Entering'). A figure then cuts away the top of the cranium from the inside ('Altering') and emerges to freedom, only to be 'recaptured' in a highlander's bearskin headwear ('Consuming'). A standing male figure in another photograph removes the whole of a seated lady's clothing in a single reveal as if he were removing a tablecloth or picking up a food dome to show a meal ('Altering'). The man puts on a Zorro-like eye-mask as if this disguises him as the woman sits in the nude, the couple re-dressing upon the approach of a police constable in the foreground of the image ('Altering'). In a seated portrait, a man's hair becomes 'wings' and his head starts to fly away ('Altering'), only to be reclaimed by an arm emerging from within his body ('Entering'). In a more daring visual gag, a sporran appears to eat away the bottom half of a soldier ('Consuming'), before metamorphosing into a young girl's hair, which in turn becomes a young girl figure reminiscent of Alice in Wonderland who is kicked by a group of seated soldiers ('Breaking') and consumed by a giant floating mouth that proclaims 'actually I find violence extremely distasteful' ('Consuming').

Gilliam's tableau gags are often constructed from a single image in which only one aspect is animated, or specific sounds become intrinsic to the joke. A frog with a man's head only moves when a tongue springs from the man's mouth to swallow a watch. His forehead then expands to show a cuckoo clock in his head, whose timer goes off, rattling his eyes. A pie is then taken from his gaping mouth as if it had been in an oven. Mouth closed, a 'Time's Up' banner emerges from his nose, and Michael Palin's voice-over – a gameshow announcer – brashly announces, 'Sorry, your time's up Mr Spume, I'm afraid you lose your three-piece suite, and your youngest daughter'. Finally, the sound of the ticking clock becomes the sound of a fuse of a bomb burning down, and the head eventually explodes altogether. This comic riff on 'time' draws on suspense and surprise, but these typical filmmaking elements are recast within the alternative logic of the context Gilliam creates, and which the animation facilitates. 'Timing' is crucial in this, and clearly Gilliam is not merely playing with typical Hollywood conventions in using time, but parodying cartoon gags that speak readily to the concept of 'timing' in the joke. This is most explicit in a joke where an ambulance takes an age to move from the background to the foreground of the image before *suddenly* knocking down a businessman, and for a policeman within – literally here 'the long arm of the law' – purloining the businessman's watch. As noted earlier this is a consequence of the 2D stop-motion technique, in which suddenness or slow motion delivers the possibility of comic outcomes – *disruptive metamorphoses* – that are formal, technical and conceptual jokes.

In Disney's 'gag-that-builds', Thomas and Johnston suggest that this is 'made up of a series of gags that increase in intensity . . . until a climactic event crowns a complete routine' (Thomas and Johnston 1987: 26). This approach invariably exploits the new logic of a situation once what was expected to happen has not occurred, and every new intervention compounds the error until one final calamity arrests the joke. Gilliam's 'gag-that-builds' does not have the logic or structure of the changing circumstance, but rather the changing association, and rarely does it build to a climax. Often, indeed, the gag leads only back to the sketch or live-action sequence in the overall programme or film, or possesses no denouement or specific 'punchline'. Gilliam's version of a 'gag-that-builds', for example, begins when three ballet-dancing admirals – the top half a cut-out of an admiral, the bottom half a cut-out of a ballet dancer – annoy another character, who responds by saying 'God if they don't stop I'll kill myself'. The man finally capitulates and does so, shooting himself in the ear, the bullet rolling one eye-ball on to the other eye-ball and out the other ear. 'For three days and nights, the displaced eye-ball plummeted earthward', intones the voice-over. 'Finally' (a caption), the eye spins and flattens into a disc when it lands on the ground, becoming the base of a bus-stop, where an old lady stands. After a bus passes here twice, on a third occasion the old lady extends her foot to trip the bus, upending it in the process, before she gets on board. The bus is then passed by a group of tourists, who are set upon by 'killer cars' hiding behind trees and in alleyways. In order to decrease pedestrian congestion, 'certain fanatical cars had taken the law into their own hands' and devoured people. 'The days of the killer cars were numbered', though, 'thanks to atomic mutation'. A Godzilla-like cat standing on its hind legs then staggers through Trafalgar Square in London in a tribute to the Ray Harryhausen's stop-motion B-movies of the 1950s in which American cities are normally destroyed by aliens or mutated creatures. The cat drives away the cars, then starts eating buildings, before a hand – a reference to 'thing' in the US sitcom, *The Addams Family* – flattens first the cat and then a group of citizens who gather to thank it for saving them.

Bodies, objects, animals and environments all take on arbitrary and incongruous qualities, merely the visual assets by which Gilliam plays out his own associative 'low-rent' spectaculars, rendering the generic, overblown and predictable as fresh ironic gags. One gag literally flows into another here, an episodic sequence of 'micro-narratives' that finds comic purchase by being rendered as the subject of a formalist controlling agency – 'the impish god' of the animator. Such control, which puts everything on an even footing, diminishes known hierarchies, established power-bases, social and cultural expectations, and oppressive habits and routines. These become a series of *disruptive metamorphoses* that rely on 'mutating' (the cat as Godzilla), 'hatching' (the bullet that produces the falling eye), 'splitting' (the dancing admirals) and 'doubling' (the eye as base, the killer cars as monstrous creatures devouring all before them). This in turn creates worlds in which suicide, accidents and violent conflict become reductive acts, made absurd by what might be termed the *filter* of the animated form in which all things are placed into the kind of relief by which they might be re-considered, and even re-appreciated. Each visual joke thus operates simultaneously as both a *dilution* of the implications of the 'reality' implied, yet an *amplification* of the possible symbolic and metaphoric interpretation of such 'reality'.

Many of Gilliam's comic riffs, therefore, are (literal) reversals of expectation or practice. For example, when Conrad Pooh (a treated photo of Gilliam himself) believes he has received a telegram, an intervening figure notes that he has actually received *a letter*, whereupon a retreating postman takes the letter away, posting the letter back into a postbox on a small island. In effect, when the letter disappears into the postbox, it is now visualised as being back in a process that is normally hidden from the public – the internalised system by which a letter goes from one person to another. In John Grierson's *Nightmail*

(Basil Wright, 1936), featuring the poetry of W. H. Auden, this is depicted, for instance, in poetic documentary form, while Gilliam uses animation's capacity for *penetration* (see Wells 1998: 122–7) – the capacity to depict interior or non-visible states, mechanisms and procedures. As Gilliam has noted:

> It's the innards of everything, whether it's people, or machines. The inner workings of things have always intrigued me. Toilets have always intrigued me. I'm curious about how things work, how the guts of a system function, and the sound of plumbing is always comic. (McCabe 1999: 36)

Once the letter enters the postbox, it is subject to the way Gilliam visualises the journey of the letter. The letter is transported by a mechanical hand from holes in the landscape into a Karel Zeman-style airship, whereupon it falls beneath a football boot, travels through the mouth of a serpent, back into a conveyor system, speeds past two nude women, and rests back on a post office counter. This reversal of the normal process puts the letter back into the hands of the live-action bowler-hatted sender (Terry Jones), making the mundane exotic, yet comically complex in its Heath Robinson/Rube Goldberg styling. The exoticism of the mundane is common in Gilliam's work, partly referring to a particularly British kind of ordinariness, but partly employing a certain comic fetishism of the *interiority* of objects and habitual processes, making them funny by pointing up their lack of exoticism by depicting them as if they were.

THE MIDWAY EXPERIENCE

Gilliam's use of the tableau gags and accumulative micro-narratives allied to the satirical context in which the Pythons largely worked place his animated sequences to some extent into the milieu of the political cartoon. Topliss has argued that

> [c]artoons tend to direct our attention to events that, for both the participant and the observer, fall between private experiences that are merely accidental and personal and public experiences in which everyone within a certain group has a share and that therefore possess a commonly recognized and well understood importance and even 'universality'. We can call these events 'midway' experiences. (Topliss 2005: 6)

Gilliam's animation plays a very important role in this regard in relation to the overall Monty Python project, in that such was the 'newness' of Python's approach to comedy on television there was no clear understanding of who the audience might be for such a show, because the satire was mostly indirect and many of the sketches grounded in unfamiliar comic strategies. The audience was being invited into an innovative creative context in which it negotiated a different space between the 'private experience' and its recognisably public referent. This was a different kind of 'midway' context in which Gilliam's surrealist turn and its satiric underpinnings did not prompt obvious points of connection in the topicality of the everyday, but rather in an assumed visual literacy – a recognition, too, that Gilliam's work was an *iteration* of script, not an *illustration* of it.

Though the visual jokes possessed enough of 'the cartoon' to hark back to the more anarchic work of Tex Avery (binocular lens bulging out like Avery's trademark bug-out eyes) and Bob Clampett (Eggs Diamond, the gangster crossed with a hen, echoing Clampett's mixed-media figures), much of Gilliam's work had different reference points and, consequently, repositioned the nature of the joke. The 'midway' experience for those familiar with cartoons, then, is in the first instance the broad recognition that these are *not* Disney cartoons, but unless there is a greater familiarity with the Warner Bros. output, there is also probably less of an understanding that Gilliam's work, at the very least, shares its urbanity and its self-conscious address of adults. Familiarity with the work of Jan Svankmajer or Karel Zeman might also offer clues to the European animation sources in Gilliam's aesthetic, most notably in its preoccupations with the grotesque, the corporeal and foregrounded fantastical artifice. Satire, of course, invites the pleasures of such decoding and, in Gilliam's case, there is a certain relish in exploring the physiological and erotic as a mode of deformation and difference, pointing to more counterculture or 'under the counter' sources. Crucially, though, if these idioms were to fully reach a new audience while brokering the 'midway', it would necessarily have to speak to mediated experience – the very act of looking and seeing in understanding contemporary visual culture. As such, Gilliam looks to contemporary advertising to reach an audience versed in watching television, and the visual iconography of the Grand Masters of art to reach the middle-class intellectuals that the Python team most resembled and spoke to.

I have already noted Gilliam's playful use of Michelangelo's *David*, but it is merely part of a significant body of visual jokes across all of Gilliam's animation that references major art works to point up the difference between high and low cultural practices. It is in undermining the assumed significance of high art with Sunday Magazine idioms that Gilliam articulates 'the midway' and offers access to amusement in the recognition of *wit*. Gilliam is 'clever', and the pleasure and fun come in the recognition of this cleverness *first*, before it is in the nuances of the subject, the joke or the object of satire. For example, in seeing the angle of a hand gesture and the position of the couple's embrace in Auguste Rodin's *The Kiss* (1882), Gilliam merely straightens the female participant's leg and adds some finger holes, and the man begins to play the woman as if she were a musical instrument. What successfully extends the gag, though, is the use of sound, in that the music played is the warped notes of a swanee whistle rather than another instrument that might have at least lent the sound more classical gravitas. The iconography of the sculpture and its significance as art is completely undermined by making the romanticism of the image the subject of mischievous 'vulgarity' by ironically *de-eroticising* the figures. There is a similar approach in most of Gilliam's use of fine art when the enigma of *The Mona Lisa* (1595) by Da Vinci is broken by portraying her in a flat cap, or by exposing her breasts; the poignancy of Da Vinci's *The Last Supper* (1490) is punctured by making the occasion just another meal, where someone says, 'That bitch, he spilled a whole bottle of chateau le tour'; the ethereal beauty of Botticelli's *The Birth of Venus* (1484) is rendered coarse by a hand tweaking Venus's nipple as if turning on a radio, reducing her to a dancing dervish; or the use of Michelangelo's Adam from *The Creation of Man* (1508–12) in the Sistine Chapel, in which he is placed in a sandwich, the implication that he is merely 'beefcake', another piece of meat. Where this becomes a culture clash of more obvious satiric playfulness is when fine art is used in the service of referencing the external world by more specific implication. The strikes that characterised the 1970s in Britain are sent up when key characters from major paintings withdraw their labour in a 'Fair Play for Paintings' strike – the peasant about to be executed in Francisco de Goya's *The Third of May 1808* (1815), the Italian banker from Van Eyck's *The Arnolfini Marriage* (1434), the future empress, the infanta Margarita from Velazquez's *Las Meninas* (1656), Jean Paul Marat from Jacques-Louis David's *The Death of Marat* (1793), and the Mona Lisa herself, all remove themselves from their frames, while the man from John Constable's *The Hay Wain* (1821) says 'there's no chance of a return to the pictures before the weekend'. Greek statues join the strike in support following a unanimous vote in which all their limbs are raised, except for one who is armless and, of course, cannot vote. Such an idea merely points up how easy it is to *devalue* things, and undermine the substance of their meaning and affect. The images essentially possess no value without the recognition of what they are worth not merely in monetary terms, but for what they actually *do* in representing the human condition in its historical circumstance. It is not hard to see the comment Gilliam makes here about the value the government might place on its working classes, but it is further an observation made in esoteric terms to speak more directly to those who might wield social and cultural power. Ultimately, the crushing foot in the Monty Python credit sequence, a detail from the corner of Bronzino's *Allegory of Love with Venus and Cupid* (1540), becomes a pertinent metaphor for the transition from the possible complacency and complicity in passive engagements with 'beauty' to the sudden violence of 'action' – a rapid and emphatic response to the 'midway' experience.

Similar techniques are used when Gilliam sends up the rhetoric of advertising – 'Whizzo Butter' enables you to 'go to heaven'; 'Crelm' toothpaste enables a lovelorn dragon to attract girls again, before eating them; packets of 'American Defence' can prevent the 'domino theory' of the collapse of one rotten tooth (through the decay of 'international communism') leading to the collapse of all the rest of the dentures; 'Dynamo Tension' promotes 'muscles pulling against muscles the natural way' in order to body-build supposedly attractive hypermuscular grotesques. Gilliam effectively parodies the promises of commercial culture, highlighting the obvious absurdities between rhetoric and reality. Fundamentally, for all its play with the physiological and the arbitrary treatment of the body, Gilliam's animation insists upon the necessity to create the Brechtian distance that promotes cerebral engagement. His 'adverts' seek to show how commercial deception is in essence the same as social and political deception. 'Purchase a Past', for example, offers the opportunity to buy 'beautifully framed photographs of other people's lives', and imagine that the people who populate them offer the possibility of a life that is better than your own. 'Cartoon Religions Ltd' insists that 'We want you to think of us as your friends', while Gilliam reveals that the vicar intoning to the public is having his brains consumed by the devil himself. Gilliam simply refuses to assume that the audience is homogeneous or will respond to lowest common denominator principles in joke-making, insisting instead that viewers will invest not merely in the immediacy of the joke, but in the value of a joke in opening up alternative points of view about the human experience. In this respect, virtually every visual joke carries with it a resonance about always questioning the things the media and other outlets present as 'a truth'. The discovery of a 'huge thumb', for example, enables the British Museum, after years of painstaking research, to reconstruct the whole animal from which it apparently came. The thumb is simply attached to a mammoth as if it were its trunk. The visual incongruity is in itself amusing, but the ultimate message is not to be deceived by the things that we see.

An Animator's Soul

> His real satiric business here is to display his wit: the reader is delighted by the ingenuity, the ransacking of natural history, military, science, medicine, folklore, philosophy, and myth to produce an interrelated series of puns. It is a bit like a virtuoso performer's cadenza, a jazz musician's improvisation, or the entries in some mad thesaurus under the heading 'Regarding the End' or 'Get in by the back door'. (Griffin 1994: 81)

Griffin, here, writes about the work of one of the greatest literary satirists, Jonathan Swift. I wish to argue that the very same view can be applied to the animated vignettes made by Terry Gilliam. In his own text, *Animations of*

Mortality, he claims to reveal the dark inner workings of the animator's soul, but instead playfully demonstrates some of the techniques of 2D stop-motion cut-out animation – 'creating nothing out of somethings', 'looking the part' or making 'meaningless political statements', for example, all in the service of 'intense religious experience' or 'sexual perversion' (see Gilliam 1978). Fundamentally, though, Gilliam makes something out of nothing, prioritises the act of looking, makes meaningful political statements, and places sex and religion in perspective as dominant and affecting social and political discourses. As the policeman, who rips open his uniform to reveal a nude woman's body, says, 'I apologise for that but I think you'll find this a bit more interesting.' It is always Gilliam's intention to surprise and shock in order to find the real interest beneath the dressings and surfaces of social, cultural and artistic experience, and as a result not merely advance the terms and conditions of satirical address, but to enhance the claims for animation as one of the most potentially subversive forms of creative expression.

Works Cited

Buchan, Suzanne (2013) 'Theatrical Cartoon Comedy: From Animated Portmanteau to the *Risus Purus*', in Andrew Horton and Joanna E. Rapf (eds), *A Companion to Film Comedy*. Chichester and Oxford: Wiley-Blackwell, pp. 521–44.

Gilliam, Terry (1978) *Animations of Mortality*. London: Eyre Methuen.

Goldmark, Daniel and Charlie Keil (eds) (2011) *Funny Pictures: Animation and Comedy in Studio-Era Hollywood*. Berkeley, Los Angeles and London: University of California Press.

Griffin, Dustin H. (1994) *Satire: A Critical Reintroduction*. Lexington: University Press of Kentucky.

McCabe, Bob (1999) *Dark Knights and Holy Fools: The Art and Films of Terry Gilliam*. London: Orion.

Pythons, The (with Bob McCabe) (2003) *The Pythons Autobiography*. London: Orion.

Sterritt, David and Lucille Rhodes (eds) (2004) *Terry Gilliam: Interviews*. Jackson: University Press of Mississippi.

Thomas, Frank and Ollie Johnston (1987) *Too Funny for Words: Disney's Greatest Sight Gags*. New York: Abbeville Press.

Thompson, John O. (1982) *Monty Python: A Complete and Utter Theory of the Grotesque*. London: BFI.

Topliss, Iain (2005) *The Comic Worlds*. Baltimore, MD: Johns Hopkins University Press.

Warner, Marina (2002) *Fantastic Metamorphoses, Other Worlds*. Oxford and New York: Oxford University Press.

Wells, Paul (1998) *Understanding Animation*. London and New York: Routledge.

Wells, Paul (2013) 'Laughter Is Ten Times More Powerful than a Scream: The Case of Animated Comedy', in Andrew Horton and Joanna E. Rapf (eds), *A Companion to Film Comedy*. Chichester and Oxford: Wiley-Blackwell, pp. 497–520.

6. FIGURES TRACED IN SHITE: THE SCRIBE, THE ILLUMINATOR AND MONTY PYTHON'S *HOLY GRAIL*

Ewan Wilson

David D. Day observed in the first edition of Kevin J. Harty's *Cinema Arthuriana: Essays on Arthurian Film* that what is '[u]ltimately at issue in *Monty Python and the Holy Grail* is our ability to know the Middle Ages at all, when every attempt we make ultimately betrays the traces of its modern manufacture' (Day 1991: 83). Indeed, the first and seemingly inevitable question at which one arrives in the examination of a film that purports to be set in the past is one of historical accuracy; regardless of the fictive nature of the narrative, the question of period authenticity is quick to arise. For their part, the Middle Ages are rarely portrayed for their own sake, often appearing instead as imagined visions of the past in service of an aesthetic or political agenda which overlooks authenticity in favour of representation. As Robert A. Rosenstone points out of such efforts,

> the focus tends to be on the creation and manipulation of the meanings of the past, on a discourse that is free of data other than that of other discourses, on what seems to be the free play of signifiers signifying history. (Rosenstone 1995: 10)

In *Monty Python and the Holy Grail* (1975), the Pythons present an absurdist retelling of Malory's *Le Morte d'Arthur* that appears, at first glance, to be little but abject silliness. However, scholars such as Day, Brian Levy and Lesley Coote (2004) and Neil Archer (2016) have made detailed examinations of the film's comedic conventions, its politics and the way in which it represents Arthur's

England, unpacking the complexities of *Holy Grail*'s specific brand of mediaevalism. For Day, *Holy Grail* highlights the difficulties of portraying the distant Middle Ages in a manner free from modern influences, particularly in a medium as modern as film; Levy and Coote's analysis draws comparison between the political stance and its comedic conventions with those present in the literature of Chaucer and Malory, ultimately arguing that the Pythons participate in an inherently mediaeval literary tradition; and Archer, in a wider discussion of parody, brings the question of 'historical verisimilitude' (Archer 2016: 60) under the scrutiny of genre convention and audience expectation. Common to these analyses of the film, and indeed to several other such studies, is an interest in the interaction between its modern and mediaeval elements. However, where the majority of the existing scholarship surrounding *Holy Grail* is concerned with the film as a modern treatment of mediaeval material, this chapter builds on Martine Meuwese's examination of 'The Animation of Marginal Decorations in "Monty Python and the Holy Grail"' (2004) to suggest that the creative practices of the film's two directors, Gilliam and Jones, are just as participatory in mediaeval tradition as is their subject matter. Drawing on the wealth of published accounts of the film's production, interviews with the Python team and J. J. G. Alexander's book-length study of *Medieval Illuminators and Their Methods of Work* (1992), it seeks to delineate the directorial styles of the two directors and draw connections between their cooperation and that of the mediaeval scribe with an illuminator, as well as the influences the film draws from cinema Arthuriana and the mediaeval epics of Bergman, Kurosawa and Pasolini.[1]

Since the early days of Python, Gilliam has been considered a member in equal weighting to his colleagues; yet as the lone American expatriate in a group of Oxbridge graduates, he has always been something of an outsider. As Cleese observes, 'he's much more like an artist in a painterly sense. He works in a studio, he doesn't work in a *team*, or didn't on Python; we worked very much in a team' (Morgan 1999: 79). This distinction between the Englishmen and the American, the writers and the artist, allows us to consider the work of the Pythons and that of Gilliam as belonging to two different traditions: the written and the visual. The Oxbridge contingent of the Pythons are heavily steeped in the written culture of Britain: Palin read history; Jones and Idle, English literature; and Cleese, law. Gilliam, on the other hand, 'just wanted to get on and paint and draw and sculpt' (Pythons and McCabe 2003: 86); he studied at Occidental College, drifting from physics to art history to political science, dipping into oriental philosophy and drama along the way. Chapman, a medic, was the outlier. Their studies were never the main focus of the soon-to-be Pythons, however; while the Englishmen brought their brand of 'literate comedy' (ibid.: 85) to the Cambridge Footlights, Gilliam immersed himself in the reinvigoration of Occidental's 'previously quite serious art and poetry journal called *Fang*, which . . . was rapidly transformed into a showcase for scabrous gags and unfettered cartooning' (Gilliam and Thompson 2015: 46). While a bent for comedy and innovation is their uniting factor, a clear divide in practice is struck between the wordsmithing of the Footlights/Revue alumni and the visual absurdism of Gilliam.

This distinction is of particular relevance to a delineation of the responsibilities of Gilliam and Jones during the production of *Holy Grail*; as its producer, John Goldstone, observes,

> Terry Jones' attitude (as opposed to Terry Gilliam's) has always been much more about performance than visuals . . . ultimately the nature of Python is more verbal than visual, and it seemed very important to make it work on a performance level and that the words were there. (Morgan 1999: 154)

Indeed, Gilliam recalls that after an argument he had with Cleese during the filming of Arthur's initial encounter with the French, '[i]t ended up with Terry talking to the guys, and me talking to the crew and the cameramen' (McCabe 1999: 56). In this division of labour, *Holy Grail* displays a level of mediaeval influence that extends beyond that of its subject matter. Meuwese identifies Lilian M. C. Randall's encyclopaedic *Illustrations in the Margins of Gothic Manuscripts* as Gilliam's primary source for the images that he employs in the animated segments of the film. As she observes:

> Gilliam's animated sequences contain many medieval visual motifs. In 'The Tale of Sir Launcelot,' this animation sequence is restricted to the Celtic-style text; the rest of the animation develops in Gilliam's own style of drawing. However, 'The Quest for the Holy Grail' contains a Romanesque Christ and a series of Gothic figures, while 'The Tale of Sir Galahad' and 'Season Animation' are also mainly populated by figures which look as though they have been borrowed directly from early fourteenth-century manuscript illustrations. And indeed, that is precisely what has happened. (Meuwese 2004: 47)

Meuwese goes on to connect Gilliam's numbering of his concept sketches for the film's animations to the numbered illustrations in Randall's book, suggesting that the relationship between Randall's text and Gilliam's appropriation of it might be compared to that of a mediaeval scribe and his source book; she writes that 'Gilliam's orientation sketches and notes may be compared to the terse instructions that a miniaturist would scribble or sketch next to the place where the illustration was to be executed' (ibid.: 54). As insightful as her observations are, Meuwese limits the scope of her study to Gilliam's use of manuscript material in his animations and neglects to consider the film as a whole, or indeed the role of the other Pythons, particularly that of Jones, within the production of the film. If Gilliam is considered a modern miniaturist, a participant in a visual tradition which spans centuries, the other Pythons, having been more directly involved in the writing of the film's script, can be viewed as akin to mediaeval scribes, represented by Jones as writer-director.

Although *Holy Grail* was written by Monty Python as a collective, and all six of the troupe are credited accordingly, this chapter's focus lies with the relationship between the film's directors and as such it shall consider Jones as chief among Python's scribes. He, more so than any other of his colleagues, is embedded in the literary and historical traditions of Britain as both a practitioner and a scholar. Post-Python, Cleese has made a long career of comedic performances while Idle has peppered his song-writing output with a handful of novels; Palin garnered a modest number of screenwriting credits, including *Ripping Yarns* (1976–9) in collaboration with Jones and *Time Bandits* (1981) with Gilliam, before embarking on a career as a travel writer and presenter for the BBC in 1989; and Gilliam, having developed a taste for the role of director but desiring complete artistic control over his projects, went on to forge a decidedly idiosyncratic career as a filmmaker. Jones, on the other hand, directed only a handful of further features, and soon returned to his passion for the mediaeval as the presenter of such BBC documentaries as *Ancient Inventions* (1998), *Terry Jones' Medieval Lives* (2004) and *Terry Jones' Barbarians* (2006), the latter two of which were later complemented with accompanying books.[2]

His is the largest of the bibliographies produced by any one Python, and his writing includes children's literature, librettos and his scholarly discussions of the work of Chaucer, *Chaucer's Knight: The Portrait of a Medieval Mercenary* (1980) and *Who Murdered Chaucer?: A Medieval Mystery* (2003). While a gifted comedic writer and actor, Jones is also a respected scholar, and Palin recalls that he 'was, from the first time I met him, a huge fan of Geoffrey Chaucer, which he took great pleasure in reciting in the original Middle English' (Palin 2012: 56). Although Jones writes of a realisation reached in the Bodleian Library during his university days that 'I didn't want to spend my life being an English academic and commentator . . . I wanted to make things and write the raw material' (Pythons and McCabe 2003: 74), his subsequent writing for both page and screen is consistently informed by and engaged with the history and literature of Britain's past. *The Complete and Utter History of Britain* (1969), for example, which Palin and Jones wrote and acted for London Weekend Television, presents a gamut of landmark moments in British history through a contemporary lens; highlights from the programme's surviving episodes include a post-Battle of Hastings sketch in which William the Conqueror gives a reporter the run-down in the manner of a post-match football interview, and Richard the Lionheart's return from the Crusades with a plethora of souvenirs and a hankering for 'a plate of egg and chips'.[3] This programme, a direct forerunner to *Monty Python's Flying Circus* (1969–74), exhibits much of the same absurdist humour that became the trademark of the Pythons, but suffers by comparison in the absence of the comedic performances of the other soon-to-be troupe members.

It was during the filming of *Complete and Utter History* that Jones was once again motivated to direct as well as to write. While working at the BBC in 1966, he was enrolled on their internal director's course, but fell ill with peritonitis shortly before the day on which he was to film his demonstration piece and was unable to complete the programme as a result (Pythons and McCabe 2003: 98–9). Subsequently, he devoted his attentions to writing jobs, although Palin recalls from the time that

> Terry was particularly keen on little films and he would have his 8mm camera, and we used to shoot little films in the back garden of his house in Claygate and rush around moving the chairs in different directions, so when he put it together, the chairs would appear to whiz around. (Ibid.: 85)

There are similar moments in *Complete and Utter History*, such as that in the 'Catechism of the Witch' sketch where Jones, in full Witch of the West regalia, 'flies' from one side of the frame to the other on his broomstick, an action achieved with stop-action trick photography. Though Jones did not direct the programme, and the absence of a script for this insert makes it difficult to determine how much of the scene's visual style was dictated by the writers, it is likely that this idea stemmed from him. In the combination of physical, slapstick humour and the earliest means of special effects is evident Jones's admiration for Buster Keaton, whom he idolises 'because he made comedy look beautiful; he took it seriously' (Morgan 1999: 10).

The question of presentation is one that was important not just to Jones, but to Monty Python as a collective. By the time *Flying Circus* had run its course, both Gilliam and Jones had developed the notion of making the jump from television to film, and consequently were acutely aware of the formal differences between the two mediums that other British comedy films of the period failed to observe. As the producer of *Holy Grail*, Mark Forstater, observes:

> British comedy films of the 1970s, unlike the TV shows, were pretty awful. Most were spin-offs of successful TV series, made for quite low budgets . . . These films were largely made for UK audiences and could only be exported to countries where the TV series had found a home . . . flat overall lighting was used to give the actors as much freedom of movement as possible, but also to avoid major lighting changes between set-ups. The Pythons' first film *And Now for Something Completely Different* (1971) fell into this category. (Forstater 2015: 15)

An amalgam of several sketches from *Flying Circus*, *And Now for Something Completely Different* (*ANFSCD*) was a feature-length sketch show which failed to make any real engagement with or exploitation of the cinematic form. The first draft of *Holy Grail* exhibits a similar lack of cohesion, being formed of two parallel grail quests – one past, one present – that eventually collide in Harrods department store. However, Forstater notes that 'the medieval story had much more potential for laughs and for medieval pastiche' (ibid.: 36), and the Pythons, too, found that there was more original humour to be mined from the court of King Arthur than from the present. By doing so, the Pythons were plumbing not just a wealth of literary and cultural material, but also the body of films which fall under the umbrellas of pastiche and cinema Arthuriana.

While Britain saw the likes of the *Carry On* franchise churn out pastiche after pastiche, parodies such as *Casino Royale* (John Huston *et al.*, 1967) and *The Producers* (Mel Brooks, 1968) gained traction in Hollywood. At the same time, however, American cinema continued to add to the body of films which Susan Aronstein dubs 'Hollywood Arthuriana', a specifically American sub-shoot of Harty's 'cinema Arthuriana'. At the tail end of the 1960s, it was Joshua Logan's musical *Camelot* (1967), an adaptation of Lerner and Loewe's eponymous stage play of 1961, that was chief in the public eye and which the Pythons lampooned most directly in *Holy Grail*.[4] While Darl Larsen refers to *Holy Grail*'s script to assert that the musical number in the film's 'Camelot' episode is modelled after 'If They Could See Me Now' from the 1966 stage play *Sweet Charity* (Larsen 2015: 244), he also notes that 'the formerly mythic denizens of Camelot had been singing and dancing for about thirteen years when the Pythons came to write their own version' (ibid.: 251). Consequently, the king's dismissal of Camelot as 'a silly place' can be understood not just as a jibe at the expense of Hollywood's tendency to look to Arthurian myth as an idealised model for society, but also at the way in which it had previously portrayed the Middle Ages. With *Holy Grail*, Jones and Gilliam strove to break away from the glamorised past presented by Hollywood, in which 'all the pores were mysteriously gone from the skin and everybody's teeth shone like Doris Day's and Rock Hudson's' (Gilliam and Thompson 2015: 172), and instead drew on the aesthetics of such mediaeval epics as Bergman's *The Seventh Seal* (1957), Kurosawa's *Throne of Blood* (1957) and Pasolini's *The Canterbury Tales* (1972).

Of the numerous influences that shaped *Holy Grail*, these three films are worthy of note because of their distinctive and evocative depictions of the Middle Ages. These films, though perhaps no more historically accurate in their construction of the past than the Hollywood features bemoaned by Gilliam, are united in the inspiration they draw not just from mediaeval art, but from a long tradition of visual culture.[5] The image of Death playing chess is just one that Bergman recalled from the walls of the churches in which his father used to preach (Bergman 1956), and the script from which *The Seventh Seal* evolved bore the title *Knight and Death*, recalling Dürer's *Knight, Death and the Devil* (Törnqvist 2012). For *Throne of Blood*, Kurosawa studied the *musha-e*, 'early picture scrolls of battle scenes', and 'decided to use black and armored walls since they would go well with the *suiboku-ga* (ink-painting) effect [they] planned with lots of mist and fog' (Richie 1996: 122). And, in *The Canterbury Tales*, Pasolini grasps 'the strong medieval connection between the sublime and the grotesque' (Blandeau 2006: 155), epitomised by the film's Boschian finale. The Pasolini film, rife with sex, filth and monstrous imagery, struck a chord with Gilliam, who would later look to the paintings of Bosch and Breugel as inspiration for the *mise-en-scène* of *Jabberwocky*. Indeed, Palin recalls viewing *The Canterbury Tales* with Jones, which 'Terry G. had recommended. Superb recreation of mediaeval England – the kind of style and quality of shooting that we must get in our film, to stop it being just another *Carry on King Arthur*' (Palin 2006: 163–4). Echoed in Palin's admiration of Pasolini's film is Jones's love of Keaton's work, and the desire to prove that comedy and artistry are not mutually exclusive.

However, the utilisation of an art cinema aesthetic was not just a means of presenting their work as a serious piece of filmmaking; it also allowed the Pythons the opportunity to make comedy out of the formal elements of the medium itself. The film's opening credits, featuring a moody, percussive score and pseudo-Nordic subtitles over a black background, plays to an audience awareness of Bergman-esque art cinema before introducing a series of jokes about renegade subtitlers. Similarly, the film's opening shot of a Catherine wheel shrouded in fog nods to *Throne of Blood*, and the revelation that the sounds of an approaching horse are produced by coconuts is made all the funnier in its absurdity. *The Seventh Seal*'s self-flagellating monks are likewise parodied, their whips substituted for boards against which they repeatedly smack their heads. Though the jokes in *Holy Grail* were generated by the Python collective and are ultimately rooted in the written word, their presentation in the visual language of art cinema is due largely, if not entirely, to Gilliam and Jones as directors. Jones has, for the purposes of this chapter, already been identified as writer-director while Gilliam's directorial duties cast him as more akin to a director-illustrator – Meuwese's 'modern miniaturist'. In their cooperative filming of *Holy Grail*, herein considered as an illuminated text, Jones and Gilliam are participants in a tradition of Arthurian illustrators who, 'by serving as authors/illustrators, explore the relational quality and ultimate interdependence of word and image . . . as Howard Pyle and Hudson Talbott did' (Lupack and Lupack 2008: 10).

It is prudent at this juncture to note that the practice of manuscript illumination is one which spans several centuries, and the relationship between and responsibilities of the scribe and the illuminator evolved over time. Jonathan J. G. Alexander offers a studious overview of the evolution of the process from the Early Middle Ages of 'about 650 to about 1100' (Alexander 1992: 72) through to the end of the fourteenth century, and it is possible to identify elements from different periods of this history that correspond to the relationship between Jones and Gilliam. He observes, for example, that 'looking at the list of illuminator's names prior to the year 900 AD given in the standard dictionary of miniaturists, almost all turn out, on closer inspection, to be scribes' (ibid.: 6), a blending of roles which is not so dissimilar to that of the writer-director or director-animator. When discussing Gilliam in this manner, however, it is useful to make the distinction between the terms 'miniature' and 'illumination', and naturally also 'miniaturist' and 'illuminator'. David Diringer connects the term 'miniature' with the Latin words *'minium'* and *'miniare'*, which relate to the use of a red paint made with ochre or lead, explaining that '[m]iniatures may be executed without the use of gold or silver while illuminations may not. Although there are illuminated miniatures – i.e., pictures finished with touches of gold to represent the lights – many miniatures are not illuminations' (Diringer 1980: 149). By dividing these two terms on the basis of their constituent alchemical metals, it is a simple matter to neatly connect the practice of filmmaking with that of manuscript illumination; the silver pigment of the page becomes the silver halide of the film stock, while the representation of light becomes the projection of light.

Applying a mediaeval model of practice to a modern form inevitably fails to produce exact parallels, but viewing the division of work within the Python troupe in this way provides an interesting insight into Gilliam's aesthetic and his evolution as a filmmaker. It has been noted above, of course, that though less visually oriented than Gilliam, Jones still had a significant role in shaping the look of the film. In the medium of film, the written word becomes the spoken word, and so, in his care for capturing the performances of his fellow Pythons, Jones's directing style is directly comparable to the care with which a mediaeval scribe prepared their page. As Alexander informs us:

> Before a scribe started to work, the page had to be ruled. It is the general, or at least by far the commonest practice throughout the Middle Ages, for this scribed ruling to dictate the format of the miniatures, borders, and initials; that is, for them at least to conform to the column of script in width and to the lines of script in height. It has been shown that in Parisian illuminated manuscripts of the early fifteenth century, the page ruling might affect not just the format of a miniature, but its internal spatial organisation and objects represented, for instance the alignment of roof-lines or the doorposts of buildings. (Alexander 1992: 40)

In much the same way that Meuwese makes the link between Gilliam's preliminary sketches and the sourcebooks of the mediaeval illuminator, a parallel can be drawn between the practice of ruling as outlined by Alexander and the preparation of a film's script. If we consider the completed film as an illuminated manuscript and the performances contained therein as its text, it follows that Gilliam's animated segments, which Meuwese suggests 'function [mostly] as comic interludes that prevent the movie from becoming boring' (Meuwese 2004: 46), become the historiated initials that begin each segment of the story. The film's script, then, is the underpinning structure that is the ruled page, a comparison which complements Meuwese's observation regarding Gilliam's orientation sketches. Again, a relatively clear division is struck between the written and visual components of *Holy Grail* and the respective directorial responsibilities of Gilliam and Jones.

Having paralleled the practices of the scribe and the illuminator with that of the screenwriter and the director, the production of *Holy Grail* can now be examined in the terms of an illuminated manuscript. The likening of the cinematic form to the plastic arts is not a new concept, as is made evident by the titles of such studies as Andrey Tarkovsky's *Sculpting in Time* (1987) and David Bordwell's *Figures Traced in Light* (2005), and the formal similarities of the *fumetti*, the comic book and the film have proven of interest to several filmmakers, including Federico Fellini, Peter Greenaway and Gilliam himself. Though a sequential art form in its own right, film is often employed as a vehicle for spoken narrative; in other words, as a form of illustration. If we return now to the idea that *Holy Grail*'s script is the equivalent to the scribe's meticulously ruled page, we can compare the scribe's preparations to that of the director. As Bordwell writes, '[f]rom the early 1900s to the 1970s, directors working in film industries were expected to turn the script into scenes, and that task involved plotting, moment by moment, the dramatic interactions of characters in space' (Bordwell 2005: 7–8). Both mediaeval scribe and contemporary director are responsible for the allocation of space in the visual embellishment of their written material, the scribe by dividing up the blank page into the territories of text and image and the director by converting textual information into spatial, visual information. The line between writer-director-scribe and animator-director-illuminator may appear to blur here as the duties of the cinematic scribe and the filmic illuminator tread the same ground, but it must again be noted that the mediaeval practices which this chapter employs as its comparative model converged in a similar manner in the tenth and eleventh centuries; as Alexander notes, 'the two practices have now drawn together, are complementary, and in practice are often done by the same person' (Alexander 1992: 10).

The most useful comparison to be made, however, is with that of the collaborative turn that the process of manuscript illumination took over the course of the eleventh and twelfth centuries. In a very similar fashion to the way that the production of a film is a process involving experts in several crafts, practitioners of illumination began to specialise in different styles and techniques and additional designers and assistant illuminators began to be incorporated into the process. Alexander writes that:

> we begin to hear of lay illuminators who are professionals working directly for a stipend in cash or kind . . . lay artists were more mobile and could import new styles from considerable distances. A typical situation seems to have been that of a master craftsman, able to execute works in different media, being called to a monastery and given board and lodging for as long as was necessary to execute whatever was required. (Alexander 1992: 12)

It takes no stretch of the imagination to apply this framework to Gilliam's initiation into the ranks of Monty Python. Though not a particularly experienced animator when he left America for the UK, Gilliam had 'worked as a volunteer for a while in a studio that did stop-motion photography (dancing cigarette packets, that sort of thing)' (Gilliam and Thompson 2015: 67), and has memories of attempting to create animations by drawing directly on the celluloid (McCabe 1999: 18). By the time he came to work on *Flying Circus*, however, Gilliam had made the leap from near silent caricaturist on *We Have Ways of Making You Laugh* (1968) to animator for the same when he offered to animate the 'terrible little punning connections' of disc jockey Jimmy Young (Christie 1999: 39). Furthermore, as the filmmaker notes, 'Terry Jones has always claimed that my cartoon *Beware the Elephants* was the inspiration for the continuous stream-of-consciousness approach in *Monty Python*; in other words, we weren't constantly stopping and starting' (ibid.: 43). Though the truth of this claim is possibly tenuous at best, it points to an early instance of Gilliam's role as a cohesive force, as the linking component between the sketches written by the other Pythons. The animations he made for *Flying Circus* function in much the same manner as they do in *Holy Grail*: as a whimsical means of getting from one sketch to another, or as the historiated letter at the beginning of each new chapter. In this way, whether considered as a cartoonist, an animator or an illuminator, Gilliam fits the profile of the mobile craftsman, plying his expertise far from home.

Even in their utilisation as a narrative glue, there is a mediaeval sensibility to Gilliam's animated segments of *Holy Grail* that extends beyond their utilisation of period manuscript illustrations. Their positioning between narrative episodes is just as important as their visual design, as is the predominance of elements such as the changing seasons and the transgression of boundaries, such as doorways and indeed the ellipsis of time itself. As Michael Camille explains:

> In folklore, betwixt and between are important zones of transformation. The edge of the water was where wisdom revealed itself; spirits were

banished to the spaceless places 'between the froth and the water' or 'betwixt the bark and the tree'. Similarly, temporal junctures between winter and summer, or between night and day, were dangerous moments of intersection with the Otherworld. In charms and riddles, things that were neither this nor that bore, in their defiance of classification, strong magic. Openings, entrances and doorways, both of buildings and the human body (in one Middle English medical text there is mention of a medicine corroding 'the margynes of the skynne'), were especially important liminal zones that had to be protected. (Camille 2015: 16)

Each and every one of Camille's instances of 'betwixt and between' are present in *Holy Grail*, multiple times over; The Black Knight, the Blind Soothsayer, Tim the Enchanter, the Cave of Caerbannog and the keeper of the Bridge of Death are all found at boundaries that Arthur and his knights must cross in pursuit of the Grail. The Historian, too, who falls victim to the one mounted knight seen in the entirety of the film, is slain by a transgression of temporal boundaries as past and present collide. Perhaps most importantly, the animations trespass on the live-action narrative at two important junctures: when God, represented in a typically Gilliam-esque visual pun by cricketer W. G. Grace, appears to present Arthur with the Grail Quest; and, secondly, when The Black Beast of Aaargh emerges from the darkness of its cave, rupturing the boundary between the 'real' and liminal spaces, as text and marginalia interact and allow the knights to escape. The betwixt and between are zones of transformation, and within the context of *Holy Grail*'s formal construction Gilliam's animations serve as the liminal zones in which one narrative episode is effortlessly transformed into another. Although only two of the film's five animated sections, 'The Monster of Aaargh' and 'Season Animation', feature two-dimensional versions of the film's characters and so have any direct involvement with its narrative, all five act as transformative boundaries between the live action episodes by disregarding even their tenuous logic in favour of sheer absurdism. Palin informs us in his diary entry from 28 November 1973 that

> much of the absurd stuff that has already been written for the *Holy Grail* film has healthy precedents (e.g. taunting one's opponents and, as a last resort, firing dead animals at them during a siege – both quoted as mediaeval tactics by Montgomery). (Palin 2006: 164)

Yet Gilliam's animations, sourced from genuine manuscripts, observe the playful and nonsensical logic of their source material rather than that of the quest narrative, thus identifying themselves as fitting squarely in the tradition of mediaeval marginalia.

Meuwese observes that the three remaining animated segments, 'The Quest for the Holy Grail', 'The Tale of Sir Launcelot' and 'The Tale of Sir Galahad', function independently of the film's plot and instead serve a structural purpose (Meuwese 2004: 55), both as brief interludes between episodes of the story and, as previously suggested, the historiated initials of new chapters of the film's text, literalised by the trope of the on-screen 'book of the film'. In addition to the frequent use of the device of the opening storybook as a starting point for several of Disney's animated feature films between *Snow White and the Seven Dwarfs* (1937) and *Robin Hood* (1973), British films such as David Lean's *Great Expectations* (1946) and Powell and Pressburger's *The Red Shoes* (1948) also employed the trope to pay homage to their literary sources. The Pythons originally incorporated the device of the storybook as a cost-effective means of quickly introducing the knights that make up Arthur's questing contingent, replacing a montage sequence that Larsen posits 'may also have been intended to be a completely animated sequence' (Larsen 2015: 226), but like many of their money-saving decisions it serves to strengthen the film as a whole. Not only does the invention of a specific source text provide the film with the sense of a loose narrative structure, it unites the Pythons' style of comedy with their source material by echoing the trend, among mediaeval authors, of citing an authoritative foreign text which they have purportedly translated. As Palin notes, 'the story could be broken down into an old university revue format – ten sketches and three songs . . . it went off in all sorts of different directions and everyone had their adventure which is very much like the Arthurian legends' (Palin 2006: 236).

Conclusion

By breaking down the division of labour between its creators to that of the primarily written and the primarily visual, Jones and Gilliam can be placed within the mediaeval tradition of manuscript illumination; by borrowing elements from a range of mediaeval films, such as the self-flagellating monks of *The Seventh Seal* and the musical revelry of *Camelot*, the Pythons engage with existing representations and appropriations of the Middle Ages on film; and, by incorporating a supposed source text into the body of the film, they draw directly on the same device of literary authority as do the likes of Chrétien de Troyes and Malory. Furthermore, in both Gilliam's appropriation of mediaeval manuscript illuminations and the Pythons' postmodern interference with the quest narrative there is an echo of the relationship between the illuminator and the text that was to be illuminated. Camille writes:

> Ironically, the medieval illuminator hardly ever read the text of a work he was formally illustrating – in the case of Bibles or Romances – where he followed earlier copies or models; but on the edge he was free to read the words for himself and make what he wanted of them. In this respect, marginal images are *conscious* usurpation, perhaps even political

statements about diffusing the power of the text through its unravelling (the word 'text' is derived from *textus*, meaning weaving or interlacing), rather than repressed meanings that suddenly flash back onto the surface of things. (Camille 2015: 42)

Though it may initially appear as mere silliness masquerading in the trappings of Arthurian legend, *Monty Python and the Holy Grail* is in fact a highly complex engagement with and continuation of a wealth of literary, artistic and historical traditions. In the same way that these mediaeval illuminators offered, in their marginalia, commentary or interpretations of the material that they were illustrating, *Holy Grail* contains and exhibits the Pythons' readings, understandings and commentaries on the plethora of influences which made their way into the film. Absurd it may be, but the Pythons' contribution to the Arthurian tradition is a well-informed one and is, in its relationship between word and image, form and content, inherently mediaeval at heart.

Acknowledgements

This work was supported by the Arts and Humanities Research Council in conjunction with the Scottish Graduate School for Arts and Humanities.

Notes

1. This term was coined by Kevin J. Harty in 1987 to designate the body of films that engage with King Arthur and his associated literature, but which may not easily be ascribed to any one genre. For more information, see Harty (2010).
2. For a detailed account of Jones's career beyond *Python*, see Kern (2017).
3. Of the seven episodes written, only the first two still exist in their entirety, the rest having been lost when the master tapes were wiped for reuse by the broadcaster. These two episodes, in both their original and broadcast versions, were remastered and accompanied by a fifty-minute feature containing the remaining film links for the lost episodes on a dual-format BRD/DVD release from Network in 2013.
4. The political import of Hollywood's appropriation of Arthurian myth, particularly in the wake of the Kennedy assassination, falls outside this chapter's remit. See Aronstein.
5. Although *Holy Grail*, and later *Jabberwocky*, made a great show of poor dental hygiene, Jones points out that 'recent excavations on preserved skeletons from the period actually reveal very strong, healthy teeth' (Morgan 1999: 145n).

Works Cited

Alexander, Jonathan J. G. (1992) *Medieval Illuminators and Their Methods of Work*. London: Yale University Press.

Archer, Neil (2016) *Beyond a Joke: Parody in English Film and Television Comedy*. London: I. B. Taurus.
Aronstein, Susan (2005) *Hollywood Knights: Arthurian Cinema and the Politics of Nostalgia*. Basingstoke: Palgrave Macmillan.
Bergman, Ingmar (1956) '[On The Seventh Seal] Text from the Presentation of The Seventh Seal Bergman Gave to his Foreign Audience', *ingmarbergman.se*. <http://www.ingmarbergman.se/en/production/seventh-seal-0> (last accessed 14 August 2017)
Blandeau, Agnès (2006) *Pasolini, Chaucer and Boccaccio: Two Medieval Texts and Their Translation to Film*, Jefferson, NC: McFarland.
Bordwell, David (2005) *Figures Traced in Light*. London: University of California Press.
Camille, Michael (2015) *Image on the Edge: The Margins of Medieval Art*. London: Reaktion Books.
Christie, Ian (ed.) (1999) *Gilliam on Gilliam*. London: Faber & Faber.
Day, David D. (1991) 'Monty Python and the Medieval Other', in Kevin J. Harty (ed.), *Cinema Arthuriana: Essays on Arthurian Film*. New York: Garland Publishing, pp. 93–2.
Diringer, David (1980) 'Introduction: The Illuminated Book', in P. A. Winckler (ed.), *Reader in the History of Books and Printing*. Englewood, CO: Information Handling Services, pp. 148–53.
Forstater, Mark (2015) *The 7th Python: A Twat's Tale*. London: Irregular Content.
Gilliam, Terry and Ben Thompson (2015) *Gilliamesque: A Pre-Posthumous Memoir*. Edinburgh: Canongate.
Harty, Kevin J. (2010) *Cinema Arthuriana: Twenty Essays*, revised edn. London: McFarland.
Kern, Kevin F. (2017) 'From Silly to Scholarly: The Complete and Utter History of Terry Jones', in P. N. Reinsch, B. L. Whitfield and R. G. Weiner (eds), *Python beyond Python: Critical Engagements with Culture*. London: Palgrave Macmillan, pp. 37–54.
Larsen, Darl (2015) *A Book about the Film Monty Python and the Holy Grail: All the References from African Swallows to Zoot*. London: Rowman & Littlefield.
Levy, Brian and Lesley Coote (2004) 'The Subversion of Medievalism in *Lancelot du Lac* and *Monty Python and the Holy Grail*', in Richard Utz and Jesse G. Swan (eds), *Postmodern Medievalisms*. Cambridge: D. S. Brewer, pp. 99–126.
Lupack, Barbara Tepa and Alan Lupack (2008) *Illustrating Camelot*. Cambridge: D. S. Brewer.
McCabe, Bob (1999) *Dark Knights and Holy Fools: The Art and Films of Terry Gilliam*. London: Orion.
Meuwese, Martine (2004) 'The Animation of Marginal Decorations in "Monty Python and the Holy Grail"', *Arthuriana* 14(4), 45–58.
Morgan, David (1999) *Monty Python Speaks!*. New York: Avon Books.
Palin, Michael (2006) *Diaries 1969–1979: The Python Years*. London: Weidenfeld & Nicolson.
Palin, Michael (2012) 'Terry Jones: The Complete Medievalist', in R. F. Yeager and Toshiyuki Takamiya (eds), *The Medieval Python: The Purposive and Provocative Work of Terry Jones*. New York: Palgrave Macmillan, pp. 55–8.

Pythons, The and Bob McCabe (2003) *The Pythons Autobiography*. London: Orion Books.

Richie, Donald (1996) *The Films of Akira Kurosawa*, 3rd edn. London: University of California Press.

Rosenstone, Robert A. (1995) *Visions of the Past: The Challenge of Film to Our Idea of History*. London: Harvard University Press.

Törnqvist, Egil (2012) 'Bergman and Visual Art Egil Törnqvist Sheds Light on a Neglected Subject', *ingmarbergman.se*. <http://www.ingmarbergman.se/en/universe/bergman-and-visual-art> (last accessed 14 August 2017)

PART THREE

CONTEXTS AND REPRESENTATIONS

7. GRANNIES FROM HELL, DARING BICYCLE REPAIRMEN, UPPER-CLASS TWITS AND 'MAKE TEA NOT LOVE': *MONTY PYTHON'S FLYING CIRCUS* AND 1960S BRITISH (POPULAR) CULTURE

Caroline Langhorst

In 'Working-Class Playwright', the hard-working, well-dressed young miner (Eric Idle) tells his cramp-suffering, swearing and London-bound Northern playwright father (Graham Chapman) that he would realise one day that 'there's more to life than culture . . . there's dirt, and smoke, and good honest sweat'. The Pythons famously addressed both mentioned aspects, the diverse strands of culture and the highly absurd and morbid nature of life, in a distinctive satirical, surrealist and subversive manner. Moreover, the selected sketch proves to be an apt example of their recurrent 'practice of inverting all roles involving social class and national and generational identities' (Landy 2005: 71). Having grown up in post-war Britain and having accordingly encountered a more critical and radical atmosphere at university, they were also 'part of worldwide cultural transformations that increasingly challenged existing social and political institutions, opening the door . . . to more critical, and perhaps cynical, approaches to questions of authority, gender, generation, sexuality, and national and regional identity' (ibid.: 19). As a result, various well-known clichés of British culture in general as well as specific pivotal cultural transformations since the post-war era are repeatedly referenced throughout the entire *Flying Circus* series: these encompass the class division, the North–South divide and related kitchen sink aesthetics and narratives (the angry young man generation and the films of the British New Wave), the generational conflict and the growing significance of youth culture and anti-authoritarian stances, the related emergence of the supposedly 'affluent', 'permissive society', the accompanying choice of alternative, non-heteronormative lifestyles, as well as the influence of American popular culture and the prevalent fear of increasing Americanisation.

Furthermore, the Pythons' lasting cult status and idiosyncratic engagement with British society and culture, their explicit focus upon the (post-)adolescent state of mind, and their alleged countercultural edge (see Mills 2014: 134) legitimate an analytical focus on the *Flying Circus* era in particular. Drawing upon previous accounts of Monty Python's roots in 1960s British (popular) culture (Landy 2005) and counterculture (Mills 2014), this chapter sets out to further examine their early years within this highly conflicted sociocultural context. As has been widely noted (see Marwick 1998; Harris and O'Brien Castro 2014), both the 1960s in general as well as British culture of the time display a very contradictory disposition that is defined by a coexistence of progressive and reactionary tendencies (e.g. empire nostalgia). Throughout the chapter, several sketches that are linked to key aspects of the era will be analysed and further contextualised with similar treatments of British culture and society in 1960s British cinema.

'Let's do it a Dada': Surrealist and Psychedelic Tendencies in *Monty Python's Flying Circus* (1969–73)

The *Flying Circus* series engages with 1960s British culture on different levels: it integrates several significant artistic influences while simultaneously explicitly addressing specific sociocultural issues of the time (e.g. the generational conflict or the affluent, permissive society) as well as including a wide range of (pop-)cultural references.[1] Mills aptly observes a coexistent affinity *for* and critical engagement *with* the counterculture in relation to Eric Idle. Accordingly, '[f]rom *Do Not Adjust Your Set* through Python and the Rutles, we have a body of work which opens a window on the 1960s roots of his comedy' (Mills 2014: 126). He then names several key influences on Idle that can likewise be extended to the *Flying Circus* series: the early 1960s satire boom (*Beyond the Fringe*), the Beatles, surrealist art and 'the Dadaist artistic movement which informed the child-like surrealism of the Python troupe' (ibid.), as well as the Bonzo Dog Doo-Dah Band. All mentioned influences further share a power structures-ridiculing degree of the Bakhtinian carnivalesque (ibid.). Accordingly, they echo the 1960s anti-authoritarian and free-spirited countercultural and psychedelic mindset. Russell Duncan further identifies '[c]anonical items associated with psychedelia: visual arts, sex, drugs, new music, and hippie fashion' (Duncan 2013: 155), while Kevin Donnelly underscores that '[t]he British variant of psychedelia was perhaps more aesthetically than politically motivated' (Donnelly 2001: 21). As Mills stresses, the 1960s psychedelic tendency also employed a surrealist element to a certain degree. At the same time, it also displays an 'indeterminacy and randomness of language' and 'bathetic discontinuity' (Mills 2014: 129), which he subsequently also applies to *Monty Python's Flying Circus*. For him, the surrealistic or psychedelic aspect even serves as the series' cornerstone (ibid.). Consequently, the *Flying Circus*'s distinctive aesthetic is therefore predominantly characterised by 'a mélange of disparate subconscious images (Terry Gilliam's cartoons) and the ridiculous (Idle's puns)' (ibid.). Additionally, the Pythons as well as the Bonzo Dog Doo-Dah Band and the Beatles '[a]ll . . . exemplify surrealism or Dadaism in a popular or low-cultural framework' (ibid.: 126).

While the *Flying Circus* series classifies as a sketch show with interlinking elements (e.g. Gilliam's animations or the 'and now for something completely different' announcer), it maintains a singular position as the sketches themselves and the series' overall structure repeatedly tend to undermine the audience's expectations. As Alexander Brock highlights, the animations 'often took an element from the previous sketch as their starting point, developed it into a mini-narrative and then led on to the next sketch. The connections occasionally followed an unexpected logic' (Brock 2016: 53). Therefore, the series applies a kind of associative 'stream-of-consciousness approach' (ibid.). This, again, is also a characteristic of the psychedelic 1960s mindset that simultaneously echoes the spontaneous nature of Surrealist automatism. Unlike their previous contribution to the satirical television programme *The Frost Report* (1966–7) and the initially rather strict televisual conventions, the Pythons were granted a certain artistic licence with regard to the *Flying Circus* series (ibid.). As a result, many sketches not only contain absurd wordplay and tongue-in-cheek double entendres, but are also devoid of a punchline while quite a few are even suddenly abandoned (e.g. the 'Strangers in the Night' sketch, in which Terry Jones plays an adulterous, promiscuous wife who is simultaneously visited by her numerous lovers, episode 10, 'Untitled').

The Pythons' absurdist-surrealist tendency is also apparent in Richard Lester's 1960s output, ranging from both Beatles films (*A Hard Day's Night*, 1964, and *Help!*, 1965) to the post-nuclear comedy *The Bed Sitting Room* (1969). Particularly the latter appears as very Pythonesque, especially since Lester fuses absurdist comic elements with tragic-nihilistic dimensions as the narrative is principally centred upon 'the theme of human alienation brought about by social annihilation' (Sinyard 2010: 74). The breakdown of social hierarchies and its absurd, at times highly bizarre consequences – a certain Mrs Ethel Shroake becomes queen and '[t]he Prime Minister is selected on the basis of his inside-leg measurement' (ibid.: 75) – are also present in *Monty Python's Flying Circus*: in the 'It's a Tree' sketch, for example, a rainforest and a bucket of sawdust express their view on teenage violence (episode 10, 'Untitled'); or in the 'Poets' sketch, each household can install its own poet of choice (episode 17, 'The Buzz Aldrin Show').

The series is also notable for its meta-humoristic tendency: frequently, the artificial nature of the sketch show is pointed out directly, 'occasionally triggered by characters complaining about the poor quality of the lines written for them . . . , apologies for repetitiveness . . . or extras who were not informed about the content of sketches they were supposed to act in' (Brock 2016: 53) (e.g. the recurrent actor dressed up as a bishop). This device had, however, also recently made its appearance in absurdist theatre, namely in the plays of Joe Orton to name one significant example. In his seminal *Entertaining Mr Sloane* (1964), Orton explicitly refers to the play's artificial disposition. Moreover, similar to the narrative structure of the Python sketches, Orton's farcical comedy is marked by a specific degree of incongruity that continuously upsets the audience's expectations. The resulting 'dislocation between language and reality is the center of what has come to be called the "Ortonesque" – an intensely farcical style characterized by fast-paced, witty word play involving elevated language applied to low and base situations' (Lawson 2003: 16). In *Entertaining Mr Sloane*, Orton even goes so far as to eventually set out 'to frustrate the expectations of the audience' (ibid.: 19) by subverting the characteristics of a well-made play and, most notoriously, by discarding the anticipated happy ending. Since Python's *Flying Circus* series also aims at – and succeeds in – inverting and exposing 'institutionalized representations of gender and sexuality as they are expressed and disseminated broadly through the culture and through the medium of television' (Landy 2005: 79), Orton's decidedly queer perspective and candid attack on bourgeois hypocrisy and outright 'refusal of society's repressive categorization of sexual conduct as "normal" or "deviant", and his mockery of its attempts to pigeonhole individuals as one or the other' (Higgins 2006: 263–4) seem particularly noteworthy.

'WE'RE DOING OUR OWN THING, MAN': THE PYTHONS AND 1960S BRITAIN

As previously highlighted, '[t]he specific cultural moment of the show's appearance was also intrinsic to its success' (Landy 2005: 15). Accordingly, '[t]he character and effects of the *Flying Circus*' comedy are best described as belonging to this broadly acknowledged moment of transition' (ibid.). By the time the programme was aired, the general mood in Britain as well as in the United States was increasingly marked by a sense of disillusionment and frustration that resulted from the dire economic status quo and what was commonly regarded as the failure of the 1960s dream of peace, love, freedom, expanded perceptual dimensions and the overcoming of social boundaries and inequalities. In Britain, a growing dissatisfaction with the Labour government (1964–70) became manifest and there were various protests against the Vietnam War, no consensus regarding Britain's entry into the European Economic Community and several strikes (ibid.). However, as Landy underlines, the actual social discrepancies were to a certain extent covered by the increase in personal income (ibid.: 16). Moreover, the notion of the era's 'affluent society' was 'directly and indirectly intertwined with media' (ibid.). Consequently, the media, whose growing impact was also intellectually acknowledged by Marshall McLuhan's various writings, contributed to the public perception of the highly conflicted decade. While its exact periodisation remains equally problematic and contested, cultural memory of the 1960s is often characterised by a tendency to mythologise the era as a 'decade of decadence and decline' (Burkett 2013: 11). Emphasising the formative role of the post-war 'youthquake' in relation to a 'wider and often mythic construction of time' (Jenss 2015: 39), Heike Jenss then refers to Colin MacInnes's portrayal of British youth culture in his seminal *Absolute Beginners* (1959). The novel 'inscribes an opposing sartorial-temporal orientation in line with the dichotomous narrative of modernity' (Jenss 2015: 39), thus simultaneously accentuating the ongoing sociocultural changes, society's transitional status and the intricate difficulty of precisely locating the beginning of 1960s culture.

As Duncan aptly observes, an 'open sore between the violent realism of established structures and the utopian ideals of a peaceful global community' (Duncan 2013: 157) was brought to the fore. Accordingly, there was a feeling that something was profoundly wrong with the system. Furthermore, the impersonal nature of the late industrial society, the generational conflict and the fear of nuclear escalation generated a 'mood of tremendous angst' (ibid.: 147) among the baby boomers as well as a growing feeling of alienation. This Cold War anxiety is then ironically approached in the 'Bicycle Repair Man' sketch (episode 3, 'How to Recognise Different Types of Trees from Quite a Long Way Away') that also playfully references the increasing impact of American popular culture as well as Britain's fear of an impending Americanisation via the comic superhero theme. Throughout the sketch, American popular culture as well as consumerist and political ideologies are conflated. At the very beginning, the omnipresence of the American capitalist mindset (the comic/pop art style inserted intertitles) and its related hegemonic status as superpower are immediately introduced through the superman dress code every man seems to adhere to. Moreover, the heroic component accentuated in superhero comics that is further connoted with a decidedly virile and active conduct is satirised by means of the male characters' attempt at an overly muscular physique (their superman uniform is, however, clearly and particularly messily stuffed with something underneath to make it look more athletic). Even earlier on, this notion of (white) American masculinity had been openly mocked in the 'Marriage-Guidance Counsellor' sketch (episode 2, 'Sex and Violence') that featured a John Wayne-echoing Southerner/Westerner who observes '[a] man's got to do what a man's got to do, and there ain't no sense in runnin'. Now you gotta turn, and you gotta fight, and you gotta hold your head up high'. F. G. Superman's (Palin) hidden 'secret identity' and double life as Bicycle Repair Man among the supermen, in turn, allude to the notorious

House Un-American Activities Committee (HUAC) and Senator McCarthy's red scare moral panic and witch hunt in 1950s America, which extended to Hollywood and the arts (e.g. Wisconsin-born filmmaker Joseph Losey, for instance, famously went into British/European exile). As his alter ego, Bicycle Repair Man, F. G. Superman sports a simple, practical worker's outfit and pursues manual labour commonly associated with communist ideology. However, the contradictory and volatile nature of the Cold War conflict – particularly in the early 1960s pre- and post-Cuban Missile Crisis of 1962 – is underscored through a juxtaposition of both clashing ideological stances: despite Bicycle Repair Man's unadorned worker attire and helpful, selfless demeanour, the over-the-top conservative, biased, and even fascist, voice-over commentary claims that he is not only always prepared to repair bicycles. Instead, Bicycle Repair Man is on a vital mission to defend Western capitalism and ultimately 'smash the communists, wipe them out'. Subsequently, John Cleese is then shown as the conservative voice-over agitator who 'articulates' his racist political views without restraint, a clenched fist and in a ranting manner, eventually resorting to crude, demonising and simplified insults such as 'dirty red scum'.

As Jeremy Varon remarks, there was a 'longing of the era's youth for a more authentic, less mediated experience of self and world' (Varon 2011: 459). Modernist alienation resurfaced in European art cinema of the 1960s such as films by the likes of Ingmar Bergman or Michelangelo Antonioni, while Guy Debord famously argued in *The Society of the Spectacle* (1967) that 'the commodity – now transmuted into "spectacle," . . . had taken over the social function once fulfilled by religion and myth, and that appearances were now inseparable from the essential process of alienation and domination in modern society' (quoted in Marcus 2004: 8). The *Flying Circus* series comically discusses the existentialist influence and mood that was also reflected in Colin Wilson's 1956 study of isolation and alienation, *The Outsider*, and cinematically evoked in culturally pessimistic British films such as Peter Watkins's *Privilege* or Don Levy's *Herostratus* (both 1967). The commodification and persistent existentialist alienation of the individual and the mechanisation of life are foregrounded in both films and the latter even eerily anticipates the digital age and social media via its intended public suicide-turned-media spectacle.

The *Flying Circus* series also recurrently engages with this aspect: in episode 5, 'Man's Crisis of Identity in the Latter Half of the 20th Century', a depressed cat suffering from 'stockbroker syndrome', 'suburban fin-de-siècle ennui', 'angst' and 'Weltschmerz' is being treated. In the 'Literary Football Discussion' sketch (episode 11, 'The Royal Philharmonic Orchestra Goes to the Bathroom'), the continental existentialist atmosphere is applied to sports: 'when Jarrow United came of age in a European sense with an almost Proustian display of modern existentialist football'. 'The Hermits' sketch (episode 8, 'Full Frontal Nudity') then ironically addresses the drop-out mentality of the hippies. It depicts gossiping hermits who live alone yet together in a secluded cave community that still echoes the heteronormative, bourgeois societal structure while seemingly pursuing alternative lifestyles. In 'The Mouse Problem' (episode 2, 'Sex and Violence'), the secret pursuit of alternative lifestyles and new perceptual dimensions – in this case, the experimentation with cheese – playfully parodies the rather difficult and closeted queer existence in British society prior to the Sexual Offences Act of 1967. Several other sketches include alternative constructions of gender: cross-dressing sailors ('Children's Story', episode 3, 'How to Recognise Different Types of Trees from Quite a Long Way Away'), the supermen in a laundrette ('Bicycle Repair Man'), Michael Palin's homicidal Sweeney Todd barber who always aspired to be a lumberjack (episode 9, 'The Ant, an Introduction'), an explicit reference to Ronnie Kray's homosexuality ('Piranha Brothers', episode 15, 'The Spanish Inquisition'), or chatty gay judges ('Poofy Judges', episode 21, 'Archaeology Today').

The tendency towards a more liberated way of living had also partly been facilitated by several political scandals of the early 1960s: both the Vassall incident and its merging of espionage, blackmail and homosexuality, or the even more seminal Profumo affair, not only provided the press with sufficient material for an intensive, even sensationalist, news coverage, but moreover exposed the duplicitous morals of the affluent elite and its cultivated intricate web of power play, sex and corruption. According to Jon Towlson, the Profumo incident 'marked the turning point from a pre-pill, pre-promiscuity age, and a time of deference to those in government, to a more permissive era – one in which the established order was being challenged' (Towlson 2014: 81). The emerging 1960s satire boom and its candid, albeit ambiguous, mockery of authority figures and British institutions then has often been considered both 'a precursor to the "swinging sixties", arriving on the heels of the relaxation of censorship occasioned by the Lady Chatterley trial of 1960' (Ward 2001: 92) and a 'symbol of profound changes in the dominant values of post-war British society' (ibid.: 91) that was influenced by Britain's ongoing search for its post-imperial position in the world. The related liberation of artistic modes of expression (free verse, musical experimentation and improvisation) is also ironically addressed in the *Flying Circus*: in the 'The Poet McTeagle' sketch (episode 16, 'Déjà Vu'), the eponymous and constantly penniless Scottish 'Lend us a quid' poet and the subsequently interviewed turtleneck-wearing playwright both ironically evoke the Beat generation as well as the Situationist fusion of everyday life and art.

'For a start David Hockney is going to design the bombs': *Monty Python's Flying Circus*, the Late 1960s and the Counterculture

As already stated, social unrest reached a new degree in the United States as well as in Europe (e.g. the 1968 student protests in Paris and their militant

'Marx, Mao, Marcuse' slogans [Duncan 2013: 149]). The increasing recourse to acts of violence on both sides also exposed the more destructive side of the era, thus demonstrating that 'the culture of peace and love was also a culture of confrontation and conflict' (Miller 2011: 87). The *Flying Circus* series similarly foregrounds the ambivalent nature of the 1960s and the counterculture: it explicitly references films such as *The Wild One* (László Benedek, 1953) starring Marlon Brando as conflicted biker leader Johnny who seemingly rebels against everything (episode 10, 'Untitled'), Lindsay Anderson's 1968-infused *If . . .* – specifically emphasising its violent climax – or John Schlesinger's melancholy *Midnight Cowboy* (1969) (both episode 19, 'It's a Living'). Additionally, it also implicitly alludes to Swinging London's infamous yet alluring crime and pop milieux-merging gangster duo, the Kray Brothers (the 'Piranha Brothers'), or cheekily calls its second episode 'Sex and Violence'. The 'Twentieth Century Vole' sketch (episode 6, 'It's the Arts') then not only mocks the then-prominent idea of the filmmaker as an individualist auteur with a specific vision as championed by the proponents of the French New Wave. It also explicitly exposes the shady, corrupt side of Hollywood's film business. In the British context, this also alludes to 1960s Soho's association with both sex and cinema (see Halligan 2003: 60). The producer's (Chapman) proposed idea of a picture also reflects the changing mores by juxtaposing the quintessential American couple of tame romantic comedies with screwball elements, Doris Day and Rock Hudson, that are still rooted in the 1950s ideal of the nuclear suburban family with the more liberated and experimental Swinging Sixties mindset: 'It's a love story. Intercourse. Italian-Style. David Hemmings as a hippie Gestapo officer. Frontal nudity. A family picture.' The references to Swinging Sixties icon David Hemmings and 'Italian-Style' lovemaking play on the permissiveness connoted by Swinging London as well as the increasingly less inhibited depiction of sexuality in European cinema. While British films such as *Darling* (John Schlesinger, 1965), *The Pleasure Girls* (Gerry O'Hara, 1965), *Alfie* (Lewis Gilbert, 1966), Michelangelo Antonioni's *Blow-Up* (1966) featuring Hemmings's by now iconic role as a fashion photographer, *Here We Go Round the Mulberry Bush* (Clive Donner, 1968) or *The Touchables* (Robert Freeman, 1968), on the one hand, display this curious mindset, on the other hand they 'do not simply celebrate freedom, superficiality, popular culture and affluence' (Luckett 2000: 233). Instead, they at times also 'conjure up a particularly bleak vision of the Swinging London zeitgeist' (ibid.).

Unsurprisingly, permissiveness and playfully naughty remarks also feature strongly in the *Flying Circus* series: whether it be the 'Marriage Guidance Counsellor' sketch (episode 2, 'Sex and Violence'), the 'Nudge Nudge' sketch (episode 3, 'How to Recognise Different Types of Trees from Quite a Long Way Away'), Eric Idle's refreshment room host Kenny Lust (episode 9, 'The Ant, an Introduction'), the naughty chemists (episode 17, 'The Buzz Aldrin Show'), the romantic date that almost turned into a 'very broad-minded' 1960s Dionysian love-in, even featuring Palin holding a goat that evokes Satyr connotations (episode 9, 'The Ant, an Introduction'), Idle's groovy, laid-back hippie who lives with his commune inside Palin's character (episode 13, 'Intermission'), multiple marriages and communal living ('They're all married and living quite well in a council estate near Dulwich'; episode 19, 'It's a Living'), or the very enamoured shadow minister and his dachshund (episode 20, 'The Attila the Hun Show'). The permissive society is also frequently directly referenced and discussed, either via interviews, talk shows or complaining letters.

The class struggle then is similarly repeatedly referenced: whereas the well-known 'Upper-Class Twit' sketch (episode 12, 'The Naked Ant') mocks the Ruling Class's delusions of grandeur and privilege, the 'Idiot in Society' sketch (episode 20, 'The Attila the Hun Show') deals with the city residents' prejudices against the rural community and clichéd notions of backwardness as well as various clichés country folk associate with their own kind. The generational conflict is then brought to the fore by the scepticism of the older, self-taught village idiots towards the college education of their graduate offspring – a diploma in Idiocy awarded by the University of East Anglia – that was enabled by the post-war social transformations. In the 'Vox Pops on Politicians' sketch (episode 21, 'Archaeology Today') that ironically applies the devoted groupie lifestyle linked to the hedonistic realm of rock 'n' roll excess to the allegedly respectable yet scandal-ridden political sphere, the interviewed parents similarly express disappointment in their wayward, hippie aesthetics-sporting children who have run away from home to obsessively follow politicians. At the same time, the privileged upbringing associated with London's elite (Eton, Sandhurst, Oxbridge, parents either bankers, aristocrats or in politics) is ridiculed. Peter Medak's 1972 comedy *The Ruling Class*, for instance, adopts a similar satirical fashion: it mocks the aristocracy via its schizophrenic protagonist (Peter O'Toole) who becomes the 14th Earl of Gurney and believes himself to be the reincarnation of Jesus before undergoing a further – albeit electroshock-induced – metamorphosis from a peaceful, nature-loving hippie 'Christ' into torture-obsessed Jack the Ripper.

Two years after the Summer of Love, psychedelic happenings and the related 'Turn on, Tune In, Drop Out' mentality, which also witnessed a public love-in in Hyde Park, and a few months after Woodstock, the Altamont Free Concert with its violent outcome likewise underscored the darker side of the counterculture. On top of this,

> the break-up of the Beatles and the expansion of the '27 Club', with the deaths of Brian Jones, Jimi Hendrix, Janis Joplin, and Jim Morrison between 1969 and 1971, marked the end of whatever 'innocence' remained in youth counterculture. (Gair 2007: 9)

The tensions and conflicts of the decade are then cinematically echoed in several by now iconic 1960s British films such as Michael Reeves's *Witchfinder General* (1968) starring Vincent Price as the ruthless witchfinder Matthew Hopkins as well as Donald Cammell's and Nicolas Roeg's *Performance* (1970)[2] with Mick Jagger as Dionysian reclusive rock star Turner. *Witchfinder General* comments upon the culture wars of the decade by explicitly relating its period setting to the contemporary conflict (Towlson 2014: 88). Simultaneously, it reflects the countercultural fascination with occultism and paganism, its related search for simpler times than the technocratic, affluent and estranged present and the prevalent yearning for a more authentic national culture (see Hunt 2002: 84). *Performance*, on the other hand, depicts the 'post-Altamont, post-Manson' (Hunt 1998: 143) status quo and prevalent atmosphere of violence and disillusion. Thus, it deconstructs the myth of the allegedly Swinging Sixties by stressing the self-destructive disposition of late 1960s culture and pop music (see Donnelly 2001: 22; Smith 2010: 55) and the counterculture's highly ambiguous and contradictory disposition that is marked both by a conflation of seemingly rebellious defiance and consumerism as well as by a reproduction of specific mainstream practices.

This latter stance is, for instance, also articulated in both the 'Working-Class Playwright' and the 'Flying Sheep' sketches (both episode 2, 'Sex and Violence') as either individualist-artistic (playwright) or career-driven and class-related (the ambitious, clever and thus dangerous ringleader sheep Harold and the equally ambitious, exploitative farmer) forces that are explicitly linked with entrepreneurial spirit and desired commercial success. British films of the time such as the Joseph Losey–Harold Pinter collaboration *The Servant* (1963) or the black comedy *Nothing But the Best* (1964) also brought this aspect to the fore: while the class struggle depicted in *The Servant* takes the shape of Pinteresque power plays with a decidedly sexual – that is, queer – tension, the latter film presents a highly ambitious young man (Alan Bates) who transcends every moral boundary – including manipulation, murder and related sexual blackmailing to keep his dark deed a secret – to get to the top. Both Python's 'Blackmail' sketch (episode 18, 'Live from the Grill-O-Mat') and the 'Secretary of State Striptease' sketch (episode 20, 'The Attila the Hun Show'), in which important politicians enter the Peephole Club's world of burlesque, also follow in this vein, thereby also evoking the previously mentioned Vassall affair.

The *Flying Circus* series' repeated fusion of surrealist, playful and satirical wordplay and a recurrent explicitly macabre humour (e.g. the 'Undertakers Sketch', episode 26, 'Royal Episode 13'; 'Falling from Buildings', episode 12, 'The Naked Ant'; 'Famous Deaths' and 'Funniest Joke in the World', episode 1, 'Whither Canada?'; or the occult practices employing police officers in episode 13, 'Intermission') then echo both dominant strands of the 1960s. This specific combination of tongue-in-cheek humour and Gothic horror had become popular with the emergence of American television series such as *The Addams Family* (1964–6), *The Munsters* (1964–6) or *Dark Shadows* (1966–71) that ironically subvert the American ideal of the nuclear suburban family. In the first sketch of episode 20, 'The Attila the Hun Show', for instance, such an alternative family image is constructed by depicting the eponymous warrior as husband and father who has just come home from 'another merciless sweep across Central Europe'.

'[B]EING ILLEGAL MAKES IT MORE EXCITING': YOUTH CULTURE, DELINQUENCY AND THE PYTHONS

In the following, the Pythons and their specific relation to the post-war youthquake will be examined. The new role of post-war youth culture and its eager embrace of rock 'n' roll music as a 'means of cultural and generational expression' (Caine 2004: 97) received different reactions from the parent generation and cultural elite who feared a considerable and presumably irrevocable decline in moral values and cultural standards. The portrayal of youth as social problem also emanates partly from the exaggerated media coverage of an alleged increase in juvenile delinquency and violent outbursts such as the 1958 Notting Hill race riots, the violent behaviour of the Teddy boys in the 1950s, or the seaside Mods vs Rockers clash in the summer of 1964. Moral panics surrounding juvenile delinquency had already peaked in the United States a decade earlier since 'the gradual relaxation of the Hollywood Production Code and the growth of independent filmmaking brought to the forefront a whole series of American movies which openly explored taboo-breaking subjects around sexuality, crime, and the use of drugs' (Biltereyst 2007: 9). Particularly, *The Wild One*, *Rebel Without a Cause* (Nicholas Ray, 1955) and *Blackboard Jungle* (Richard Brooks, 1955) 'directly confronted the issue of postwar youngsters' crime and gang life, initiating cycles of teen-pic exploitation films often called juvenile delinquency movies (Gilbert, 178–195; Doherty, 1–18; Shary 2002, 82)' (Biltereyst 2007: 9). *The Wild One*, for instance, even 'had been considered too risky for general distribution in post-war Britain and was banned by the British Board of Film Censors until 1967' (Tebbutt 2016: 98).

A close reading of the sketch 'Hell's Grannies' (episode 8, 'Full Frontal Nudity') aims to demonstrate how the *Flying Circus* series engages with different aspects related to youth culture and juvenile delinquency as well as the counterculture. The moral panic surrounding juvenile delinquency, for instance, is then openly parodied in the sketch. It starts with a kitchen sink atmosphere evoking shot of a bleak district in Bolton (Greater Manchester) and the northern city is introduced by the news presenter's (Eric Idle) voice-over as 'a frightened' place that is burdened by the 'fear of a new kind of violence which is terrorising the city'. Then two young men (played by Chapman and

Jones) appear who are subculturally dressed in cuffed jeans – like Brando in *The Wild One* – and short jackets. Shortly afterwards, the audience's expectations are subverted by a suddenly introduced narrative twist: aggressive old women with a high-pitched mean giggle emerge from behind the trees and start attacking the two men while the voice-over announces, 'Yes, gangs of old ladies attacking defenceless young men.' The old ladies in entirely black attire then go on prowling the streets and repeatedly either pushing away or attacking other people. Very briefly, the eponymous 007 theme song from *Thunderball* (Terence Young, 1965) is played to mockingly underscore their 'menacing' demeanour. Even more ironically, two apparently frightened leather-clad bikers (Jones and Cleese) are interviewed: they state that it was a quiet place before the old women appeared and that it is now simply no longer safe to leave the house. This is an ironic inversion of the clichéd moral panic surrounding motorcycle gangs. The biker phenomenon was particularly present in 1960s American cinema, including Roger Corman's *The Wild Angels* (1966), Richard Rush's *Hells Angels on Wheels*, Anthony M. Lanza's *The Glory Stompers* (both 1967) and Dennis Hopper's *Easy Rider* (1969). A prominent British example would be the cult horror/biker film *Psychomania* (Don Sharp, 1973) that ironically and playfully fuses the lust for ultimate mayhem and destruction depicted in American exploitation biker films with British occultism and paganism, a devilish butler figure and a rural setting.

The sketch further encapsulates both the 1950s moral panics atmosphere surrounding juvenile delinquency as well as its further development during the 1960s. The, in this case 'senile', delinquents are described derisively as 'old hoodlums' and 'layabouts-in-lace' who preferably attack telephone kiosks, shamelessly graffiti walls with imperative slogans ('Make tea not love'), and are – according to an exasperated police officer (Chapman) – generally causing nothing but mischief, especially on pension day when they immediately 'blow it all on milk, bread, tea'. They also tend to behave aggressively during 2pm matinée screenings, especially if *The Sound of Music* (Robert Wise, 1965) is being shown. 'Hell's Grannies' embarks upon an ironic play with cultural myths about both the youth culture of the day as well as the 1960s counterculture. The slogan 'Make tea not love' represents an explicit tongue-in-cheek mockery of the hippie mantra 'Make love, not war' while at the same time bringing both the Summer of Love and John Lennon's and Yoko Ono's famous bed-ins for peace to mind, which are, in turn, openly parodied in episode 24, 'How Not to Be Seen' (Idle's Lennon: 'I'm starting a war for peace!') and the Rutles' mockumentary *All You Need Is Cash* (Eric Idle and Gary Weis, 1978). The actually conservative and repressive message conveyed via 'Make tea not love' as well as the rather Puritan nature of the grannies' alleged excesses (milk, bread, tea) or their cinematic preferences (*The Sound of Music*) again expose the previously highlighted conflicted disposition of the countercultural mindset. The mentioning of the eagerly awaited pension day also hints at the new significance of leisure time for post-war adolescents as well as a growth in job opportunities and a resulting increase in affluence.

At the same time, however, the authority figure's (Chapman's police officer) slight expression of outrage with regard to the grannies' 'hedonistic' profligacy ironically alludes to the increasing drug excesses of the mid- to late 1960s. As David Simonelli observes: 'By 1968, Britain had developed an alternative youth culture based around rock music, Romantic values, the experience of drugs, and a general desire to explore the limits of human experience' (Simonelli 2013: 139). Particularly William Blake and his notion of excess as well as nineteenth-century works of art by the likes of Charles Baudelaire (*The Flowers of Evil*, 1857–68), Arthur Rimbaud, Joris-Karl Huysmans (his seminal *Against Nature*, 1884) or Oscar Wilde (both fin-de-siècle London and Wildean wit are playfully addressed in the 'Oscar Wilde Sketch', episode 39, 'Grandstand') seemed to appeal to the curious 1960s mindset that, in the aftermath of Aldous Huxley's *The Doors of Perception* (1954), yearned for the psychedelic discovery of new perceptual and sexual dimensions. These artists also had a considerable impact upon singer-songwriters such as Bob Dylan, Jim Morrison or Leonard Cohen. In the British context, the Rolling Stones represented the darker, Dionysian side of the counter-culture since 'they reignited rock'n'roll's associations with delinquency that had been reconfigured in the mid-decade's optimism' (James 2016: 255). Simonelli then underscores that the Stones were turned into 'clear targets of press and public fears' as well as the 'embodiment of youth culture's evils' (Simonelli 2013: 116). While Mills describes Eric Idle's friendship with George Harrison (Mills 2014: 131), it may also be noted that Keith Richards also 'spent much of his time with Peter Cook and members of the Python crew' (Sandford 2012: 291).

The ironic hint at the grannies' unruly behaviour in the cinema also references the tumultuous reception of *Blackboard Jungle* in the United States, continental Europe and the UK. In Britain, this kind of mayhem tended to be predominantly blamed on the Teddy boys at the time (see Tebbutt 2016: 98). Moreover, however, the fact that the delinquents who adopt such conduct are senior citizens in this case then results in an ironic inversion of the era's fascination with youthfulness and its 'idealized and romanticized view of childhood and adolescence' (Mills 2014: 133). Idle's news presenter, who has just embarked upon a moralising lecture on the grannies' outright 'rejection of the values of contemporary society: They see their children grow up and become accountants, stockbrokers', is then quickly and irreverently silenced by the mischievous old ladies and therefore unable to reach a final verdict on the matter.

Conclusion

As the preceding analysis has hopefully demonstrated, Python's *Flying Circus* era is deeply intertwined with the post-war sociocultural transformations, various twentieth-century artistic strands (Surrealism, Dadaism) and, more specifically, 1960s (British) culture. Particularly the 1960s influence becomes manifest on different levels: the aesthetic-stylistic level (*Flying Circus*'s surrealist and psychedelic tendencies), the impact of the sociocultural background, the 'youthquake' and the countercultural mindset and the encounter with both American and British popular culture. The series also generally employs many references to films and music of the time. As the close reading of 'Hell's Grannies' then set out to highlight, *Monty Python's Flying Circus* engages with the sociocultural context of the 1960s and its popular culture in a very nuanced manner. Despite its stylistically spontaneous absurdist-surrealist tendencies, the cultural references are, in fact, thoroughly situated in the sketches' respective structural composition.

Mills further claims that 'Idle and the Pythons are cut from the same material as the rock bands of the 1960s. They are iconoclastic, surrealist, absurdist, and youthful' (Mills 2014: 134). Therefore, like the Beatles and the Rolling Stones, the Pythons are also 'informed by a hippie culture: they are a symbol of a youth-obsessed decade' (ibid.). Idle confirms this remark by stating that the group 'addresses the post-adolescent state. It's anti-army, anti-authority, anti-teachers, anti-church, anti-mothers, anti-fathers, anti-aunties' (quoted in ibid.). At the same time, however, like the Oxbridge-educated members of *Beyond the Fringe*, the creative driving forces behind the British New Wave or the 1960s counterculture, the Pythons belonged to the very bourgeois patriarchal system they set out to criticise. Accordingly, they echo the initially mentioned contradictory coexistence of progressive and conservative tendencies (e.g. the counterculture's conflation of rebellious defiance and a consumerist stance, its penchant for alternative lifestyles that still do not completely break free from heteronormative norms as mentioned in relation to the 'Hermits' sketch, the fusion of art and entrepreneurialism as evident in the 'Poet McTeagle' sketch, the 'Working-Class Playwright' and the 'Flying Sheep' sketches, or the repeatedly addressed generational conflict) that characterised 1960s British society to a certain extent. Nonetheless, given the sheer abundance of (popular) cultural references, further examinations of the Pythons' distinctive relation to 1960s culture or specific aspects thereof would prove very insightful.

Notes

1. These, to name only a few examples, include contemporary artists such as David Hockney, singers such as Petula Clark, actors such as Marlon Brando or Paul Newman, film directors such as Stanley Kubrick, Lindsay Anderson, John Schlesinger, Sam Peckinpah, Pier Paolo Pasolini or Alfred Hitchcock, or sex symbols of the time such as actress Raquel Welch.
2. The film was originally shot in 1968.

Works Cited

Biltereyst, Daniel (2007) 'American Juvenile Delinquency Movies and the European Censors: The Cross-Cultural Reception and Censorship of *The Wild One*, *Blackboard Jungle*, and *Rebel Without a Cause*', in Timothy Shary and Alexandra Seibel (eds), *Youth Culture in Global Cinema*. Austin: University of Texas Press, pp. 9–26.

Brock, Alexander (2016) '"The Struggle of Class against Class Is a What Struggle?" *Monty Python's Flying Circus* and Its Politics', in Jürgen Kamm and Birgit Neumann (eds), *British TV Comedies: Cultural Concepts, Contexts and Controversies*. Basingstoke: Palgrave Macmillan, pp. 51–65.

Burkett, Jodi (2013) *Constructing Post-Imperial Britain: Britishness, 'Race' and the Radical Left in the 1960s*. Basingstoke: Palgrave Macmillan.

Caine, Andrew (2004) *Interpreting Rock Movies: The Pop Film and Its Critics in Britain*. Manchester: Manchester University Press.

Donnelly, Kevin J. (2001) *Pop Music in British Cinema: A Chronicle*. London: British Film Institute.

Duncan, Russell (2013) 'The Summer of Love and Protest: Transatlantic Counterculture in the 1960s', in Grzegorz Kosc, Clara Juncker, Sharon Monteith and Britta Waldschmidt-Nelson (eds), *The Transatlantic Sixties: Europe and the United States in the Counterculture Decade*. Bielefeld: Transcript Verlag, pp. 144–73.

Gair, Christopher (2007) *The American Counterculture*. Edinburgh: Edinburgh University Press.

Halligan, Benjamin (2003) *Michael Reeves*. Manchester: Manchester University Press.

Harris, Trevor and Monia O'Brien Castro (2014) *Preserving the Sixties: Britain and the 'Decade of Protest'*. Basingstoke: Palgrave Macmillan.

Higgins, David (2006) 'Joe Orton: Anger, Artifice and Absurdity', in Mary Luckhurst (ed.), *A Companion to Modern British and Irish Drama 1880–2005*. Oxford: Blackwell Publishing, pp. 258–68.

Hunt, Leon (1998) *British Low Culture: From Safari Suits to Sexploitation*. London and New York: Routledge.

Hunt, Leon (2002) 'Necromancy in the UK: Witchcraft and the Occult in British Horror', in Steve Chibnall and Julian Petley (eds), *British Horror Cinema*. London and New York: Routledge, pp. 82–98.

James, David E. (2016) *Rock'N'Film: Cinema's Dance with Popular Music*. Oxford: Oxford University Press.

Jenss, Heike (2015) *Fashioning Memory: Vintage Style and Youth Culture*. London and New York: Bloomsbury.

Landy, Marcia (2005) *Monty Python's Flying Circus*. Detroit, MI: Wayne State University Press.

Lawson, D. S. (2003) 'The Creation of Comedy in Joe Orton's *Entertaining Mr. Sloane*', in Francesca Coppa (ed.), *Joe Orton: A Casebook*. London and New York: Routledge, pp. 15–20.

Luckett, Moya (2000) 'Travel and Mobility: Femininity and National Identity in Swinging London Films', in Justine Ashby and Andrew Higson (eds), *British Cinema, Past and Present*. London and New York: Routledge, pp. 233–46.

Marcus, Greil (2004) 'The Long Walk of the Situationist International', in Tom McDonough (ed.), *Guy Debord and the Situationist International: Text and Documents*. Cambridge, MA: MIT Press, pp. 1–20.

Marwick, Arthur (1998) *The Sixties: Cultural Revolution in Britain, France, Italy and the United States, c.1958–c.1974*. Oxford: Oxford University Press.

Miller, Timothy S. (2011) *The Hippies and American Values*, 2nd edn. Knoxville: University of Tennessee Press.

Mills, Richard (2014) 'Eric Idle and the Counterculture', in Tomasz Dobrogoszcz (ed.), *Nobody Expects the Spanish Inquisition: Cultural Contexts in Monty Python*. Lanham, MD: Rowan & Littlefield, pp. 126–35.

Sandford, Christopher (2012) *The Rolling Stones: Fifty Years*. London: Simon & Schuster.

Simonelli, David (2013) *Working-Class Heroes: Rock Music and British Society in the 1960s and 1970s*. Lanham, MD: Lexington Books.

Sinyard, Neil (2010) *Richard Lester*. Manchester: Manchester University Press.

Smith, Justin (2010) *Withnail and Us: Cult Films and Film Cults in British Cinema*. London and New York: I. B. Tauris.

Tebbutt, Melanie (2016) *Making Youth: A History of Youth in Modern Britain*. Basingstoke: Palgrave Macmillan.

Towlson, Jon (2014) *Subversive Horror Cinema: Countercultural Messages of Films from* Frankenstein *to the Present*. Jefferson, NC: McFarland.

Varon, Jeremy (2011) 'After "The Fall": Politics, Representation, and the Permanence of Empire in the Cinema of Peter Whitehead', *Framework: The Journal of Cinema and Media* 52(1), 458–79.

Ward, Stuart (2001) *British Culture and the End of Empire*. Manchester: Manchester University Press.

8. THE PARROT, THE ALBATROSS AND THE CAT: ANIMALS AND COMEDY IN MONTY PYTHON

Brett Mills

Introduction: The Parrot

The most famous sketch in the history of Monty Python is that commonly known as 'the dead parrot sketch' (also known as 'the pet shop sketch' and 'parrot sketch'). It has a disarmingly simple premise: a customer (John Cleese) returns to a pet shop to complain that the parrot he has recently bought is dead. The comedy arises from the shop owner's (Michael Palin) refusal to accept that it is no longer alive, and a battle of wordplay ensues as the customer uses an increasingly complex array of terms to describe the animal's deceased state while the shop owner offers a variety of rationales for the bird's lack of movement. The sketch quickly moves beyond this set-up, with the customer being advised to visit the pet shop's complaints department, and, after a detour into a sequence where he is confused about being in Bolton or Ipswich, the sketch ends as many others in Monty Python do; with Graham Chapman's army captain entering the scene and complaining that everything has now gone too silly, and that the programme should move onto something else. The sketch is the UK's favourite sketch from across the whole of the troupe's output (Jefferies 2014), and was voted as the second greatest comedy sketch in the history of British television in one poll (BBC News 2005) and first in another (BBC News 2004). Its iconic status as an 'old friend' (Wilmut 1980: 205) of Monty Python fans was confirmed when, in order to promote the troupe's comeback performances in London in 2014, a fifty-foot-long fibreglass model of the deceased bird was unveiled in the city (Rucki 2014).

While the comedy of the sketch is dependent upon the linguistic playfulness and absurdity of the two participants' responses, coupled with the contradiction of Cleese's strained exasperation and Palin's cunning benignity, it is also important that the sketch is about a parrot. Indeed, in outlining the development of the sketch, Cleese has stated that it began as being about a shifty car salesman, before he and his co-writer (Graham Chapman) thought such a setting not inventive enough. When it was decided a pet shop would instead be more productive, the next step was to decide upon the animal being returned:

> What animal, then? A cat? No, dead kitties are not funny. A mouse? Wouldn't work: too small, and too vulnerable. Something big? A dog? Could work, but people are fond of dogs. Imagine banging a dead dog against a counter to wake it up – you could get lynched. A parrot . . . ? Yes! Nobody's going to get upset about the death of a cartoon creature like a parrot – except, perhaps, its owner . . . (Quoted in Lockett 2014)

While revealing an interesting insight into the decidedly mechanical nature of the creative process, Cleese's recollection also indicates an awareness of the sociocultural meanings of a variety of animal species. That a cat would not be funny, that a mouse is 'too vulnerable', that a sketch about a dead dog raises fears of lynching, points to the differing meanings contemporary Western television audiences assign to an array of animals. Furthermore, this process indicates the particular relationships that exist between comedy and animals, whereby the use of non-humans for humorous purposes – especially if those animals are dead – is socially regulated in terms of offence. The funniness of the sketch is therefore dependent on picking the right animal, and the right animal is dependent upon cultural connotations of the selected non-human, both within society as a whole and in comedy in particular. In order to delineate the functions to which comedy can put animals, this chapter examines the use of animals in the output of the Monty Python team to delineate the humorous functions animals can and cannot play within the kinds of comedy they produce. It works from the assumption that the purposes to which humans put animals reveal something significant about human–animal relations; furthermore, that when those purposes are – as here – comic, they help highlight those assumptions and, in some places, interrogate them. Indeed, some of the comedy in Monty Python works precisely by refusing to conform to standards of broadcasting decency which, for 'the parrot sketch', meant that fears of lynching result in the impossibility of 'the dead dog sketch'. By this account, comedy is a useful mode for thinking through the complex and contradictory understandings humans have of animals, especially given that it is precisely those complications that humour can draw upon so productively for its matter.

Marcia Landy argues that the Pythons' use of animals for comic purposes arises from the unsettling nature of 'unpredictable transformations' that 'ridicule the cultural restraints placed on the human body and on all forms of language' (Landy 2005: 63). These restraints apply to cultural understandings of animals too, and thus the humour arises from the rejection of those societal norms. By this account, such representations of animals in comedy could be seen to function in a powerful way, critiquing and destabilising human–animal relationships. A reading such as this could align with emerging debates about the representations of animals within culture, particularly given that culture relies on language, and 'language [has] denied animals throughout the history of much philosophy' (Lippit 2015: xiv). This has resulted in conceptualisations of animals as lacking in the kind of subjectivity deemed to define the human; and the consequence of this is that animals within cultural representations are forever objects rather than subjects. We can then see 'people's framing of animals in visual culture' (Malamud 2012: 2) as a powerful contributor to humans' treatment of animals in the lived world. Indeed, humans encounter animals as representations far more often than they do as living beings; it is not unlikely that many people who have seen 'the parrot sketch' might never have encountered an actual, living parrot. Thus, human–animal relationships are ones dominated by representations, to the extent that those relationships are ones *of* representation.

The particularities of those representations are inflected here via the comic nature of the programme under discussion. Indeed, the relationships between animals and comedy are acute, for there is

> a common view that almost anything to do with animals is somehow funny, or at least likely to be funny. This funniness in animal representation – a release from the usual constraints of meaning – may range from the endearingly amusing to the surrealistic and bizarre. (Baker 2001: 23)

What this suggests is that animals function as a representational category which can be used for particular purposes within human cultures, and those purposes rely on an understanding of animals as 'somehow funny'. This funniness is dependent on their non-human status, and that distinction is enough to render animals funny. What this means is that comedy functions as a space within which the human norm is repeatedly reinscribed, via the representation of the other which is not human: the animal. That a culture should find animals *intrinsically* funny points to the certainty of human–animal distinctions, with humour used to police and naturalise those distinctions.

Given this 'common view' of animals' funniness, it is not surprising that animals recur across Monty Python's oeuvre beyond the 'Dead Parrot Sketch'. In *Monty Python's Flying Circus*, these include: 'Mouse Organ' in which Terry

Jones hammers mice to make music, 'Albatross' in which John Cleese attempts to sell that bird in a manner more akin to ice-cream, the linked 'Flying Sheep' and 'French Lecture on Sheep Aircraft' in which sheep suddenly become airborne, 'Confuse-A-Cat' in which a vet advises a couple worried about their cat's lack of movement to confuse it more, 'Gorilla Librarian' featuring a gorilla at a job interview, and 'Crunchy Frog', where that animal's inclusion in a box of chocolates is deemed problematic. In the Monty Python films, animals often appear for comic purposes too, from *Holy Grail*'s killer rabbit of Caerbannog to the recurring fish tank in *The Meaning of Life*. There are *Flying Circus* episodes called 'The Ant: An Introduction' (series 1, episode 9), 'It's the Arts (or: the BBC Entry to the Zinc Stoat of Budapest)' (series 1, episode 6), 'The Naked Ant' (series 1, episode 12), and 'Owl Stretching Time' (series 1, episode 4). The latter of these was a suggestion for the title of the programme itself, and many others of these similarly refer to animals, including 'A Horse, a Spoon and a Bucket' and 'The Toad Elevating Moment'. That the eventual title itself includes an animal – and that the troupe are often referred to as 'the Pythons' – demonstrates the recurring interplay of comedy and cultural understandings of animals.

This plethora of animal representation also indicates the variety of ways in which humans use animals – both in representations and in the lived world. In the 'dead parrot sketch' the animal is a domesticated pet; in sketches featuring sheep those animals are farmed, prior to their being turned into meat; the humour in the 'gorilla librarian' sketch relies on the typical understanding of that animal as wild; and whereas the killer rabbit of Caerbannog is also a wild animal, its wildness is of a kind not expected for a rabbit. So, some animals are pets, some are wild, some are farmed, some are meat. The category 'animal' is a baggy and loose one, encapsulating a variety of meanings. This evidences human cultures' contradictory understanding of animals, and the title of Hal Herzog's book *Some We Love, Some We Hate, Some We Eat* aims to capture that '[t]he way we think about other species often defies logic' (Herzog 2011: 1). The case studies examined below draw on those contradictions, looking at representations of animals as meat and as pets. Yet those contradictions remain framed within the broader category of 'the animal', and so this variety is evidence of the breadth of that category, rather than a destabilisation of it. Animal representations can be used for multiple purposes, yet they never fundamentally trouble human–animal hierarchies.

Eating Animals: The Albatross

The sketch 'Albatross' is set in a cinema where, in common with contemporaneous theatrical norms, there is an intermission between the various films being shown. John Cleese is dressed as a female ice-cream seller, replete with tray upon which it is typical for that product to be available. But instead of calling 'ice-cream' to attract customers, the seller instead yells 'albatross', and there is a large bird of that kind lying on the tray, taking up all of its space, one of its wings raised in the air. Terry Jones plays a cinemagoer, who goes up to the seller to enquire about the availability of choc-ices. The seller replies that they only have the albatross, and continues to yell the bird's name across the cinema to attract more customers. Jones asks what flavour the albatross is, and whether it comes with wafers. Cleese, irate, answers that it is sea-bird flavour, and, 'Course you don't get bloody wafers with it.' After asking the price, Jones buys two, and Cleese then moves on to the other wares for sale, this time exclaiming, 'Gannet on a stick.' Later in the episode Jones reappears, once again sitting in the cinema audience, this time with the albatross on his lap. It is a short sketch, lasting less than forty seconds, and it is this brevity that signals its usefulness for thinking about the cultural understandings of animals. After all, such a concise sketch has no time to set up complicated ideas or work through a complex narrative, and so must instead rely on normalised sociocultural contexts in order for its comic meaning to be apparent.

As such, the sequence aligns neatly with the incongruity theory of humour. This theory argues that comedy arises because '[w]e live in an orderly world, where we have come to expect certain patterns among things ... We laugh when we experience something that doesn't fit into these patterns' (Morreall 1983: 15–16). This conceptualisation of humour is commonly traced back to Immanuel Kant, who argues that *'[l]aughter is an affectation arising from the sudden transformation of a strained expectation into nothing*' (Kant [1790] 1931: 233). Important here are two ideas. Firstly, that comedy requires its incongruities to be presented and understood suddenly; a punchline that is slowly worked out, or laboriously explained, is rarely funny. Secondly, comedy turns such expectations into 'nothing'; that is, these are not incongruities that result in fear or horror or disgust. By this account, comedy is a relatively benign phenomenon, its pleasure dependent upon its resolution resulting in 'nothing'. The incongruity theory was also expounded by Arthur Schopenhauer, who argues that

> The cause of laughter in every case is simply the sudden perception of the incongruity between a concept and the real objects which have been thought through it in some relation, and laughter itself is just the expression of this incongruity. (Schopenhauer [1819] 1970: 76)

For Schopenhauer, comic incongruity does not result in 'nothing', but '[r]ather we get something that we were not expecting' (Morreall 1983: 17). This formulation argues that the incongruous nature of comedy allows it to present ideas, concepts or representations beyond those of our expectations, and thus it can constitute a considerable force for reconceptualising how the world is thought about. Yet in order for it to do this, it must draw on, and establish, those expectations which are to be overturned or reformulated. So, whether comedy results in 'nothing' or 'something', it is a form of communication whose incongruities can only be meaningful if it draws on expectations assumed to be shared by its audience. And it is because of this that we can examine comedy to make explicit those expectations and, by extension, a wide range of sociocultural norms.

But the structure of comedy is more constrained than that which is produced by presenting incongruities. After all, not everything that is incongruous is funny. Kant's assertion that comedy results in 'nothing' begins to point towards the necessity for comic incongruities to be unthreatening in order to be pleasurable. But in addition to this is the necessity for a 'logic of the absurd' in which 'the state of affairs portrayed is simultaneously highly implausible and just a little bit plausible' (Palmer 1994: 96; also see Palmer 1987). The 'logic' Palmer refers to is one that both enables the incongruity to be resolved, but also points towards the possibility of the incongruity occurring in the first place. As such, jokes typically require set-ups and punchlines, whereby the set-up offers a logical world of expectations, while the punchline delivers an incongruity that is sudden, unexpected, unthreatening and – importantly – in some way makes some kind of sense according to the rules established by the set-up. It is the relationship between the set-up and the punchline that constructs an event as a joke; one without the other is not comic. But important here is that set-ups themselves typically draw on sociocultural norms in order to establish the 'logic' of the world in which the punchline is both incongruous and 'a little bit plausible'. It is because of this that comedy can be examined for its indication of sociocultural norms, for they are vital to both parts of the process; they are drawn upon in order for the set-up to be established efficiently, and they are troubled or overturned by the punchline. It is precisely because both parts of the comic moment rely on expectations and norms for their effects that, even if a joke unarguably questions those norms, it is possible to argue that humour is never truly radical. After all, comedy can never move into an arena where those norms are truly abandoned, for then there would be nothing upon which the 'logic of the absurd' could be established.

For the 'albatross' sketch, it's clear the cultural assumptions this logic relies upon. Indeed, these assumptions are so specific that the sketch can become unintelligible when viewed from outside the required context. The sketch is not required to explain to its contemporaneous audience that intermissions at cinemas take place, or that during those intermissions sellers proffer ice-cream; the mere presentation of it as fact would resonate with the viewing audience at the time. But that this is merely a cultural norm is evidenced in that viewers watching the sketch now might be confused by what is taking place, given that intermissions and ice-cream sellers are largely absent from contemporary multiplexes. And there are other cultural norms the sketch relies on too. The offering up of an albatross adheres to the 'logic of the absurd' Palmer proposes, in that while the seller is not vending what is typically expected, it is 'possible' that an alternative to ice-cream could be such a bird. While large and unwieldy, it is conceivable that it is edible, and the sketch relies on this logic for Jones's line, asking what flavour it is, to make sense. This line is comic because it is both incongruous to ask about the flavour of an albatross, and logical given that it's a question a consumer might ask of a new product they're thinking of trying.

As noted above, the gestation of the 'dead parrot' sketch required thinking through the 'right' animal for the comedy to work. Here, too, it is unlikely that any animal would work. And this is because different kinds of animals are categorised in different ways by contemporaneous human cultures, via a 'discourse of lines' (Johnson 2012: 56) that chops up lived reality via taxonomies such as species. As such humans engage in a 'social construction of nature' (Eder 1996 [1988]) that builds a clear line between humans and other beings, then dividing those beings into subcategories that can be, as Herzog (2011) notes, loved, hated or eaten. The 'logic of the absurd' that enables an albatross to be comic in this sketch is one that relies on the idea that an albatross *could* be in the 'edible' category, even though it typically is not understood to be as such. It is thus incongruous in that it is not what is usually for sale at a cinema, but also incongruous as not something eaten by humans at all; but it is logical that it could be for it is a bird and thus sits within the same category of chickens, ducks and geese. To be sure, it is larger and more unwieldy, but it is not impossible to imagine eating an albatross at a cinema in the way in which, for example, a giraffe might be. And these two layers of incongruity are necessary; after all, a seller at a cinema offering lamb would be incongruous but much less funny, given that lamb is an animal that is understood as edible. So, it is the albatross's possibility of edible-ness that enables the logic to function, and it is this logic which means the ensuing conversation between Cleese and Jones about the animal's taste makes (comic) sense.

But telling here is that all of this relies on the idea that it is normal and mundane for humans to eat other animals. After all, part of the humour rests on Cleese's repeated yells of 'albatross' and his disinterested expression while doing so, in the manner of such sellers selling ice-cream in the real world. By making this an albatross, that mundanity becomes marked, the comic absurd resting on the incongruity between the unexpected animal and the normality with which Cleese presents it. But for this to work it has to be something that is reasonably edible, and thus it has to be an animal. After all, it would be incongruous if Cleese's seller was proffering something resolutely inedible, such as a toaster, or a helicopter or an umbrella. This means the albatross sits in the category of 'potentially edible' because it is a bird, and human cultures categorise birds as something with the potential to be consumed even if – as in this case – it is an animal typically not eaten. And so the sketch signals how animals function as objects to be consumed by humans, their status as living beings rendered absent through 'mechanisms of erasure and alienation' (Stibbe 2012: 3) that normalise animals as food.

Pets: The Cat

Another category that cultures place animals into is that of pets. The anger of Cleese's character in the 'dead parrot sketch' arises less because the animal is dead, and more because its lack of life means that it cannot function as a pet in a manner promised by the financial transaction that led to his ownership of it. As such, it is significant that the sketch is in a pet shop, for a skit about a dead parrot in the wild would necessarily work quite differently. It is the shopkeeper's failure to supply a product that fulfils its purpose that motivates the initial anger of Cleese's character, and the shopkeeper's subsequent disregard for the conventions of dealing with complaining customers that enables the sketch to continue. The scene therefore relies on cultural understandings of pets, and the capitalist structures that enable animals to be bought and sold. That the sketch's initial setting was a car shop, which was later changed to a pet shop, shows how within these terms an animal is understood as interchangeable with a vehicle. The 'logic of the absurd' that the sketch relies on, then, is one that does not query the notion that animals can be bought and kept as pets; in presenting the collapse of this transaction as comic it upholds the notion of animals as objects.

After all, '[i]t is by "disavowing" animals that we construct ourselves [as humans]' (Fudge 2008: 7). That is, categorising animals as objects to be bought and sold powerfully distinguishes them from humans, who are commonly not understood as objects in this way. It is through placing animals within regimes of financial transaction that 'man [*sic*] instils or claims in a single stroke *his property* . . . and his *superiority* over what is called animal life' (Derrida 2008 [2006]: 20). Human cultures have had to work hard in order to assert and normalise this superiority, and the boundaries between the human and the non-human have not always been stable, as the history of slavery attests (Spiegel 1988). While humans have always interacted with other beings, the idea of keeping animals as pets – rather than as livestock or hunting partners – became widespread in the UK only in 'the mid-nineteenth century, [when] a positive cult of pet keeping arose in Victorian society' (Fagan 2015: 259). The movement of animals into the home as pets over the last couple of centuries has coincided with humans having fewer interactions with other beings as wildlife or livestock. This means that '[e]verywhere animals disappear' (Berger 2009: 36), to be replaced by representations of animals in cultural forms such as art or wildlife documentaries. Alongside these, animals continue to live alongside humans within the interaction of pet-keeping, a human–animal relationship whose norms something like the 'dead parrot sketch' can rely on for its humour.

Important in these human–animal relations is that 'pets exist for human pleasure and convenience. Fond as owners are of their animals, they do not hesitate to get rid of them when they prove inconvenient' (Tuan 1984: 88). The activity of pet-keeping is one whose primary driver is the desire of the human, and it is not a relationship that an animal enters into through choice. While it is certainly the case that pet-owners attend to their pets' needs, these must function within the dominant needs of the human. As such pet-keeping can be seen to evidence a 'psychology of dominance and affection' (ibid.: 167) by which humans justify the dominance over animals they choose to keep in their homes via displays of affection. And that dominance is most evident in that 'English law views animals simply as the property of human owners, only trivially different from less mobile goods' (Ritvo 1987: 2). The transformation of other living beings into property establishes a hierarchical power relationship normalised and enacted by pet-keeping.

The failure of that power relationship can function as the incongruity that comedy exploits. So, in the sketch 'confuse-a-cat', a suburban couple peer worriedly out of the living room window at the cat sitting motionless on their lawn. A vet arrives, and it transpires that the couple have sought the medical expert's help because the cat, as the wife explains, 'Doesn't do anything. He just sits out there on the lawn.' The vet goes on to diagnose the cat as exhibiting '[t]otal physical inertia. Absence of interest in its ambience . . . Failure to respond to conventional external stimuli . . . To be blunt, your cat is in a rut'. The couple react fearfully, and the vet continues: 'It's the old stockbroker syndrome. The suburban *fin de siècle* ennui.' His prescription is to call the company Confuse-A-Cat Ltd, who arrive in a large van from which several white-coated performers emerge. They are managed by an army general, who orders them to build a stage in the couple's garden, directly in the eye-line of the cat. Once it's built they perform a sequence of nonsensical and non-realist tableaux, in which boxers, a policeman, Napoleon and a penguin on a pogo stick interact. Editing means that characters vanish in a moment, and reappear elsewhere. The performance ends with the actors taking a curtain call, and the couple and the army general turn their attention to the cat. The cat slowly gets up, walks past the humans and into the house. The couple enthusiastically thank the general, who modestly notes that they were simply doing their job. Captions on-screen then state that Confuse-A-Cat Ltd is associated with other animal-startling companies, such as Amaze-A-Vole, Puzzle-A-Puma and Bewilderbeest. This is overlaid with rousing military music, as the general looks determinedly into the middle distance.

The sketch's comedy relies on the idea that to make such an effort in order to solve the problem of a cat not doing much is absurd. This is evident in the performance style that runs throughout, in which Graham Chapman's vet and John Cleese's general deliver their lines in excessive earnest. It is also captured in the suburban couple's worrying, in which Terry Jones and Michael Palin clutch at each other as if receiving devastating news. This is significant in that it means the narrative is rendered comprehensible because of the humans' interpretation of the cat's behaviour. The couple's concern arises because the cat is failing to behave as is required in a pet-keeping household. While the vet's diagnosis blames the couple for their failure to confuse and excite the cat as required by responsible owners, the cat's behaviour is a problem for those owners rather than the cat itself. There is nothing in the sketch that suggests the cat itself finds its situation to be a problem. Indeed, it is precisely the humans' overreaction that constitutes some of the comic meat. But it also means that the sketch re-enacts the idea that animals are meaningful only inasmuch as they conform to humans' expectations of them. It is because the couple cannot interpret their cat's behaviour that they call the vet; it is they who have the problem. Solving the cat – via an absurd theatrical performance – is actually about solving the couple's problems within the human–animal relationship. It is they who are grateful at the end of the sequence, because the cat no longer troubles the pet-keeping norm. Important here is that the cat is perceived to respond appropriately to human stimuli, and thus the idea that a cat (or any other pet) should be objectified by human activity constitutes the resolution to the problem the sketch dramatises. This evidences this interplay of dominance and affection, where the couple believe they have demonstrated their affection by getting help for their cat, but the outcome that resolves the problem is one that reasserts humans' dominance over other species. Thus '[p]ets can support a hierarchy that reassures us [humans] of our status in the world' (Fudge 2008: 21), where that status is one in which a pet is knowable and controllable.

Like the parrot and the albatross, the cultural conceptualisations of particular species is important to the comedy in this sketch. While there are a number of animals that are commonly kept as pets in the UK, this sketch relies on the cat-ness of this cat. Cats are contradictory animals, bringing the 'inaccessible, unrestrained, wild' (Lorenz 2002 [1949]: 162) attributes of non-humans into the home in a way that helps reassert the controlled human-ness of the domestic space. So this wildness is

> also the very reason why the cat is so 'homely', for somebody or something can only be 'at home' whose profession lies outside; and the purring cat on the hearth betokens for me the symbol of homeliness just because he is not my prisoner but an independent being of almost equal status who happens to live in the same house that I do. (Ibid.)

Cats are pets that are not conceived of as enthusiastically interacting with their human cohabitees in the way dogs do. The 'confuse-a-cat' sketch draws on this, for there is an incongruity in worrying about a cat behaving distantly, given that that is what cats are understood to do. A sketch about a dog with 'suburban *fin de siècle* ennui' would work quite differently, for a dog sitting in a garden distractedly staring into space would be understood as genuinely problematic and of concern. Furthermore, a dog failing to react to the theatrical performance presented to it would similarly have a different meaning to this cat doing the same. It is significant that while the sketch ends with a list of companies who engage in the activity of confusing other species, this is not behaviour that is enacted with the sketch. A sketch about 'Amaze-A-Vole' would not function in the same way, partly because voles are not typical domestic animals, but mainly because it is not a species for which human cultures have defined expectations, and thus there is little for the 'logic of the absurd' to draw upon. The jokes here are far more about the wordplay that extrapolates the linguistic structure of 'confuse-a-cat' and applies it to other animals, alongside the absurdity of there being so many companies engaging in similarly redundant activity. This is one of the ways in which animals 'disappear' (Berger 2009: 36), becoming nothing other than species able to be employed in a comic list.

But the bored cat is instead depicted, and in its behaviour it could be read as comically troubling the structures of 'affection and dominance' that pets are ensnared in. It is in refusing to be active, and in troubling its owners' expectations of it, that it actually engages in a form of agency. The comedy of the sketch arises because it disturbs the human–animal interaction by evidencing that a cat has a subjectivity, even if that subjectivity results in it doing nothing. Indeed, the power of that subjectivity is most acute in the cat's *in*activity, given that pets' continued status as domestic animals is dependent on their engaging in behaviour deemed acceptable and pleasurable to humans. It refuses to be a pet, and is instead a cat: the Confuse-A-Cat company returns it to a pet. Or, more accurately, given that it is impossible to know whether the cat's eventual movement is a consequence of the performance in front of it or merely a coincidence, Confuse-A-Cat instead offers the cat's owners the possibility that they have regained mastery over the animal in their house. What constitutes a narrative resolution here is the reassertion of 'status' (Fudge 2008: 21) for the humans, which shows how this comic sketch relies on the normalised idea of human–animal hierarchies for its humour. So, while the sequence might lampoon fretting pet-owners, and depict cats as having agency, its narrative structure – and therefore comic success – relies on unquestioned notions of the human domination of animals as pets. It is this contradictory nature – in which the narrative appears to offer quite a different reading to the comic moments – that renders comedy such a difficult mode to make sense of.

Conclusion: Animals and Comedy

This difficulty, though, is one that does not negate the humour's reliance on cultural understandings of humans and animals for its potency. In 'confuse-a-cat', the notion of animals as pets is not troubled, even if the sketch relies on the idea that suburbia might be a boring place for a cat. The humour concerns the excessive techniques use to re-enthuse the cat; there are no jokes that trouble the idea that cats can be the property of humans, or that trouble the concept of 'cat' in the first place. This is made explicit in the 'dead parrot sketch', in which the humour is dependent upon a failure of the successful commercial transaction expected in a pet shop; Cleese's character asserts his right to own a parrot, and this assertion is not critiqued by the sketch. Similarly, while the 'albatross' sketch finds humour in the 'wrong' kind of animal being offered for consumption, this 'wrong-ness' is reliant upon the idea that there are 'right' animal-related foodstuffs to be offered for consumption in a cinema.

These are sketches, then, in which human characters assert their right to have particular relationships with animals, and this relationship is one centred on concepts of ownership, particularly via commercial transactions. In all the sketches, the comedy arises from the failure of successful commercial, transactional activity, with the animals merely objects that enable that failure to be explicit. The specificity of their animal-ness – whether as members of species, or as individuals – is absent, and they function merely as signifiers of the expected norms of human dominance over animals. There are other sketches, though, which might suggest a depiction of animal agency. For example, both the killer rabbit of Caerbannog and the gorilla librarian depict specific, individualised animals whose agency is precisely the meat of the comedy. However, still what the comedy offers here is an incongruity between expected animal behaviour and that which the sketch depicts. More importantly, though, this incongruity is depicted in a manner that situates the viewing audience as aligned with the human characters in the sketch. It is the human characters' reactions to the actions of the rabbit and the gorilla that offers the 'empowered gaze' in which 'the practice of looking is at the heart of both our sympathy for and our oppression of the animal' (Baker 2001: 15). So, while such sketches might be seen to offer up *the dance of relating* (Haraway 2008: 25) that animal advocacy supporters argue is necessary in order for more morally appropriate human–animal relations to come into being, they do so within contexts that are human-centric. After all, the comic nature of this material is made for human consumption, and so must align with communicative strategies that are comprehensible for that audience. While Marcia Landy might argue that the animal-related comedy seen in sketches such as those outlined above are forms of 'unpredictable transformation' indicative of a troubling of 'assumptions about human uniqueness and rationality' (Landy 2005: 63), the only cultural strategy on offer for this activity is a human-centric one. That the comedy's offering up of the absurd logic of human–animal relations might be seen to critique that 'uniqueness and rationality', it can do so only via discourses that construct the viewer as avowedly rational, with that rationality enacted via the process of reading these sketches as funny.

Furthermore, the status of this cultural material as *television* is significant. Television's social role is predicated on the notion that there is a relatively coherent idea of the public that it serves, and it is for this reason it is a mass medium. Comedy often inscribes that collective public within its textual elements, with the laugh-track functioning as a signal to the viewer at home of how others reacted to what is being depicted. Monty Python has a laugh-track, and in doing so evidences to its viewers not only how these sketches should be understood, but also evidences that they were understood as such by real people. But this collective can only ever be anthropocentric; the laugh-track is a tool by which human cultures signal their collective certainties about what is and is not funny. It is then humans that decide that a dead parrot is funny, that an albatross for sale is funny, that a bored cat is funny. And humans signal their assent to this delineation through the laugh-track that evidences it. So even if the content of some of these sketches might trouble assumptions that underpin human–animal relations, they do not – and cannot – trouble the authority humans give themselves to offer up representations of others, and to come to a consensus about the meaning and value of those representations. This means that the animals on display here can only ever be comic objects, whose representation serves no purpose that is not anthropocentric.

Works Cited

Baker, Steve (2001) *Picturing the Beast: Animals, Identity, and Representation*. Urbana and Chicago: Illinois University Press.

BBC News (2004) 'Python Dead Parrot Is Top Sketch', *BBC News*, 29 November. <http://news.bbc.co.uk/1/hi/entertainment/tv_and_radio/4052641.stm> (last accessed 1 August 2017)

BBC News (2005) '*Little Britain* Tops Sketch Poll', *BBC News*, 3 April. <http://news.bbc.co.uk/1/hi/entertainment/4406377.stm> (last accessed 1 August 2017)

Berger, John (2009) *Why Look at Animals?* London: Penguin.

Derrida, Jacques (2008 [2006]) *The Animal That Therefore I Am*, David Wills (trans.). New York: Fordham University Press.

Eder, Klaus (1996 [1988]) *The Social Construction of Nature: A Sociology of Ecological Enlightenment*, Mark Ritter (trans.). London: Sage.

Fagan, Brian (2015) *The Intimate Bond: How Animals Shaped Human History*. London: Bloomsbury.

Fudge, Erica (2008) *Pets*. Stocksfield: Acumen.

Haraway, Donna J. (2008) *When Species Meet*. Minneapolis: University of Minnesota Press.

Herzog, Hal (2011) *Some We Love, Some We Hate, Some We Eat: Why It's Hard to Think Straight about Animals*. New York: Harper Perennial.

Jefferies, Mark (2014) 'Monty Python's Dead Parrot Sketch Voted Favourite Python Comedy Routine of All Time', *The Mirror*, 11 July. <http://www.mirror.co.uk/tv/tv-news/monty-pythons-dead-parrot-sketch-3844947> (last accessed 1 August 2017)

Johnson, Lisa (2012) *Power, Knowledge, Animals*. Basingstoke: Palgrave Macmillan.

Kant, Immanuel (1931 [1790]) *Critique of Judgment*, J. H. Bernard (trans.). London: Macmillan.

Landy, Marcia (2005) *Monty Python's Flying Circus*. Detroit, MI: Wayne State University Press.

Lippit, Akira Mizuta (2015) 'Medium Foreword', in Michael Lawrence and Laura McMahon (eds), *Animal Life and the Moving Image*. London: British Film Institute, pp. xi–xvi.

Lockett, John (2014) 'John Cleese Explains the Origin of the Dead Parrot Sketch', *Vanity Fair*, 7 November. <https://www.vanityfair.com/hollywood/2014/11/monty-python-dead-parrot-sketch> (last accessed 1 August 2017)

Lorenz, Konrad (2002 [1949]) *Man Meets Dog*, Marjorie Kerr Wilson (trans.). London: Routledge.

Malamud, Randy (2012) *An Introduction to Animals in Visual Culture*. Basingstoke: Palgrave.

Morreall, John (1983) *Taking Laughter Seriously*. Albany: State University of New York Press.

Palmer, Jerry (1987) *The Logic of the Absurd: On Film and Television Comedy*. London: British Film Institute.

Palmer, Jerry (1994) *Taking Humour Seriously*. London: Routledge.

Ritvo, Harriet (1987) *The Animal Estate: The English and Other Creatures in the Victorian Age*. Cambridge, MA: Harvard University Press.

Rucki, Alexandra (2014) 'Giant "Dead Parrot" From Monty Python Sketch Unveiled on the Southbank', *Evening Standard*, 14 July. <http://www.standard.co.uk/news/london/giant-dead-parrot-from-monty-python-sketch-unveiled-on-the-southbank-9605453.html> (last accessed 1 August 2017)

Schopenhauer, Arthur (1907 [1819]) *The World as Will and Idea*, vol. 1, R. B. Haldane and J. Kemp (trans.). London: Kegan Paul, Trench, Trübner and Company.

Spiegel, Marjorie (1988) *The Dreaded Comparison: Human and Animal Slavery*. London: Heretic Books.

Stibbe, Arran (2012) *Animals Erased: Discourse, Ecology, and Reconnection with the Natural World*. Middletown, CT: Wesleyan University Press.

Tuan, Yi-Fu (1984) *Dominance and Affection: The Making of Pets*. New Haven, CT and London: Yale University Press.

Wilmut, Roger (1980) *From Fringe to Flying Circus: Celebrating a Unique Generation of Comedy, 1960–1980*. London: Methuen.

9. 'POLITICAL CORRECTNESS', REVERSAL AND INCONGRUITY: DYNAMICS OF HUMOUR IN *LIFE OF BRIAN*

Kathleen J. Cassity

Does so-called 'political correctness' cause people today to take offence too easily, to the point of stifling the collective comic muse? Does comedy from prior eras, such as the work of the Monty Python troupe, often fail to hold up for the same reason? In short, has the polarised sociocultural climate of the 2020s rendered humour impossible, especially when it is deliberately irreverent as is the case with Monty Python's body of work?

On the surface, it may seem easy to answer a quick 'yes' to all of the above. One does not need to delve very far into social media or online publications before encountering some version of the sentiment, 'We can't tell jokes any more because people today are too easily offended', and much recent humour scholarship focuses on this issue. At first glance, John Cleese would appear to agree with the frequently articulated belief that 'political correctness' has stifled comedy, having posited that today's social norms may have a censorious effect on comic production. In his 2015 autobiography *So, Anyway . . .*, Cleese hypothesised that much of the Monty Python troupe's work could not be produced today due to a zeitgeist of 'political correctness' that represses humour.

However, a more nuanced understanding of the dynamics and power relationships shaping comic cultural production suggests a situation that is both more complex and more optimistic. In this chapter, I will interpret selected scenes from *Life of Brian* (1979) in order to demonstrate that while some aspects of Monty Python's comedy may initially appear at odds with shifting social norms, this is not universally the case. In fact, much of that film's humour still resonates today, largely because much of its humour stems from incongruity and reversal rather than superiority. While some might write off attention to power differentials in superiority-based humour as mere 'political correctness', I would argue that inattention to power dynamics does indeed pose an ethical problem. Fortunately, superiority-based humour directed at those with less power and/or status is not the only potential source of humour. Even when some aspects of comedy from earlier eras are deemed to be problematic in retrospect, other sources of humour, such as incongruity and reversal, not only allow earlier comedies to withstand the test of time, but at least some aspects of those comedies may become even *more* relevant in light of cultural and historical developments.

I focus here on *Life of Brian* because, on several fronts, it lends itself particularly well to analysis from a twenty-first-century perspective. First, while this film has arguably been the most controversial of the Monty Python troupe's body of work – a status it held even prior to its highly publicised and picketed release – the aspects that garnered widespread disapproval have shifted in the subsequent forty years. Where concern over blasphemous depictions of the divine provided the source of the original controversy, contemporary culture is more likely to locate problems in the film's portrayal of human beings from marginalised groups. Second, *Life of Brian* is often considered to be Monty Python's emblematic work, braiding together many of the themes explored earlier in the troupe's sketch comedy and in the *Holy Grail* film. Finally, *Life of Brian* lends itself particularly well to illustrating both incongruity and reversal as sources of humour – strategies which continue to make the film largely salient today despite some of its dated aspects. As Danielle Bobker states, it is possible to move towards a 'humor-positive frame' when comedy stems from incongruity rather than from superiority, and when comedy that does depend on superiority 'punches up' rather than 'punching down' in terms of power (Bobker 2017). *Life of Brian*, for the most part, engages both of these dynamics, rendering its satirical critique of status-quo power relations still relevant in many respects today. Considering the power dynamics at play in this film provides a framework for understanding why not all comedy – even that from an earlier era – is equally open to charges of 'political incorrectness', even as we recognise *some* earlier comedy as problematic from a contemporary social justice perspective. (Here it should be noted that both problematic and acceptable sources of humour may be located in the same cultural production.) Fortunately, when it comes to comedy, derisive jokes that poke fun at the less privileged are not the only option. Understanding the dynamics at play allows comedy to remain thinkable even in our current polarised, sometimes too-humourless world.

Before turning to my reading of the film, it is helpful to provide a brief contextual summary of comic theory. For all the contemporary complaints about 'political correctness' rendering humour obsolete, the assumption that humour is inherently problematic from a moral standpoint is clearly not new. For well over two millennia, thinkers from Aristotle and Plato to Hobbes and Konrad Lorenz have posited humour as inherently unethical, based on the underlying assumption that laughter always and necessarily stems from a sense of 'superiority'. As Morreall summarises this longstanding philosophical assumption: 'The oldest, and probably still most widespread theory of laughter is that laughter is an expression of a person's feelings of superiority over other people' (Morreall 1983: 4). Plato viewed laughter as a condition in which 'our attention is focused on vice' (ibid.), and Morreall adds, 'Aristotle agreed with Plato that laughter is basically a form of derision' (ibid.: 5). This theory of laughter as necessarily derisive would remain dominant for many centuries, with Hobbes positing that laughter arises from 'a sudden glory arising from some conception of some eminency in ourselves, by comparison with the infirmity of others' (quoted in ibid.). Voltaire broke from centuries of conventional thought by positing a completely different view, that 'laughter always arises from a gaiety of disposition, absolutely incompatible with contempt and indignation' (ibid. 8). Yet, as Morreall points out, Voltaire's stance is, like the superiority theory of humour itself, incomplete: 'What is wrong with this response to the superiority theory is that it denies an obvious fact – that people sometimes [do] laugh in derision at other people' (ibid.: 8). The laughter of derision, Morreall emphasises, has always been with us. Where the superiority theory fails, however, is in its attempt towards totalisation – the claim that *all* laughter is necessarily derisive. (This assumption has also contributed to centuries of venerating the serious/tragic above the comic.)

While much humour indeed derives from superiority, what these thinkers failed to consider is the importance of power dynamics in determining humour's ethical implications. When a 'joke' derives from an assumption of superiority on the part of someone with relative power and status and is targeted towards someone with less of both, the humour may quickly become sadistic. Shifts in our collective cultural thinking, both in the United States and globally, have generated greater awareness of this potential sadistic streak – even as some complain that attention to power dynamics constitutes a stifling form of 'political correctness'. Despite that widespread complaint, I would argue that any attempt at humour that kicks those who are already down is not funny. Yet considering superiority out of context, without attention to the power dynamics at play, does not alone determine whether an attempt at humour is likely to be deemed offensive. Here it is important to ask contextual questions: who holds power, status and privilege over whom? Do those power dynamics reverse or reinscribe existing sociocultural norms? What broader social purpose is being targeted by the humour? When 'superiority' is invoked as a means of questioning rather than reinscribing status-quo power relations, the effect can be to bring differentials into sharp relief, in the process affirming the humanity of those in power-down positions and making visible a power asymmetry that was previously taken for granted. (Whether this reversal results in meaningful and lasting social change or simply provides a 'release valve' for the built-in tensions surrounding hegemonic social roles is, of course, a question open to discussion.)

Reversal can be understood as a form of incongruity, which Morreall identifies as one of the most potent sources of comedy. Drawing upon Schopenhauer and Kant, Morreall explains incongruity as an unexpected disruption in expectations: 'We live in an orderly world, where we have come to expect certain patterns among things, their properties, events, etc. We laugh when we experience something that doesn't fit into these patterns' (Morreall 1983: 16). While Kant and Schopenhauer differed in how they conceptualised the mechanisms of incongruity, Morreall succinctly summarises a key principle uniting them both: 'What causes laughter, if you will, is a mismatch between conceptual understanding and perception' (ibid.: 18). As Bobker puts it: 'Today humor philosophers are most convinced by the idea, first fully elaborated in the 18th century, that laughter is a response to incongruity: something familiar suddenly looks strange, and the resulting sense of surprise pleases us' (Bobker 2017). Reversal of power dynamics, similarly, surprises by offering 'just the opposite of what everyone is expecting'. Reversal is often more pointed than other forms of incongruity, since it has the potential to uncover implicit biases and cultural assumptions. Since power dynamics are often invisible to those in a privileged location, humour and satire often use reversal as a strategy to render those dynamics visible – an approach that, of course, harkens back to Jonathan Swift and that continues to be prevalent today.

While some humour in *Life of Brian* may be found problematic by contemporary viewers (as I will demonstrate shortly), a substantial portion of the film's humour draws on the dynamics of incongruity and reversal of culturally hegemonic power dynamics. Consequently, *Life of Brian* can still stand today as a salient critique of human folly and hypocrisy, the blindness and pervasiveness of power, and the dangers of mob mentality.

Take, for example, the 'stoning' sequence near the beginning of the film. In a humorous instance of dramatic irony, the predominance of women in the crowd is obvious to anyone with full sensory capacity. When the Priest (played by Cleese) asks the obvious question, 'Are there any women here today?', he appears to be fooled when the assembled women respond by suddenly dropping their voices into the lower male register. The joke here is not so much on women as on the arbitrariness and the blindness of a patriarchal society that excludes women for no other reason than 'It is written, that's why!' The scene marks a recognition that such arbitrary rules are often broken, while mocking the gullibility of those who enforce the status quo (in this case, the Priest). The power dynamics then invert literally, as the mob summoned by the Priest against the accused blasphemer turns its frenzied mentality against the Priest and hurls its stones at him instead. The arbitrariness of 'It is written, that's why' is capable of being inverted, with the enforcers of arbitrary power suddenly as vulnerable to capricious regulations as the masses were previously. (Unfortunately for Brian and the other victims of the Roman imperialist regime, no such inversion takes place at the end of the film.)

A similar dynamic is at play in the scene where the nearly inarticulate 'cave man' jailers in the dungeon turn out to be acting. The joke, once again, is on the easily fooled establishment that exploits the working class (whom it perceives, incorrectly, to be stupid and disabled) in order to perform its enforcement function. The clandestine intelligence of the jailers suggests a larger-picture reality that does not align with hegemonic beliefs about what various social classes are capable of achieving. Ruptures, fissures, dissent and disobedience seep through the accepted narrative, once again revealing social roles (whether dictated by class, race, ethnicity or gender) to be arbitrary and socially constructed rather than essentialised. In this scene, the two jailers who are assumed by the establishment to be sub-human are actually demonstrating far more wit and intelligence than their overlords, finding enjoyment in mocking those ostensibly 'above' them by over-playing roles that they – and only they – know to be artificially imposed.

Similarly, towards the end of the film when the crowd publicly mocks Pilate (played by Michael Palin) for his speech impediment, Pilate mistakenly believes that he is being revered. Throughout this scene, he remains clueless that, far from being the target of anyone's admiration, he is in fact the butt of a massive collective joke. While it may be possible to interpret this scene as mocking the differently abled and therefore falling under the umbrella of problematic superiority, I would argue that both Pilate's self-delusion and his all-encompassing power – one man in charge of millions with the power to make life-or-death decisions and eliminate those who do not comply with his mandates – would mitigate that interpretation. (Given the rise of dictatorially inclined national leaders around the globe who often persist in believing themselves to be widely popular despite the fact that grasping and maintaining their power has necessitated a considerable amount of chicanery, this scene is perhaps even more relevant today than when the film was released.) When Pilate's 'very good friend in Rome', Biggus Dickus (played by Graham Chapman), arrives on the scene and reveals that he speaks with a lisp, it becomes clear that, despite the pretentions of the ruling class to godhood, they are in fact not only human and flawed, but self-deluded as well. Brian (also played by Chapman), of course, is also clearly imperfect and mortal, especially when juxtaposed alongside the Christ for whom he is continually mistaken. Unlike the ruling class, however, Brian remains keenly aware of his own mortality – even as those around him continue in their collective delusions and insist on venerating him to a status that he is ill-equipped to assume.

A clear example of reversal takes place earlier in the film, when the Legionaries attempt but ultimately fail to restrain their laughter in the face of the phallocentric, imperial social order represented by Pilate. Here, the troops inform Pilate that they doubt the would-be revolutionary Brian's claim to Roman paternity, since his absent father's purported name, 'Naughtius Maximus', is clearly a joke name, 'like Biggus Dickus'. That name, Pilate counters, is *not* a joke; the Romans in power apparently take their phallocentrism seriously. Pilate makes it clear that he expects an answer of 'No' when he then asks his assembled troops, 'Do any of the rest of you find anything funny about the name Biggus Dickus?' Here the complete ridiculousness of Pilate's unchecked power and fragile masculinity breaks through in laughter that the assembled Legionaries attempt yet fail to suppress – a semiotic eruption through the symbolic walls, to invoke a Kristevian analysis – leading to one of the film's funniest moments while at the same time demonstrating both Pilate's fragility and his self-delusion.

Both in this and in the later 'Release Roger' scene, everyone aside from Pilate and Biggus seems to understand the absurdity of life and their own relatively minor place in the larger scheme of things. The dictatorial authority figures, blind to their own unpopularity as well as to the arbitrariness and ultimate cruelty of the absolute power they hold, stand alone in their oblivion. Yet the social order is not upended in a permanent or meaningful way, as this scene underscores a grimly serious point: while the mobs and even his own troops may ridicule him, Pilate will continue to hold absolute power, even to the point of being able to grant life or death, over those beneath him. The mob may have the ability to mock their leader, and, due to his own delusional narcissism, to protect themselves temporarily from his wrath by engaging in collective plausible denial for comic effect. Yet ultimately the mob lacks the power to overthrow Pilate, as we see in the rows and rows of crosses bearing the unjustly crucified that become visible as the film's credits roll. This harsh reality, while anything but funny, underscores the fact that *Life of Brian*, despite being released forty years ago, still has much to say to contemporary viewers; and, while it is presented as a comic film, some of its most compelling messages are profoundly serious.

For all its critique of power, however, 'the masses' are not idealised in *Life of Brian*, given that the dangers of mob rule and the folly of blindly following one's tribe provide some of the film's most frequently recurring themes. One memorable example includes the ease and speed with which Brian's followers divide into conflicting factions when deciding whether to 'follow the gourd' or 'follow the shoe'. The gullibility, mob mentality and easy divisibility of the crowd are satirised when the already-factionalised mob follows Brian into the desert, and when they gather below Brian's window the following morning after his amorous tryst with Judith (played by Sue Jones-Davies). Here, incongruity is at play in the tension between the idealistic hopes of the crowd venerating the hapless, obviously mortal Brian as a god, and their own collective inability to achieve any kind of transcendent ideal due to their propensity for infighting and their gullibility.

Incongruity can also be located in the internal hypocrisy of those who gather into self-righteous social groups at multiple points along the political spectrum. Some examples are fleeting, such as the 'Popular' Front of Judea with its membership of one. Another example occurs when competing anti-imperialist groups finally appear to grasp that they are more likely to achieve their aims against Rome if they cease their internecine quarrelling long enough to fight against the 'real enemy' – only to reaffirm their 'splitting' tendencies when they unite just long enough to identify the 'real enemy' as 'the Judean People's Front!' Hypocrisy intertwined with bureaucracy provides fodder for satire when, after agonising for several minutes about the need to take action rather than getting mired in discussion, Judith breaks into the revolutionaries' headquarters to announce that Brian has been arrested – to which the revolutionaries respond, 'Right! This calls for immediate discussion!' In this manner, as Michael Palin stated in David Morgan's *Monty Python Speaks!*, *Life of Brian*'s satire was pointed not only towards religious excess but was targeted just as sharply at the factionalised leftist political groups that existed in England at the time the film was made (Morgan 2019: 196).

On this point, numerous scholars have argued that *Life of Brian* is not satirising Jesus Christ at all nor sincere followers of the faith; the satire instead is on the gullible, the hypocritical and the self-deluded. Here, the incongruity lies between the human desire for a divine transcendent and the human flaws that prevent us from getting anywhere near that ideal. As Bill Gibron pointed out in *Pop Matters*:

> The only time Christ Himself is depicted in the film is during the Sermon on the Mount, and then it's the audience who is the butt of the joke, as they misunderstand and misapply His poetic words. The movie treats the Son of God as an unfathomable good, while those who would follow Him are depicted as merely human by nature and design. (Gibron 2004: 3)

When Jesus speaks early in the film (and one time only), the incongruity lies between the profundity of his words and the inability of his audience to hear them ('blessed are the cheesemakers'). The joke here is not on Jesus, but on everybody else.

Incongruity abounds in what is perhaps the film's most iconic scene, when a naked (that is to say, clearly mortal) Brian lazily yawns as he parts the curtains at the window after a night of debauchery with his love interest Judith – only to discover that a huge crowd has gathered beneath his house to 'worship' him as a deity. Compelled in his state of surprise to speak back to the masses, Brian informs them that 'You don't need to follow me – you don't need to follow anybody!' When Brian insists to the crowd, 'You're all individuals!' the crowd responds in unison, 'Yes, we're all individuals!' to which one lone voice counters, 'I'm not!' This amusing ironic moment is just one line of dialogue in a scene rich with incongruity, most notably the very physical bodies of Brian and Judith juxtaposed against the sacred notion of an entirely spiritual Messiah. A further incongruity sparks humour in the film's arguably most iconic line, delivered by Brian's equally mortal mother (played by Terry Jones): 'He's not the Messiah! He's a very naughty boy!' Still more incongruities lie in Brian and Judith's perceived privacy against the masses gathered outside, and in the crowd's expectation of hearing a profound sermon rather than Brian's crudely vernacular stab at existential philosophy. This scene also includes a notable instance of reversal, with Graham Chapman's full-frontal male nudity inverting the conventional cinematic male gaze.

The film is rife with other examples. There is the Centurion's attempt to police Brian's graffiti not by threatening his arrest for defacement of public property but by correcting his Latin grammar (in the manner of an English public-school headmaster). There is the overall ordinariness of Brian, who consistently serves as a conventional foil against which the absurdity surrounding him plays out. Not least of all, there are the thwarted expectations of rescue in the crucifixion scene, which lead to a denouement that, despite the film's status as a comedy, is devastatingly tragic in terms of plot trajectory. Brian's helplessness ultimately reveals a recognition of one's own limitations in the larger scheme of things, bringing to mind Morreall's observation that the comic mindset involves a certain distancing: 'To have a humorous attitude toward some issue is to be distanced from its practical aspects' (Morreall 1983: 122). That sense of critical distance lends a comic effect to a scene that would be devastating in another context: Brian's inability to remove himself from the cross despite his innocence. As an individual, Brian is helpless to change his fate; to solve his extremely consequential, life-or-death problem will require the cooperation of community, which he is ultimately unable to receive. Brian is rendered helpless both by the pervasiveness of imperial power and by the lack of solidarity displayed by those around him. The final message of the film, then, is deeply serious, harshly critical both of status-quo power relations and individualistic self-centredness. Despite being wrapped in a comical package, the plot trajectory of *Life of Brian* is tragic, the message sombre.

The classical tragic trajectory, in fact, is a key element in most of Monty Python's body of work. In the Pythonesque world, situations rarely reach resolution and comic set-ups almost invariably devolve into unresolved chaos. (One exception is Eric Idle's more recent stage play *Spamalot*, which offers the expected – though self-consciously and meta-theatrically artificial – happy ending.) The pervasiveness of the tragic ending in Monty Python's work is itself an example of incongruity, since the classical definition of 'comic' implies a happy resolution typically culminating in marriage. Even the comic ending of *Spamalot* is written with such a self-conscious intertextual nod to audience expectations ('a Broadway wedding!') that it can still be interpreted as mocking the audience's expectation for comic resolution. In the majority of Monty Python's oeuvre, there are no happy endings, just spiralling chaos. Perhaps it is this dynamic that continues to keep at least some aspects of the troupe's work culturally relevant today; whereas a comic resolution implies finality, the unresolved chaos of a classically tragic ending is, though unpleasant, never entirely finalised. Becoming is emphasised over being and process over product, suggesting that, for all the difficulties in the world, we are not yet finished – and neither are the incongruities that continue to provide us with the possibility of humour.

The emphasis on incongruity and reversal throughout this chapter is not intended to obscure the clearly problematic aspects of humour in *Life of Brian* that may be poorly received by many contemporary audiences. This point resonates with multiple current cultural conversations regarding to what extent we can/should accept art forms from earlier times as products of their time, or whether such a 'presentist' approach to interpretation unfairly imposes our current value systems upon an earlier social order. (The discussion of how the song 'Baby, It's Cold Outside' should be interpreted in the post-#metoo era comes to mind here.) This longstanding and broad debate clearly touches on much more than Monty Python. What are we to make, for instance, of Shakespeare's Shylock? Is *The Merchant of Venice* anti-Semitic, or does it actually expose anti-Semitism? What of *Othello*? *Huckleberry Finn*? *To Kill A Mockingbird*? Do creative works such as these that shape sweeping social injustices into an artistic frame primarily serve to question and challenge those injustices? Or, by giving injustice the status of art, do works such as these risk reinscribing that injustice?

Three scenes readily come to mind as potentially challenging from this standpoint. First is the dialogue regarding 'What have the Romans ever done for us?', which can easily be interpreted as an apologetic for empire – a potential ethical problem, given that the script was written by those from the imperial centre. (At times in his autobiography, in fact, Cleese appears tone-deaf to the implications of a British man, from the centre of a once-major empire, bemoaning his 'inability' to poke fun at those from a formerly colonised and impoverished country, and at the struggles of assimilation experienced by people from the former colonies who have immigrated to Britain.) However, as some sketch comedy regarding Brexit has demonstrated, in a world where Britain arguably no longer occupies the colonial centre, the implications of this scene can also be reversed. (See, for example, the *Guardian* video featuring Sir Patrick Stewart, along with several recaptioned 'Brexit' versions of this scene on YouTube.) Another problematic instance can be found in the 'Big Nose' scene near the beginning of the film – arguably the film's most tedious and least amusing sequence. This exchange could certainly be interpreted as anti-Semitic, though, alternatively, it could be interpreted as a critique of anti-Semitism given the complete unlikeability of the character giving voice to the ugly stereotype. Since the villain here is himself sporting a rather large nose, this scene can also be interpreted as yet another instance of hypocrisy, one of many moments in the film in which unlikeable characters who easily find fault in others appear to be blind and deaf to their own flaws.

In the scene where Stan/Loretta (Eric Idle) has to keep reminding the revolutionaries to include women in their liberatory plans, some may find nothing funny nowadays about Stan/Loretta's assertion that he wants to be a woman because he 'wants to have babies'. With issues surrounding the struggles of transgendered people coming to the fore, this scene may feel less than humorous for anyone who has faced that challenge. At the same time, this scene does serve to point out one of the often-noted limitations of revolutionary groups: male dominance and the mimicry of hegemonic power relations even in groups that claim a liberatory agenda. Here, the anti-imperialists are made up almost entirely of men (with the exception of Judith, whose presence primarily serves the purpose of providing a love interest for Brian). The revolutionaries are imagining a 'freedom fight' waged by, and entirely on behalf of, men – something only Stan/Loretta has the wherewithal to point out. Viewed from this vantage point, the scene can be interpreted as foreshadowing the growing awareness that even in ostensibly marginalised groups, dominant power structures such as patriarchy and heteronormativity are often at play.

Perhaps the most problematic scene from a contemporary perspective is the response of Brian's mother to his question as to whether she was raped by his Roman biological father, Naughtius Maximus: 'Well, at first, yes . . .' Since rape is clearly no laughing matter, this line may cause many a contemporary viewer to cringe. The too-often-accepted narrative of women as 'wanting it' even when they say 'no', and of powerful men not taking 'no' as meaning 'no', has only just begun to receive the attention it deserves. It is long past time that we address this issue head-on and cease accepting abuse of power and coercion in sexual situations; understandably, many viewers may find there simply is no interpretive frame that can salvage a rape joke. A possible alternative reading, for those so inclined, would be that the character of Brian's mother is unscrupulous and absurd in every way and thus not remotely believable. (Nor, of course, is the character of Brian's mother even played by a woman.)

While it is possible to argue for more palatable interpretations of certain scenes, many viewers may well find certain aspects of *Life of Brian* to be cringeworthy from a contemporary perspective. Nevertheless, I would argue that the majority of the film's humorous scenes – and the overall interpretation of the film if it is considered as a whole – derive comic effects from incongruity and reversal, in the process delivering a message that continues to be pertinent today, especially in light of recent political and social developments.

The times we are currently living in, on both sides of the Atlantic and globally, are undeniably challenging. Some would argue that humour has no place in today's world: how can we be laughing in the face of pending disaster, increasing inequality, dehumanisation and unleashed bigotry? I would argue, however, that it is in times like these that we need comedy more than ever – not of the sadistic variety where the powerful invoke their own superiority, but in the forms of incongruity and reversal. Despite his own tendency to complain about 'political correctness', Cleese himself demonstrates an awareness of the role of power dynamics when he states:

> Not that laughter can't be unkind and destructive. Like most manifestations of human behaviour it ranges from the loving to the hateful. The latter produces nasty racial jokes and savage teasing; the former, warm and affectionate banter, and the kind of inclusive humour that says, 'Isn't the human condition absurd, but we're all in the same boat'. (Cleese 2014: 103)

Cleese's latter statement may sound contradictory to his prior assertions, in that if humour is to be inclusive and filled with 'warm and affectionate banter', derogatory humour targeting those with less power and privilege – the sort that he earlier writes off as mere 'political incorrectness' – is just the kind of 'nasty' or 'savage' comedy that should be avoided. But, like all of us mortals who are 'in the same boat', Cleese is hardly alone in having some blind spots. Often the distinction between humour and disparagement can be difficult to discern; there can be a fine line between the two, and, as society changes, those lines are not only blurring but constantly shifting. Consequently, many of us experience an ongoing tension between the desire to move towards a more equitable world and the comfort of the familiar. It is especially difficult for those who are not targeted by derogatory humour in power-laden contexts to perceive how that 'humour' may be received by someone with a different identity and social location. Perceptions of whether an utterance that the speaker calls 'humorous' is funny or cruel will differ, depending on the subject position of the audience for that supposedly funny joke.

In counterpoint to the narrative that comedy is being 'ruined' by 'oversensitive' neurotics, easily offended 'snowflakes' and so forth, a growing body of contemporary humour scholarship addresses issues such as cultural, racial and gender power dynamics in humour. Many both within and beyond the scholarly community argue that it is long past time that society opens its eyes to various forms of bigotry and cease accepting the systematic ridicule of marginalised populations in the name of comedy. As William Cheng argues in 'Taking Back the Laugh: Comedic Alibis, Funny Fails':

> Within neoliberal logics, people who endure systemic oppression (blacks, queers, crips) – who might have the *least* reason to lighten up arbitrarily – tend to be the ones who are *most* exhorted to gain a sense of humour, to take a joke, and to laugh things off. (Cheng 2017: 530)

From an ethical perspective informed by awareness of power dynamics and social inequities, it is difficult to view sensitivity to bigotry and disapproval of disparaging humour towards the oppressed as a negative. It may also be difficult to feel sympathetic to the complaints of those with the social position of the Python troupe: Oxbridge-educated Anglo-Saxon males (some of whom have been knighted), located at the cultural centre of a nation that, until relatively recently, imperialised and controlled much of the globe.

It may also seem falsely nostalgic to claim that Pythonesque comedy was deemed more acceptable in the past, since anyone old enough to remember the original release of *Life of Brian* will recall the outcry that accompanied its release. As is well known by Python followers, the original filmmaker halted production of the film due to the controversial nature of its subject matter, and it was only thanks to George Harrison's intervention and financial backing that the film could be made at all (Benko 2012: 3). Even then, the film's release was met with boycotts, censorship, negative press and widespread disapproval. When it came to Monty Python's short-form work, the surviving members of the troupe revealed in an interview with *The Telegraph* that the BBC occasionally censored their sketch show back in the 1970s (Stadlen 2013). As Freud (for all his limitations) pointed out nearly 100 years ago in *Jokes and Their Relation to the Unconscious*, the 'tendentious joke' is hardly new. However much we might long to harken back to a previous 'golden age' of comedy, even in Monty Python's heyday much of the material they produced was – in Cleese's terms – 'not allowed'.

Here it should be noted, however, that the source of *Life of Brian*'s offence in the late 1970s was much different from what is likely to generate offence today. The aspects of the film that triggered the most acrimonious critiques upon its release were focused not on gender roles, imperialism or rape jokes, but almost entirely on whether it was appropriate for a comic film to invoke a satirical approach to the gospel story. Interestingly, much recent scholarship on the film has been produced by religious scholars who explore various ways in which *Life of Brian* reinscribes the story of Jesus (see, for example, the 2015 edited collection *Jesus and Brian: Exploring the Historical Jesus and His Times via Monty Python's Life of Brian*, along with Benko's article and my own in the *Journal of Film and Religion*). While undoubtedly there are many Christian believers who would still interpret the film as blasphemous, the more salient critiques today appear to be not so much about the film's depiction of Jesus (who, as Gibron points out, is only seen once in the film and is depicted as an 'absolute good'), but where the film pokes fun at certain aspects of human identity.

Conclusion

Objections to certain forms of humour, along with public discussion about what constitutes appropriate and inappropriate jokes, are certainly not unique to the current era. Contexts shift between cultures and across time, and highly contextualised humour often does not travel well, especially as social norms evolve. As Lauren Berlant states:

> Although having good humor is often considered a virtue and a relief, we would not always want the state of humorlessness to be replaced by whatever appears as the generosity of humor . . . How do we, how can we, distinguish foolish righteousness from principled commitment? Context is everything. Perspectives vary. (Berlant 2017: 314)

Even Cleese's apparently contradictory statements capture the tension in play during this polarised moment: what kind of humour is deemed 'acceptable' in a world of seemingly ever-shifting cultural values, and who gets to make that determination? As a society, we are currently grappling with an increased awareness of inequity and oppression, along with an intense (and presently hegemonic) backlash to that heightened sensitivity. For many of us today, laughter only feels safe when we are securely located within our own 'in-group'; in more heterogeneous social spaces, polarisation often gives rise to humourlessness, and lack of humour both creates and is created by intransigence, the insistence of the 'rightness' of one's position. As Berlant states, '[h]umorlessness involves the encounter with a fundamental intractability in oneself or in others' (ibid.: 308).

This intractable 'humorlessness' worldview stands in opposition to the 'deeply comic worldview' described by Morreall in *Taking Laughter Seriously*:

> Having a sense of humor . . . involves a flexibility and openness to experience which a fundamentally serious person lacks. In part this flexibility comes from the realization that what is important is relative to the situation someone is in and to his point of view . . . Indeed, relativity itself gives a humorous cast to our lives as a whole. (Morreall 1983: 123–4)

The rigidity that Morreall attributes to the contrasting 'serious' worldview explains the dichotomy noted by Berlant: 'Humorlessness is associated both with political correctness and with the privilege that reproduces inequality as a casual, natural order of things. Humorlessness wedges an encounter in order to control it, creating a buttress of immobility and impasse' (Berlant 2017: 308). Thus, lack of humour, as Berlant points out, is not the sole province of supposedly 'over-sensitive' marginalised people who are often targeted by jokes told by the more powerful and privileged at their expense. Humourlessness can also be located in those *with* power and privilege, for whom much is at stake if they perceived the social order to be threatened, whether by humour or by anything else.

Once again, the operative variable here is one of *power*: it makes inherent sense for those with little power and status to react negatively against humour that ridicules and perhaps even dehumanises them. Furthermore, the defence of 'we were only kidding – don't you have any sense of humour?' is often used to silence appropriate objections on the part of the marginalised. As Cheng points out, '[c]omedians and laughers, after all, often demand get-out-of-jail-free cards by professing something to be just a joke' (Cheng 2017: 532).

Amidst these challenges, I would argue, ethical humour – humour that does not depend on disparagement of the disadvantaged or through replication of current power relations – is more necessary than ever. If the comic worldview is inherently flexible and if humourlessness stems from intractability, it stands to reason that if we are going to progress past our current cultural impasse, we need a reprieve from that intractability and rigidity. In short, now as never before, we need humour. What we do not need, however, is more humour that kicks those who are already down. To dismiss such a position as mere 'political correctness' is at best tone-deaf, at worst deliberately cruel.

Fortunately, other forms of humour are available and always have been. While not 'perfect' in these terms, much of Monty Python's work still resonates today. The Pythons' work has been deeply influential, changing comic expectations and conventions in significant ways. While some aspects of their comedy may reveal cultural blind spots, examples abound – both in *Life of Brian* and elsewhere – of incongruities and reversals that not only amuse us, but that have the potential, even decades after their original production, to question and challenge multiple aspects of the status quo.

Works Cited

Benko, Steven (2012) 'Ironic Faith in Monty Python's Life of Brian', *Journal of Religion and Film* 16(1), article 6. <http://digitalcommons.unomaha.edu/jrf/vol16/iss1/6/> (last accessed 26 August 2019)

Berlant, Lauren (2017) 'Three Monologues and a Hairpiece', *Critical Inquiry* (23)2, 233–49.

Bobker, Danielle (2017) 'Toward a Humor-Positive Feminism: Lessons from the Sex Wars', *Los Angeles Review of Books*, 17 December. <https://lareviewofbooks.org/article/toward-humor-positive-feminism-lessons-sex-wars/#!> (last accessed 26 August 2019)

Cassity, Kathleen (2016) 'Not Alone: "Ironic Faith", the Comic Worldview, and Process Theology in *Monty Python's Life of Brian*', *Journal of Religion and Film* (16)3, article 11. <https://digitalcommons.unomaha.edu/jrf/vol20/iss3/11/> (last accessed 7 October 2019)

Cheng, William (2017) 'Taking Back the Laugh: Comedic Alibis, Funny Fails', *Critical Inquiry* 23(2), 528–49.

Cleese, John (2014) *So, Anyway. . .* New York: Crown Books.

Gibron, Bill (2004) 'Monty Python's Life of Brian', *Pop Matters*, 29 April. <http://www.popmatters.com/review/monty-pythons-life-of-brian-2004/> (last accessed 26 August 2019)

Green, Michelle (1991) 'The Mouth of Texas', *People*, 9 December. <http://www.people.com/people/archive/article/0,,20111466,00.html>, pp. 1–4.

The Guardian (2016) 'Patrick Stewart Sketch: What Has the ECHR Ever Done for Us?', 26 April. <https://www.youtube.com/watch?v=ptfmAY6M6aA> (last accessed 30 September 2019)

Life of Brian script (1979) Available at <http://www.intriguing.com/mp/_scripts/briafilm.php>

Morgan, David (ed.) (2019) *Monty Python Speaks, Revised and Updated Edition: The Complete Oral History.* New York: Dey Street Books.

Morreall, John (1983) *Taking Laughter Seriously.* Albany, NY: SUNY Press.

Stadlen, Matthew (2013) 'Monty Python Interview: "We Were Censored by the BBC"', *The Telegraph*, 9 December. <https://www.telegraph.co.uk/culture/comedy/10500459/Monty-Python-interview-We-were-censored-by-the-BBC.html> (last accessed 26 August 2019)

Taylor, Joan E. (ed.) (2015) *Jesus and Brian: Exploring the Historical Jesus and His Times via Monty Python's Life of Brian.* London: Bloomsbury Academic.

PART FOUR

CULT, FANDOM AND PYTHON

10. PHILOSOPHY, ABSURDITY, WASTE AND *THE MEANING OF LIFE*: A CULT FILM, OF SORTS

Ernest Mathijs

– *Baby, life's what you make it*
                      Talk Talk, 'Life's What You Make It' (1985)
– *Oh well, there we are, here's the theme music*
                      Monty Python's The Meaning of Life (1983)

Monty Python's The Meaning of Life (1983) reflects life and behaves like a cult film, of sorts. The film is structured like receiving bad road directions. It starts with a firm belief in (certain kinds of) logic and progress as it moves stubbornly straight and linear from birth to death. Junction after junction, *The Meaning of Life* puts morality at the centre of life – the difference between right and wrong, good and bad, or as Douglas Adams put it in his introduction to *The Hitchhiker's Guide to the Galaxy*, 'wrong for good' (Adams 2002: vii). On its way, *The Meaning of Life* confronts and ridicules binary oppositions (the individual vs bureaucracy, religion vs materialism, austere vs orotund). Then, the film gradually and inevitably loses track of itself as it cuts cultural topics up into fragments and snippets, and finally it weaves itself into an endlessly circular, head-scratching knot – with an exclamation mark. Like most road directions, it finishes abruptly: time is up, a switch is flicked off, and a solid effing rant about the state of entertainment today ends it all.

This chapter analyses *The Meaning of Life*'s move from logic to loss not as an admission of cynicism or a manifesto of nihilism, or a 'well, what the heck', namely that nothing matters. Rather, this chapter holds that *Life* presents the absurdity and wastefulness of life as a philosophy that worms its way into all facets of understanding our time on earth by glorifying it not as depression but *joie de vivre éclatante*. In that philosophy, happiness and cruelty are neighbours and they are *both* to be approached with exuberance, and they all lead to waste – but that waste is good. In conjunction with philosophical commentary, and in an effort to simultaneously narrow it down to its textual moments and intricacies, as well as situate it in a wider perspective of cinema, comedy and culture at the time, this chapter aims to sketch instances and connections that clarify the peculiar position of *The Meaning of Life* as a wonkily structured wagging finger at the seriousness profundity assumes. In literary scholarship, this chapter's approach comes close to the terminology and methods Mikhail Bakhtin proposes in *The Dialogical Imagination* (1982 [1975]), especially with regard to 'utterances' (intertextual units). To put it at its most direct: *The Meaning of Life* explodes through a whole lot of utterances.

One more note on methodology: as the majority of this chapter combines textual interpretation with an analysis of cultural contexts, I could not resist applying a technique that *The Meaning of Life* uses too, as do its inspirations and points of reference, and that is to employ quotations from all around popular culture to illustrate how tangled up in circuits of culture this Python film is (a bit like the beginning of the segment called 'Death'). If that makes the reading of this chapter a bit more of an endurance test, then please imagine some theme music alongside it.

Philosophy

In contradiction to its own declaration in a segment on Middle Age, *The Meaning of Life* does not use philosophy as 'an attempt to construct a viable hypothesis to explain the meaning of life', at least not directly. If one puts it all in one broad claim, Python's examination of the meaning of life is not that different from that of Terry Eagleton, who uses pictures from the film as illustrations in his short philosophical tractate *The Meaning of Life* (2007). For Eagleton, life is what you make it and, in its materiality, in its process and practice, there is a movement towards happiness (not individual but communal happiness, untainted by ideology or consciousness, but with a moral compass – an Aristotelian set of virtues). Substitute happiness for enjoyment (and ignore the few quibbles Eagleton has about the 'passing' nature of pleasure – he equates it with a night on the town, which is, by the way, also a strong feature of how the Pythons end their film), and substitute his admission that life is 'what it all adds up to' with Python's last sentence of the film 'there we are', and the notion that life is *to be had*, there and then, *as it passes*, seems about the only reasonable answer. It is similar to the conclusion Siegfried Kracauer comes to, in his propositions for a 'wait-and-see' attitude as a form of openness that is as close to a meaning as life can come (Kracauer 1995).

Life is not a purely individual pursuit either, Python's *Meaning of Life* claims. Like Kracauer's and Eagleton's considerations, it is firmly placed in a social context. Life is with people, in constellations sometimes called families, neighbourhoods, communities, parties, constituencies, populations, with dynamics that help propel life. And because it occurs in groups, life bounces off other people. In doing so, it can, according to Henri Bergson (1900), create a variety of reactions, one of which is laughter. Most of this laughter is a reaction to oddities and accidents, unplanned occurrences and utterances, that people through structure hope to solve (or at least mute). In that sense, comedy is a coping mechanism that helps life make meaning (see Noel Carroll in *Comedy Incarnate* [2009]). *The Meaning of Life* offers plenty of such moments of being-together. Some of them take on the form of large choreographies, such as the Roman Catholic song and dance that ends up involving an entire working-class neighbourhood in Yorkshire (and then some). Others, like the small grouping of fish in a tank, stay small. Together, however, these scenes knit a whole that offers not only solace (the coping) but also an imaginary direction to life. As Michel Maffesoli (1988) observed, social gatherings become a structure for their own sake.

So, in spite of openness, waiting and coping, *The Meaning of Life* also firmly imposes a grouped structure, a strict script, chronological and categorical. Life is presented in stages. Moreover, as this structured living comes with stresses (responsibilities, duties, regimes, . . .), it also shows itself from a side that is perverse – a side that seems to go against the aforementioned path towards happiness. One of these sides is cruelty. According to André Bazin (2013 [1976]), in his analysis of cruelty in the films of Luis Buñuel, Alfred Hitchcock and Preston Sturges (among others), there exist several kinds of cinematic cruelty. One is happenstance cruelty, accidents. A hurtful pratfall would be an example, the kind of slapstick and circus comedy Carroll describes as physical humour, in which bodily hurt and smarts are possibilities – they happen, to no-one's fault. There is little of that in *The Meaning of Life*. Python's *Flying Circus* series and *The Holy Grail* deal with it on occasion, but it is pushed to the sidelines here. One example worth mentioning is the death of young Jenkins' mother, which is announced only in passing. We do not even get to know what she died of.

The second kind of cruelty is deliberate. It is intended to harm but it can stand outside of morality – it is meant to hurt but not to punish. If one follows Bazin's philosophical and Christian inspirations to their source here, we can even distinguish between amoral and immoral cruelty. The first is meant to just hurt. The second is meant to hurt because it is enacted out of a belief system, and it usually comes through a structure of 'correctional execution' (see Mathijs 1994, for a detailed discussion of the connections between Bazin's analysis of cruelty in cinema, and philosophies of morality). We witness a lot of deliberate hurt in *The Meaning of Life*. In the first few minutes, a fish gets offered as food in a restaurant. 'Hey, look,' some other fish in a tank say, 'Howard is being eaten'. 'Makes you think,' they contemplate. Further on in the film, another restaurant guest is persuaded to eat a mint after having consumed so many courses everyone knows he is about to explode. And so he does (I will expand on this scene further on). Pranks are played; people are tripped up. These examples show cruelty that may be mischievous but that exists outside the distinction between good and evil. Other scenes show cruelty as a result of efforts to enforce a belief system. The revolt of the pirates against The System in the prologue to the film is one example: there is the cruelty of the corporate system the workers labour in, and there is their cruelty as they, once liberated, maraud, execute victims and loot. And there is the corporate boardroom's debate about 'viewpoints', later on in the film, which aims to implement penalties for not wearing enough hats. Their meeting is interrupted by pirates. But as these try to enter the boardroom, the pirate building/ship is violently flattened by a skyscraper. The reason? To enforce the progress of the film (which it presents as its own morality).

We find this metaphor or trope of immoral cruelty in other British comedy of the time, and also in literary efforts that infuse the science fiction genre with philosophical aspirations (and there is quite a bit of science fiction in *The Meaning of Life*). The closest point of reference here is writer Douglas Adams. The successful and cult-like reception of *The Hitchhiker's Guide to the Galaxy* (1979), as a science fiction story with a philosophical overtone, revolves around the search for the meaning of life by groups (aliens this time) who use cruelty (the blowing up of a planet) as a means to administer a viewpoint. Earth has to go simply because of some administrative plans, made in the name of a belief about progress – no matter who is hurt. *The Hitchhiker's Guide to the Galaxy* goes a long way in following the philosophical implications of cruelty and institutionalised violence, even if it does so tongue-in-cheek (one can easily read it as a philosophical manual the same way Robert Pirsig's *Zen and the Art of Motorcycle Maintenance* [1974] had been received, or Ursula K. Le Guin and Italo Calvino's stories – though the influence of those was not as direct as Adams's novel). Its cheery preoccupation made the novel a pressing cultural phenomenon, which, one could argue, the Pythons used as a source of inspiration. Terry Jones makes this closeness apparent when he recalls that near the inception of *The Meaning of Life*, 'Douglas Adams phoned me up and said he'd just written a book called 'The Meaning of Liff'. I said: 'Oh no! Our film is going to be called *The Meaning of Life*' (Michael 2013). Of course, the film comments on this: a tombstone in the title sequence of *The Meaning of Life* references the (shall we say) coincidence when it misspells its own title as The Meaning of Liff. The mistake is erased by a strike of lightning but the nudge is made. Reference aside, *The Hitchhiker's Guide to the Galaxy* and *The Meaning of Life* both direct attention to immorality as a logical consequence of belief systems and the practices of oppression they employ. *The Meaning of Life* resists acceptance of this consequence quite angrily, as the unravelling of most sketches in the film shows, but it also does not know how to redirect that frustration.

In fact, the film cannot decide whether to offer a critique of cruelty or, as the flattening of the pirate ship/building implies, use it for its own purposes. It takes a detour, and then another one, and then another one, as if it drags, as Pier Paolo Pasolini puts it (in a critique of Calvino), 'everything with itself in a completely illogical dimension that solves problems by diluting them infinitely, destroying them until they're rotten and it's their turn to be surreal' (Pasolini 1973: 121). This indecision makes shaky the philosophical foundation of *The Meaning of Life* (life happens, it moves to happiness, and structure is what we hold on to, to get there even if it brings some 'necessary violence' with it). Philosophically speaking, then, *The Meaning of Life* is unsteady. Its disbelief in a vast structure or worldview (or even worldviews, plural) makes it so it can only rely on morality. That morality is unmasked as suspicious, subordinate to influences that disguise it as coincidences but that, like towels and fish in *The Hitchhiker's Guide to the Galaxy*, add up to as much of a structure as anything else – fragile at best. As the beginning of *The Meaning of Life* shows, fish's navigation systems (or, in this case of tank fish, the lack thereof) are the only compass left. It offers only flow, not solid ground. But hopefully that flow drifts towards happiness.

The Absurd and the Poetic

In its slide away from philosophy as a model, towards philosophy as flow, and even beyond that, beyond philosophy, *The Meaning of Life* makes what Jörg Aufenanger (1984: 159) has called, via Roland Barthes, a turn away from modelling, towards chronicling the myths of everyday life – but in an order that disrobes them rather than confirming them as building blocks for understanding life. Life is not meaningful as such but instead filled with rituals, and, as Graham Chapman's character remarks in the segment called 'The Miracle of Birth', it is increasingly stocked with 'apparatus', equipment that goes 'ping', which seem to write their own myths. But these rituals do not explain anything. Instead, they show themselves to be accidental, contingent and morally empty. They are not good or bad, just nonsensical. As *The Meaning of Life* proceeds, this becomes abundantly visible. After the hospital scene in which a child is born, scenes of childhood and youth in a church and a school, in congregation, in sports are organised around rituals and for-the-sake procedures. In these, the Pythons puncture holes, first sparingly, then increasingly so. The frequency of interruptions mounts, and with few or no exceptions, segments end either again in dance and song, what Barbara Ehrenreich sees as the collective joy around rituals (Ehrenreich 2006), or in mayhem and chaos – in anarchy. Within a few minutes of screen time, the film jumps from a well-structured classroom to a rugby game that ends in wild jostling and equally wild celebrations to a war conflict in which all sense of direction is gone. As the camera zooms out of the absurdity of a situation in which troops tried to maintain etiquette while under bombardment, only waste remains. In another example, a scene on sexual education brims with absurdity, as rituals (the sex act, in-class discipline) fight with each other over dominance of a situation that has already stopped making sense well before that. Throughout, there persists a philosophy that maintains that rituals, even in their randomness, have purpose.

As has been noted in Rick Hudson's chapter in this volume, the Pythons' attitude here is similar to that of Luigi Pirandello. In his evocation of the absurdity of roles, be they performative ones, on stage (as in Pirandello's most famous play, *Six Characters in Search of an Author* [1921]), or in more mundane sketches of daily life (in *Eleven Short Stories* [1994]), Pirandello's characters uphold the notion that there is some sort of extrinsic reason for why we do what we do, even if it is unintelligible, and even if it is a merely instrumental one (like 'marching up and down the square', as one vignette in the film has it). Virtually every segment in *The Meaning of Life* has a moment in which the Pirandellian attitude takes centre stage, when 'everyday trivia' that potentially distract from the narrative become the focal point of that scene, for no reason other than to offer a pivot around which a wonky structure, completely random or irrational, can be built, and kept. The film's short (and interrupted) excursion into systems of belief via energy physics, in which wearing a hat is proposed as a boardroom topic for vital discussion, is such a moment of structured absurdity. Yet another example finds a team of organ transplanters cutting out a person's liver simply because they can and it says so on the donor card. Violence ensues, with blood galore, but because it is part of a structure that seems self-explanatory (the card says so), the lookers-on (the family) as well as the perpetrators (who banter about) accept it – absurd but all right.

'The Middle of the Film', an intermission-type segment that interrupts what had been somewhat of a flow to the story as it makes its way from school through various stages of the military and empire-building, exemplifies this best. Stylistically, it resembles the cinematography, *mise-en-scène*, design and make-up of *The Rocky Horror Picture Show* (Sharman, 1975), a film that at the time was at the centre of cult cinema (see Weinstock 2007). Announced as a game to find the fish (which no one ever does), it just shows a seemingly improvised act of freakery and alienation, without structure whatsoever, but awash with exuberance, dance (mime- and magician-like movement is perhaps more accurate) and innuendo. In its absurdity, this scene goes beyond the Pirandellian attitude of 'holding on to nothing', because it has not even an imaginary centre of organisation. If it is a ritual or procedure (and as a 'game' it is supposed to have one), it does not reveal

PHILOSOPHY, ABSURDITY, WASTE AND *THE MEANING OF LIFE*

Figure 10.1 *Monty Python's The Meaning of Life* (1983) and *The Rocky Horror Picture Show* (1975): *joie de vivre éclatante*.

itself. It is therefore nonsensical, anarchistic; it only vaguely suggests there is any meaning to be derived from how it behaves yet it seems confidently fuelled by some dynamic. Pasolini (1976), in his description (and practice) of poetry and his search for pure language and dialects in danger of losing their cultural function, and Thomas Pynchon (1973), in his explorations of explosive frames of reference in which everything refers to everything to the extent that language and existence act without any gravitational pull, offer such instances as 'orgies' in which happiness erupts blindingly bright as *joie de vivre éclatante*. Consider the computer-animated body, built from a grid that appears in the middle of the Milky Way, whose vagina explodes a case in point. Much like *The Rocky Horror Picture Show*, and with Pynchon and Pasolini, the Middle of the Film is the moment when *The Meaning of Life* creates its own poetry.

BUREAUCRACY, HYPERBOLE AND WASTE

The Meaning of Life was financed by Universal, and it was the highest-budgeted Python film to that date. Though, as we shall see, this brought with it certain production logistics, it also brought opportunity for experimenting with set pieces that could be properly prepared and rehearsed. Blowing up those set pieces allowed Python to be at its most Pythonesque (which is, in this case, to be understood as self-aware of its own style). Some of the influences for such experimenting have been mentioned above, and Calvino, Pasolini and

Pynchon, and, above all, *The Hitchhiker's Guide to the Galaxy*, must count as profound points of reference. As with *The Rocky Horror Picture Show*, there is not only a shared resistance to oppressive systems that regulate moral behaviour, ideology and gender and the conduct of sexuality, as well as a desire to expose the hypocrisy of these doctrines (the Roman Catholic segment followed by the Protestant Conversation is a good example), but there is also a stylistic overlap in the segmenting of a narrative into vignettes, some flowing neatly from one another, and others intercalating the main narrative more abruptly. Among the reasons why *The Meaning of Life* is considered a cult film, these similarities certainly carry weight. A lot of the stylistic flavour of *The Meaning of Life* comes of course from the Pythons' earlier work. As detailed in other chapters in this collection, musical set-piece interventions, brusque changes in pace and tone that pervert the logical progression of time, voice-over commentary that contradicts or otherwise reframes the visual flow, and crazy and absurd animated bursts (courtesy of Terry Gilliam) are key staples of the Python aesthetic, and we find them in abundance here as well. A British middle-aged couple's visit to an event-restaurant where philosophy is on the menu is a classic Python sketch (complete with Cleese's aplomb and 'Oh, I see, very well then'-esque reactions to silly dialogue).

One of the stylistic techniques *The Meaning of Life* applies that constrains it is its internal bureaucracy. The structure of the film, even though it gets blown to bits, does survive the madness and mayhem of exuberance that it endures – after all is done, it is still a story about one's life trajectory, and the idea of a path, a route, is pervasive throughout the film's vignettes and asides. Michael Palin, in an interview, describes it as follows: 'That harked back to Python's love of bureacracy [*sic*]: you know, people coming round from the council, 10 of them, with different bits of paper' (Michael 2013). Even though Palin adds that, in his view, *The Meaning of Life* has only a shell structure ('the loosest structure, which will be the meaning of life'), he acknowledges that the film's vast budget brought with it its own administrative demands, from which it then had to break loose. *The Meaning of Life* comments on this in its prologue, *The Crimson Permanent Assurance* short feature that precedes the long feature. In it, the workforce of an insurance company, most of them it seems of near-retirement age (the age when insurance becomes a more pressing concern, one is led to think), and 'strained under the yoke of their oppressive corporate management', revolt against their labour conditions. They take over the building in which they work, and, with the building dressed as a pirate ship, the clerks set sail from London to New York, to overtake Wall Street's bankers. The bankers fight back but the pirate-accountant prevails and they leave Wall Street behind as a wasteland . . . only to drop off a cliff – end of short feature.

When considered in some detail, that bureaucracy is twofold. On the one hand, it is similar to what Karl Mannheim (1929) points to as bureaucracy as an ideology. It is a way of organising life and beliefs about life and its inspirations that supersedes any and all other considerations for worldviews. It is encapsulated in 'ways to do things' that become their own command, simply because they offer practical ways of living life – so much so that life is what happens when you're making other plans (to paraphrase an overused quotation). For instance, it meant that the Pythons were now parcelling out and scheduling their time commitments. Whereas with previous films each member of the team was always on hand, with *The Meaning of Life* members only showed up on schedule, when needed (Michael 2013). For an art form like comedy (especially in its troupe form) that relies on group dynamics, this meant the structure *became* the film's meaning – spontaneity traded for production efficiency. One implication of this was a more rigorous division of labour (one that is cheekily implied at the beginning of the short feature via a cardboard-clipped time sheet). If, at times, as some reviewers remarked, the film appears a bit laboured, then bureaucracy can certainly be pointed at as a cause (McNally 2012). Gilliam, who was in charge of *The Crimson Permanent Assurance*, explains how the division of labour, which he calls 'they didn't know how I worked so I got to do it' (Christie 1999), led to him going vastly over budget to make it an outstanding and grandiose critique of bureaucracy, only to see the protocols of audience previews reduce the segment's significance (and its power as a critique of bureaucracy): 'It had a completely different style from the Python material,' he observes, 'the laughs aren't immediate.' After Gilliam suggested it become the main feature's accompanying short, 'it gave us the chance of allowing it to come back and "attack" the main film' (ibid.: 108).

On the other hand, this bureaucracy offered the perfect background against which to fire off critiques on structure, which is already indicated in the short prologue and, further, as the film progresses from birth to death, following life's trajectory. The seven core segments of the film, The Miracle of Birth, Growth and Learning, Fighting Each Other, Middle Age, Live Organ Transplants, The Autumn Years, and Death, are commented on by insertions that become increasingly wild and nonsensical (though they do present a lyricism not seen too often in earlier Python work). As McNally (2012) puts it: 'The tone and style of each sketch changes, but the comedy hits higher and higher speeds with such perennials as John Cleese's Sex Education Class, Over-Appreciative World War I Soldiers and Fishy, Fishy, Fishy, Fish!' The *Hollywood Reporter* (Osborne 1983) wrote that the film disintegrates into a 'hodgepodge of vignettes', an accurate observation of the film's disintegration into wildness. As hinted at in the discussion of the film's employment of notions of absurdity and poetry as deviations from the straitjackets of structure, it blows protocols, routines and rituals out of the water. Two techniques of representation typical for cult cinema that, in fact, border on what *is* representable demonstrate this: hyperbole and waste.

If hyperbole already was a well-established tactic in comedy, especially in the humour of Python's immediate predecessors Peter Cook, Dudley Moore and Peter Sellers, the Pythons turned it up a notch or two – making, in a way, hyperbolic silliness the rhetorical centrepiece of many of their sketches (see Jeffrey Weinstock's chapter in this volume). To that, the Pythons also add visual hyperbole aided by the increased permissibility of the time. Nudity, violence, evocative choreography and hallucinatory *mise-en-scène* (helped by cinematography that was a lot more daring in its angling, movement and use of wide-angle lenses than what was present in the Pythons' television work) make *The Meaning of Life* more provocative, and yank it out of any regime of representation. This is reflexively commented on in the film's ending (fittingly announced as 'the ending of the film'), and its snipe at popular culture of the time, and beyond. In this epilogue, a lady presenter, somewhat resembling the archetype of the well-meaning yet finger-wagging Auntie BBC, laments this hyperbolic overkill: 'Family entertainment? Bollocks. What they want is filth. People doing things to each other with chainsaws, . . . armed bands of theatre critics exterminating mutant goats. Where's the fun in pictures?' It is an apt comment on the ways in which hyperbole blew aesthetic rules out of existence and equally a smart reflection on then-popular genres experiencing some sort of hyperbolic renaissance: the horror film, science fiction and grotesque realism, from mondo films to Pasolini's *Salo* (1975).

Hyperbole becomes waste in *The Meaning of Life*. The crazy abundance of elements stuffed into a scene leads to an explosion of utterances, instances and mentions that make up a dense and unruly pile of unnecessary detail from which the story, and the film, needs to discharge. A lot of this is visualised via food and body fluids. Prompted by theories of pollution and purity, Mathijs and Sexton (2011) make the case that displays of traffic of food and fluids from the inside of the body to the outside present instances of transgression that are typical for cult cinema. *The Meaning of Life* sprays these instances around in abundance. Blood, urine, spit, semen, drool and slime all make noted appearances, as they are tied to absurd considerations of etiquette, sex-education, politeness and hospitality, and made to illustrate the idea that whatever flows from the messy insides of people to the highly controlled presentation of self that is one's outside, challenges good behaviour until it blows up.

The inevitable exemplar of this, and indeed the one scene in *The Meaning of Life* that is never left unmentioned, is the 'Mr. Creosote' scene. In it, an overweight patron in a posh restaurant overeats until he is so filled he looks ready to explode. In their very depiction of Mr. Creosote, the Pythons already cross boundaries of taste. He is shown as hyperbolically obese, with spilled food scraps dribbled and drivelled down his expensive suit. After a copious dinner, and in spite of his reluctance, the maître d' persuades him to consume just one more 'wafer-thin mint', after which he literally explodes. Litres of minestrone soup are blown across the screen. There is hardly any better indication of an utterance in

PHILOSOPHY, ABSURDITY, WASTE AND *THE MEANING OF LIFE*

Figure 10.2 Hyperbole and waste at work in *The Meaning of Life*.

the history of film than this one. Robert Osborne in the *Hollywood Reporter* said it was 'unbelievably crass' (Osborne 1983), and warned that its inclusion in the film requires audiences to 'unbend'. Vincent Canby (1983) in the *New York Times* called it 'out of proportion' and Roger Ebert (1983) adds that 'we get gallons of vomit, streams of it, all a vile yellow color, sprayed all over everybody and everything in a formal dining room. . . . It's a barbed, uncompromising attack on generally observed community standards'. Most reviewers comment on how Monty Python's attempt to demonstratively purge itself by pushing puke into cinemagoers' view helps it rise above vulgarity (it's more like vulgarity XXL), but that it also blows up any possible understandings. Tellingly, most critics do not get further than to merely describe what's happening, as if nothing else can be said. And that is exactly it. Nothing can be said about the scene. It is waste and waste only. In that sense, the 'Mr. Creosote' scene goes beyond what Bakhtin (1965) describes as potentially grotesque or carnivalesque – beyond attempts to offer a safe space to unbounded celebrations of life outside structured and regulated normality. Instead, by not adding anything to the plot, or the poetics (it is beyond absurd), or the structure, or the bureaucracy or the philosophy of the film (it does add its *flow* but only visually), it is pure waste.

Conclusion

History, as it is, has not been terribly kind to *The Meaning of Life*. The reason for that is Python's own myth. At the time of its release the film was applauded, and even won a prize at the Cannes festival. But it was also found to be exasperating; at least that was the consensus among anglophone reviewers. Home nation reviews that had been critical of Monty Python's output, especially with regard to *Life of Brian*, were unexpectedly mild in their assessment. For instance, *The Telegraph* called it a 'curious hit-and-miss affair' (Chilton 2014). It seemed most reviewers avoided the bait of 'controversy' the film itself dangled in front of them. Outside the English-speaking world the reception was decidedly positive, especially in France and Latin America. Nowadays, the status of *The Meaning of Life* seems overweight, at least as a bearer of Python's legacy. Though the film frequently features in generalist overviews of the canons and cults of cinema (see Mathijs and Sexton 2011), it also sits there uneasily. For instance, French and French (1999) give their 'cult Python' vote to *Life of Brian*, and Soren McCarthy (2003) and Mathijs and Mendik (2011) prefer *The Holy Grail*. For Neil McNally (2012), too, the film is not quite as good as the others. Some of the Pythons themselves have commented on how the writing and the logistics of the film and its ambitious theme made them run out of steam (see Jones *et al.* 2009). And virtually all sources that discuss the oeuvre of Python in this era present Gilliam's *Time Bandits* (1981) and *Brazil* (1984), or the *Crimson* short that precedes the feature (which was by his hand), or still Terry Jones's *Erik the Viking* (1989), as films that more legitimately capture the aesthetics of the legacy of Python – its whimsicality, exuberance and silliness – what I called above its *joie de vivre éclatante*. *The Meaning of Life*, then, is Python's final aria, to be over with it.

The Meaning of Life retains a tongue-in-cheek irony as to its own seriousness. In that sense, it is perhaps tempting to see it connected, in one way or another (perhaps as an aside, similar to how scenes in the film move into each other?), to postulations of the end of philosophy or of postmodern theory (and anti-theory), common in the early 1980s (see the description in the last chapter of Aufenanger 1984). As Patrick West observes in a review of the work of French philosopher Jean Baudrillard, much of philosophy of the time concentrated on how symbolic and sign value (the worth of something through its appearance) is central to the kind of 'rituals of gift exchange' and 'conspicuous consumption of useless goods' that made 'waste and excess . . . a central value of commodities' (West 2011). It is an observation that, as this chapter has hopefully shown, sits at the centre of *The Meaning of Life* (West also makes an explicit reference to Monty Python, albeit to *Life of Brian*). If one looks at it like that, *The Meaning of Life* fooled philosophy by offering it a symbolic carrot at a time when philosophy was desperately looking for one. The carrot suggested that the film's 'everything's waste' idea could be co-opted into schemata and models of life's meaning as a sometimes bureaucratic ritual of wasteful gifts – such as mints – that 'just keep the whole thing going' but are otherwise meaningless. But, in making that offering, *The Meaning of Life* also forces philosophy to tie itself into a knot of irrelevance by foregrounding the kind of ironic playfulness that amounts to silliness and absurdity ('there it is, nothing is real. And even that's not real. See what I did there?').

Beyond postmodernism, *The Meaning of Life* continues to baffle critics. Eagleton, who ambitiously took his book title from the film, is one of the very few who hold it for what it is (as I showed above). But Eagleton's reviewers fail to see that (look for instance to Dempsey 2010). To this day, the Pythons *still* fool a critical establishment slavishly eager to champion them as prophets. *Harper's* solemn publication of John Cleese's 'Sermon' (2019) is but one example (and one in which Cleese cheekily references *The Meaning of Life* in anything but name), as is the seriousness surrounding Michael Palin's documentary travel series, or even his appearance in *Death of Stalin* (Iannucci, 2018) – another film about laughter and murder taken way too seriously by those in the serious-business. The only difference is that, as Eric Idle observes, it is now no longer in their hands: 'I think I've done my bit. I'm interested in my life, whatever is left of it' (Deb 2018).

For many, *The Meaning of Life* is indicative of the 'ending of Python', its ramshackle assembly and overblown style not a show of firepower but of exhaustion, as if the machine had run out of fuel. As such, then, the link between *The Meaning of Life* and the rest of the Python oeuvre is that it functions as a tail, a loose end. True, it shares with *Life of Brian* a sense of impertinence – as if there is a pinch of meanness to it, and that the aforementioned exhaustion is also, slightly, one of frustration (perhaps a frustration within the troupe). But in essence it stands alone, as a big landfill at the edge of town. That view is backed by the fate of some contemporary films Pythons were involved in. *Yellowbeard* (Damski, 1981), *Brazil* and *Erik the Viking* also appear to indicate Monty Python's time was simply up. In spite of the involvement of Pythons, these films did not fare too well. In the end, *The Meaning of Life*, and the comparisons it draws with philosophy, kinds of cruelty, absurd realism and poetry, contemporary comedy and other Python-influenced projects, paint it as overly ambitious – perhaps not by design, but certainly in its eventual appearance and, yes, meaning. It is Python's rock opera or concept album (Pink Floyd or The Who, anyone?) going over the top. That said, the film's trajectory from logic to loss, and its insertions, at increasingly higher rhythm, of increasingly more absurd vignettes, give the in-between segments a degree of anarchic freedom, as if *The Meaning of Life* goes rogue at the cost of its own game plan and team structure. It is in this waste that its value lies.

Ultimately, *The Meaning of Life* refuses to be taken seriously. It is irreverent because its behaviour shows it couldn't possibly be in earnest. As a confirmation of the fluidity of comedy at large and as a hyperbolic gesture, as well as, to stick with *The Meaning of Life*'s own ending, a solid rant on the state of entertainment today, it remains the perfect Python endnote. 'Now everybody –'

Figure 10.3   The end of *The Meaning of Life*: a solid rant on entertainment today.

Works Cited

Adams, Douglas (1979) *The Hitchhiker's Guide to the Galaxy* (2002 omnibus edition). London: Pan Macmillan.
Aufenanger, Jörg (1984) *Filosofie*. Munich: Bertelsmann.
Bakhtin, Mikhail (1965) *Rabelais and His World*. Bloomington: Indiana University Press.
Bakhtin, Mikhail (1982 [1975]) *The Dialogical Imagination*. Austin: University of Texas Press.
Bazin, André (2013 [1976]) *The Cinema of Cruelty*. New York: Skyhorse Publishing.
Bergson, Henri (1900) *Laughter: An Essay on the Meaning of the Comic*. Paris: Alcan.
Canby, Vincent (1983) 'The Meaning of Life', *New York Times*, 31 March. <https://www.nytimes.com/1983/03/31/movies/monty-python-the-meaning-of-life.html> (last accessed 31 December 2018)
Carroll, Noel (2009) *Comedy Incarnate*. London: Wiley-Blackwell.
Chilton, Marti (2014) 'Monty Python's The Meaning of Life Review', *The Telegraph*, 20 April. <https://www.telegraph.co.uk/culture/film/filmreviews/10765951/Monty-Pythons-The-Meaning-of-Life-review.html> (last accessed 29 December 2018)
Christie, Ian (ed.) (1999) *Gilliam on Gilliam*. London: Faber & Faber.
Cleese, John (2019) 'A Divine Pat', *Harper's Magazine*, 4 February. <https://harpers.org/archive/2018/11/a-divine-pat-john-cleese/> (last accessed 4 February 2019)
Deb, Sopan (2018) 'For Eric Idle, Life's a Laugh and Death's a Joke, It's True', *New York Times*, 26 September. <https://www.nytimes.com/2018/09/26/books/eric-idle-always-look-bright-side-life-monty-python-spamalot.html> (last accessed 26 September 2018)
Dempsey, Ernest (2010) 'The Meaning of Life by Terry Eagleton', *Philosophy Now* 78, December. <https://philosophynow.org/issues/78/The_Meaning_of_Life_by_Terry_Eagleton> (last accessed 4 February 2019)

Eagleton, Terry (2007) *The Meaning of Life: A Very Short Introduction*. Oxford: Oxford University Press.
Ebert, Roger (1983) 'Monty Python's *Meaning of Life*', *Chicago Sun-Times*, 1 April. <https://www.rogerebert.com/reviews/monty-pythons-meaning-of-life-1983> (last accessed 31 December 2018)
Ehrenreich, Barbara (2006) *Dancing in the Streets: A History of Collective Joy*. New York: Metropolitan Books.
French, Karl, and Philip French (1999) *Cult Movies*. London: Pavilion Books.
Hunter, I. Q. and Laraine Porter (eds) (2012) *British Comedy Cinema*. Abingdon: Routledge.
Jones, Bill, Alan Parker and Ben Timlett (2009) 'Monty Python: Almost the Truth – The Lawyers' Cut' (Documentary, 6 episodes, 107 minutes).
Kracauer, Siegfried (1995) *The Mass Ornament*. Boston, MA: Harvard University Press.
McCarthy, Soren (2003) *Cult Movies in Sixty Seconds*. London: Fusion Press.
McNally, Neil (2012) 'Looking back at Monty Python's *The Meaning of Life*', *Den of Geek*, 15 June. <https://www.denofgeek.com/movies/monty-python/21662/looking-back-at-monty-python%25E2%2580%2599s-the-meaning-of-life> (last accessed 24 November 2018)
Maffesoli, Michel (1988) *The Time of the Tribes: The Decline of Individualism in Mass Society*. London: Sage.
Mannheim, Karl (2013 [1929]) *Ideology and Utopia*. Abingdon: Routledge.
Mathijs, Ernest (1994) 'André Bazin: Filmkritiek en kunst', *MediaFilm* 208, 61–74.
Mathijs, Ernest and Xavier Mendik (2011) *100 Cult Films*. London: Palgrave Macmillan.
Mathijs, Ernest and Jamie Sexton (2011) *Cult Cinema*. Boston: Wiley-Blackwell.
Michael, Chris (2013) 'How We Made *The Meaning Of Life*', *The Guardian*, 30 September. <https://www.theguardian.com/film/2013/sep/30/monty-python-meaning-of-life> (last accessed 26 December 2018)
Osborne, Robert (1983) 'Monty Python's *The Meaning of Life*', *The Hollywood Reporter*, 31 March. <https://www.hollywoodreporter.com/review/monty-pythons-meaning-life-review-1983-movie-1097286> (last accessed 13 October 2018)
Pasolini, Pier Paolo (1973) 'Italo Calvino's Invisible Cities', in Jack Hirschman (ed.), *In Danger: A Pasolini Anthology*, San Francisco: City Lights Books, pp. 116–22.
Pasolini, Pier Paolo (1976) 'The Cinema of Poetry', in Bill Nichols (ed.), *Movies and Methods*, vol. 1. Berkeley: University of California Press.
Pirandello, Luigi (1994) *Eleven Short Stories*. New York: Dover Publications.
Pirandello, Luigi (1997 [1921]) *Six Characters in Search of an Author*. New York: Dover Publications.
Pynchon, Thomas (1973) *Gravity's Rainbow*. New York: Viking Press.
Weinstock, Jeffrey (2007) *The Rocky Horror Picture Show*. London: Wallflower Press.
West, Patrick (2011) 'I Am the Simulacrum of Myself', *Culture Wars*, 16 December. <http://www.culturewars.org.uk/index.php/site/article/i_am_the_simulacrum_of_myself/> (last accessed 4 February 2019)

11. IN PRAISE OF SILLINESS: THE CULT OF PYTHON

Jeffrey Andrew Weinstock

Comedy's Neglect

While scholarship on cult film, television and media has blossomed in the twenty-first century, comedy in general and Monty Python in particular have largely been neglected by cult media scholars. True, following on Susan Sontag's famous essay on the subject, some attention has been paid by film and television critics to camp – both the retrospective campiness of classic Hollywood films and the obvious intent to elevate bad taste into an art form in films such as those by John Waters (see Sontag 1964). Comedy and cult has been touched on as part of the discussion of mockumentary's parody of the documentary (with an emphasis on *Spinal Tap* [Rob Reiner, 1984]; see, for example, de Seife 2007), and certainly cult scholarship has addressed films with comedic elements – typically those that we might describe as black comedies that combine the absurd and ridiculous with the gruesome (see, for example, Egan 2011). As I've addressed elsewhere, however, scholarship on cult media has tended to keep a wide berth around the unapologetically silly (see my essay 'Bubba Ho-tep' 2015). There are those it seems who study comedy, and those who study cult film, TV and media, and it appears seldom the twain do meet.

My suspicion is that this neglect of comedy on the part of those who study cult media in its various forms is because silliness along the lines of dead parrots, silly walks, killer jokes and unexpected inquisitions, rather than pointed political comedy or satire that has attracted some attention from scholars, lacks the frisson of the transgressive or just the out-and-out weirdness that those who study cult media (myself included) tend to enjoy. People consume cult films for many reasons, of course; however, I would hazard that the pleasure in doing so often clusters at least in part around the sense of sophistication or superiority that accompanies consciously adopting an antagonistic position in relation to established social norms and conventions: the consumer of the cult film feels pleased to be able to appreciate that which goes beyond or violates the conventions of the mainstream Hollywood film and the presumed provincialism of its audience. This appreciation may involve watching classic films 'differently' – calling out their queer subtexts, for example, or mocking what seems absurdly saccharine or primitive from a contemporary perspective – or embracing the strange, gross, ghoulish or 'bad'. There is a kind of aggressive posturing towards the mainstream associated with cultivating non-normative tastes, and to deploy one's tastes as a marker of one's independence and individuality (as a 'refusal' in the sense developed by Dick Hebdige in connection with social subcultures; see Hebdige 1979) is to offer a kind of critique or implicit rebuke of society that positions one as superior: one possesses the intellectual capacity, requisite sensitivity, specialised knowledge – and often endurance – to appreciate and derive enjoyment from that which confuses, disgusts or outrages the less sophisticated. Part of the cult fan's pleasure then is connected to a sense of superiority that comes from mocking the provincialism of the mainstream.

The pleasure of studying cult film, television and media to a certain extent mirrors the pleasure of participating in the cult itself (and often the two overlap as scholars choose objects of focus they enjoy). Like cult film fans, cult film scholars – sometimes at least – seem to savour their outcast status as they focus their attention on 'questionable' texts and argue for their meaningfulness and importance. The scholar perhaps differs from the fan most often only in the degree to which they overlay a more sustained intellectualisation atop the experience of viewing genres often dismissed as frivolous or trash or juvenile. And, indeed, those who study cult film can often seem like wizards as they recuperate gruesome horror, bad taste and/or sheer absurdity as canny social commentary, and make sense of the surreal. The analysis of the horror film is a case in point as film critics have repeatedly and often persuasively analysed cinematic monsters as metaphors for pervasive cultural anxieties. *The Babadook* (Jennifer Kent, 2014), for example, is an allegory for grappling with depression. *Get Out* (Jordan Peele, 2017) – which, granted, wears its metaphoric status on its sleeve – is an allegory of the American history of white usurpation of black bodies. Zombies reflect anxieties about viral contagion and global pandemics. Werewolves are metaphors for the concealment of a shameful secret such as homosexuality. And so on. Using a kind of Freudian dream logic, critics of cult media and genre fiction have frequently made compelling cases that that which we don't like, which is unpleasant, which scares us or disgusts us, can be interpreted as the condensation and displacement of both idiosyncratic and widely shared anxieties and tabooed desires. Interpreting such media and our response to it is then regarded as telling concerning both intra-psychic processes and the cultural imaginary.

Ironically, given comedy's second-class status, it would seem ideally suited as an object of scrutiny for film scholars who make their livings excavating the depths of neglected or dismissed genres – showing us the meaning against the tendency to dismiss something as gratuitous or frivolous, pornographic, or simply gross. But this wizardry curiously seems to reach its limit where comedy is concerned – the right spells can't be found to master the Knights Who Say Ni or a dynamite carnivorous rabbit – and my suspicion again is that this is because silliness, associated with childishness, is often felt to be the antithesis of cult film sophistication. The same scholars who will insist on the social significance of *I Spit on Your Grave* (Meir Zarchi, 1978) and *Cannibal Holocaust* (Ruggero Deodato, 1985) refuse to visit Camelot because it is a silly place.

To a certain extent, this dismissive attitude reflects a deeply engrained critical and cultural tendency to consider comedy as less real or important than drama. The standard assumption is that Shakespeare's tragedies are where the real grandeur lies and present the true test of the thespian. One is hard-pressed to find too many comedies included as part of the secondary school curriculum anywhere (my recollections of works from high school English class are unrelentingly bleak – *The Grapes of Wrath* anyone?). In the history of the Academy Awards to date, going back to their beginnings in 1928, only seven 'comedies' have won best picture. Even fewer Pulitzer Prizes for Literature have gone to comedies. Drama in general is considered to have more depth, to be more real, to be weightier and more meaningful. In contrast, films and programmes that seek to elicit laughter and particularly those that wrap things up neatly with a happy ending (which not all comedies do, of course) are considered more surface and characterised as fantasy.

There are in fact multiple levels of irony at play here that extend beyond the idea of critics who specialise in neglected genres neglecting a neglected genre. The first is that, despite popular perception, comedy is never straightforward or depthless. As Andrew Stott explains and I will address more fully below, comedy is inherently social and, like horror, presupposes shared understandings of social norms that are then suspended, inverted or abandoned (Stott 2014: 8). Just like horror and science fiction – and drama and romance and all other genres for that matter – comedy requires interpretation and contextualisation to be understood. Indeed, to recognise something as funny in the first place presupposes certain cultural understandings of what makes something funny or not. And while silliness may connote a childish *naïveté* and lack of guile, cinematic silliness as the product of conscious deployment (rather than accident or incompetence) is itself a sophisticated manipulation of culturally embedded expectations. Further, the performance and consumption of silliness by adults is itself on some level transgressive given cultural mandates concerning 'mature' deportment. Put differently: kids being silly means one thing, adults being silly signifies entirely differently.

To be fair, I expect most scholars and cultural critics – of cult media and beyond – will grant these claims; so the question remains: what explains the neglect of comedy by cult film scholars in general, and Monty Python in particular? (And not least among the many ironies here is that, in my experience, cult film scholars and academics in general almost universally express a fondness for Monty Python!) Is it that comedy is considered too mainstream? It should be pointed out that this hasn't stopped criticism of the *Harry Potter* and *Star Wars* and comic character franchises from becoming cottage industries. Is it that comedy just isn't outré enough to allow for academic wizardry? Is it that, despite an understanding by scholars that all texts require interpretation to be meaningful, the cultural bias against comedy prevails and comedy is still considered to have less depth – to be less meaningful – than other genres? Does some of the hesitation to address comedy simply have to do with the awareness that, while humour is complicated, nothing is less funny than a joke explained – or less interesting than the tedious bore who explains it?

The neglect of Monty Python by scholars of cult media is especially curious given the commonplace acceptance of Monty Python as a focus of cult veneration. Robert Hewison, for example, writes in his overview of the history of Monty Python and censorship that, in Great Britain, '*Monty Python* quickly became a cult . . . Its energy and enthusiasm transmitted itself to the audience, who rejoiced in the absurdity of it all' (Hewison 1981: 8). Marcia Landy, in her excellent book on *Monty Python's Flying Circus*, quotes a similar history of the programme by reviewer Andrew Cliff from 1989: 'Monty Python is 20 years old . . . For a while the show languished on the BBC's second channel . . . Soon it had a cult following' (Landy 2005: 100). That cult then spread to American shores: 'Many young Americans saw it [the *Flying Circus*] and believed in it to the extent of its becoming a campus cult' (Wilmut quoted in Landy 2005: 26). Landy then comments on this, writing,

> the term cult suggests a particular type of devoted, collective, and intense emotional reaction usually associated with fandom. The *Flying Circus* appealed to young people and to disaffected groups for its irreverence toward authority and for its unconventional uses of television – it exposed the existence of deeply felt desires for alternatives to social and cultural conformity in the United Kingdom, America, and elsewhere. (Ibid.: 26)

Python, it appears, was cult almost from the get-go, which is acknowledged by critics of cult film even as they then swiftly move on to discussions of other cult media. Mathijs and Sexton devote only half a paragraph to Monty Python in their authoritative textbook, *Cult Cinema: An Introduction* (2011), writing primarily in relation to *Monty Python and the Holy Grail* (Terry Gilliam and Terry Jones, 1975) and *Life of Brian* (Terry Jones, 1979) that '[f]or some, Monty Python is ridiculous, for others silly, for others yet it is ultra-clever, and for many it is all of that – cult because of how it unhinges notions of humor' (Mathijs and Sexton 2011: 227). Leon Hunt in his *Cult British TV Comedy: From Reeves and Mortimer to Psychoville* considers *Monty Python's Flying Circus* as sketch comedy's 'canonical object' (Hunt 2013: 100) – and then offers no analysis of it at all, except to briefly note concerns about the 'tastelessness' of a particular sketch ('The Undertaker's Sketch' from 1970; see ibid.: 204–5). There is no inclusion of *Holy Grail* or any other Python film in the Wallflower Press 'Cultographies' series of books on cult films (which frankly boggles the mind), nor does Hoberman and Rosenbaum's oft-cited *Midnight Movies* (1991) mention Monty Python at all among its discussion of 100+ cult films. Gregory A. Waller does mention *Monty Python and the Holy Grail* in his discussion of midnight movies, but only to contrast it against the unique status of another cult film – *The Rocky Horror Picture Show* (Jim Sharman, 1975)! He explains,

> As further proof of its special status, *Rocky Horror* had by the mid-1980s been singled out and accorded the status of cultic and cultural phenomenon by the American media and analyzed by academic scholars in a way that *Monty Python and the Holy Grail* and [Cheech and Chong's] *Up in Smoke*, for example, had not. (Waller 1991: 173)

And this absence of analysis remains the case: with the notable exception of Landy, whose concern is less with considering the cultic qualities of Monty Python than with offering an overview of the television series' history and emphases, Jeffrey S. Miller's consideration of the American reception of *Monty Python's Flying Circus* in *Something Completely Different: British Television and American Culture*, and Justin Smith's brief consideration of *Holy Grail* in *Withnail and Us: Cult Films and Film Cults in British Cinema*, it seems to have been Python's fate to be frequently mentioned by film and media critics as a focus of cult veneration but little discussed – indeed, to the best of my knowledge, to this date there has been no sustained analysis of the cultic qualities of *Monty Python's Flying Circus* or the films, or sociological consideration of the Monty Python cult.

This neglect of Monty Python by cult film scholars is even harder to comprehend once one notes that the Pythons across their oeuvre demonstrate precisely the kinds of characteristics that cult film scholars tend to highlight in their analyses. Writing of the *Flying Circus*, but generalizable to all the Pythons' work, Landy observes, for example, the various ways that the Pythons consciously and cannily foregrounded and manipulated televisual and cinematic conventions and upended cultural expectations. She notes that the Pythons experimented with continuity and segmentation, resulting in a self-reflexive and critical treatment of televisual media (Landy 2005: 2–3; see also Miller 2000: 130–3). She calls attention to their mix of 'high and low culture' which combined allusions to literature, philosophy and history with slapstick and nonsense (Landy 2005: 3). She argues that 'Python cultural politics played on the absurdity and abuses in language, social institutions, and media' (ibid.: 30), and so on. The frisson of the transgressive, the cultural commentary and the out-and-out weirdness many cult film scholars look for is certainly there but, with the Pythons, we have the curious case of paradigmatic cult media that has received very little scholarly attention, arguably due to the primary association with silliness and the entrenched bias against comedy. Hence this chapter: What I will attempt in the space left to me is to take a shot at redressing this omission by considering some of the cult film qualities of Monty Python with a focus on *Holy Grail*; then I will briefly address another under-theorised area: the role of cultural difference in cultic veneration.

COME AND SEE THE VIOLENCE INHERENT IN THE SYSTEM!

Analysis of what makes something a cult film has arguably often suffered from the same malady that has in some cases afflicted considerations of humour: *the search for the definitive conclusion.* Just as the factors that cause someone to receive something as funny can vary considerably based on background, context and disposition, the factors that result in a film developing a cult following can vary. Indeed, it is a tricky endeavour to try to draw specific conclusions about a category that can encompass *Casablanca* (Michael Curtiz, 1942), *The Rocky Horror Picture Show*, *The Evil Dead* (Sam Raimi, 1981) and *This Is Spinal Tap*. The best we can do as far as an overall generalisation is perhaps Telotte's conclusion that what cultists enjoy in a film is a 'comfortable difference' that suggests 'something unusual, noteworthy, and valuable not just about the movies, but about their own character, too' (Telotte 1991: 5). However, before turning to the specific cultic qualities of *Monty Python and the Holy Grail* from 1975, I would like to suggest one cult film criterion that, while not applicable in every case, seems to me to apply in many of them – and certainly where the Pythons' programme and films are concerned: quotability.

To some extent, my proposition here is related to Umberto Eco's assertion that cult films are defined by their lack of organic unity, which Eco describes as 'glorious incoherence' (Eco 1985: 4). Eco writes,

> I think in order to transform a work into a cult object one must be able to unhinge it, to break it up or take it apart so that one then may remember only parts of it, regardless of their original relationship to the whole. (Ibid.)

Eco's proposition is that a precondition for an object to become one of cult veneration is a certain looseness of organisation in which the seams show, so to speak. To quote selectively from a film seems to me to fall into the category of 'breakability'; however, I would also argue that it acts as an unhinging that functions as communal shorthand for calling to mind what Eco calls a 'completely furnished world' (Eco 1985: 3). The quotation wrenches something out of context for the purpose of communal re-establishment of precisely that context.

Quotability is obviously not a contributing cultic factor in all cases or to the same extent – it will apply less to silent films (although one may perhaps quote intertitles), and certain films may be defined more immediately by other factors: striking shots and scenes, music, effects and so on. Nevertheless, one marker of fandom that applies as equally to *Spinal Tap* and *The Princess Bride* (Rob Reiner, 1987) as it does to *The Shining* (Stanley Kubrick, 1980) and *They Live!* (John Carpenter, 1988) is the ability to quote key lines as a form of bonding with other like-minded fans. To fans of these films, 'This one goes to eleven', 'As you wish', 'Here's Johnny!' and 'All out of chewing gum' are passwords that admit one to a select community. Quoting a line to someone else who grasps the allusion and shares the speaker's enthusiasm establishes a bond. And one quotation begets many: if you are fan of one or more of these films, you may now be mentally rehearsing other lines. In this way, a universe is reconstructed out of pregnant shards, each of which carries with it the DNA of the whole. The breakability of the film into individual lines allows for its communal reconstruction – as well as for the communication of a kind of shared affect of affectionate or passionate regard.

This seems to me central in discussing Monty Python, whose programme and films are particularly notable for their profusion of oft-quoted lines. Considering *Holy Grail*, the list of oft-quoted lines is extensive indeed: 'just a flesh wound', 'taunt you a second time' (and the entire French soldier's monologue), 'I'm not dead yet', 'Ni!' 'Holy Hand Grenade of Antioch', 'a shrubbery', 'some farcical aquatic ceremony', and so on. Fans of the programme and the films will be able to supplement this brief list with other favourites – and then to recite the scenes more fully. What I am therefore suggesting is that one important factor that precipitates cult fandom at play in *Monty Python and the Holy Grail*, the other Python films, *Monty Python's Flying Circus*, and film and television in general is the presence of striking lines of dialogue that can be detached and deployed as both a signal of affinity and invitation to reconstruction. In this way, quotability helps establish what Nöel Carroll refers to as a 'community of laughter' (Carroll 2014: 85). With precisely this point in mind, Justin Smith notes in his brief consideration of *Holy Grail* how 'the Pythons' transgressive humour gave a generation of adolescents scripts to memorise, rehearse and intone like the mystic liturgy of some obscure, clandestine sect' (Smith 1984: 121).

Given, however, that most films have a significant amount of dialogue, this raises the obvious question of what makes a line striking enough to be detachable. Again, there is no single answer to this question. A line may be memorable for its delivery, its gravitas or its eloquence. In the case of *Holy Grail*, however, detachable lines are generally memorable for their absurdity within the context of silly scenes, accentuated in some cases by the ridiculousness of their delivery. As such, the question of memorable lines dovetails with considerations of the film's humour and 'glorious incoherence'.

Monty Python and the Holy Grail is a film with only the barest thread of continuity linking together its twenty-three disparate scenes, all of which can essentially stand alone as comic sketches as Arthur (Graham Chapman) or Galahad (Michael Palin) or Lancelot (John Cleese) or Sir Robin (Eric Idle) or a combination encounter various odd situations. Many of the scenes, such as Arthur's confrontation with the Black Knight (Cleese), Sir Robin's encounter with the three-headed giant, Galahad's visit to Castle Anthrax or Lancelot's 'rescue' of Herbert (Terry Jones) could be reordered or even omitted without any significant harm to the integrity – such as it is – of the film. In this sense, the film very much reflects Eco's proposal that a precondition for becoming a cult film is its glorious incoherence: cult film as 'a disconnected series of images, of peaks, of visionary icebergs' (Eco 1985: 4). Like an episode of *Flying Circus*, *Holy Grail* can be broken up into different stand-alone scenes connected by certain general conceits and occasionally interrupted by the equivalent of 'now for something completely different'.

Within each scene, the emphasis is on provoking laughter from the audience – in the service of which goal the troupe uses every device at its disposal ranging from slapstick to caricature to inventive wordplay, but clustering around the device of incongruity or ironic inversion. Some of the jokes are what Freud would call 'tendentious' – that is, jokes that are hostile or obscene; others are what Freud would call 'innocent' with humour derived from its 'play on words or transposition of concepts' (see Stott 2014: 184). Let us propose that the successful joke is one that evokes the intended amusement or laughter from its audience; successful jokes are then apt to be repeated to or referenced with others who share similar affection for the film. With this in mind – and bearing in mind the maxim that a joke explained is the least funny thing possible – let us consider two oft-quoted scenes: Arthur's confrontation with the Black Knight and Arthur's encounter with the peasants Dennis (Palin) and the unnamed woman (Jones).

The Black Knight scene, which would seem to fall into Freud's category of the tendentious, derives its humour from the grotesqueness of the Black Knight's injuries, the slapstick nature of the battle between the Black Knight and Arthur, the absurd incongruity between the Black Knight's evaluation of his status and his actual health, and the surrealness of his continuing to fight when deprived of limbs. After refusing to step aside and allow Arthur to pass, the Black Knight

IN PRAISE OF SILLINESS

attacks Arthur and relatively quickly has his arm cut off, causing a grotesque stream of blood to spout from the wound. This could of course be a tragic scene, but the Black Knight refuses to acknowledge the injury. When asked again to stand aside, the Black Knight responds with ''Tis but a scratch.' When Arthur replies in disbelief, the Black Knight claims 'I've had worse' and the two engage again with the result being the severing of the other arm and more spurts of blood. Again, the Black Knight refuses to acknowledge what is clearly evident both to Arthur and the viewer, insisting the injuries are 'Just a flesh wound.' Following a methodical progression, the Black Knight loses first one leg and then the other, but, impossibly, fails to acknowledge his defeat. As Arthur and his companion Patsy clip-clop off, the scene ends with the Black Knight's taunt, 'Running away, eh? You yellow bastards! Come back here and take what's coming to you. I'll bite your legs off!'

The Black Knight's denials punctuate absurd exaggeration with understatement, provoking laughter through incompatibility. For fans of Monty Python, ''Tis but a scratch' and 'Just a flesh wound' serve as shorthand for the ridiculousness of the entire scene in which one combatant, defying the laws of reality as we know them, continues to fight although successively deprived of limbs until he is left as an inconvenienced but still feisty torso, neck and head. Indeed, the fight itself would be ridiculous absent the dialogue – the severed limbs, spouting blood

Figure 11.1   Just a flesh wound: *Monty Python and the Holy Grail* (1975).

and unconvincing effects participate in Bakhtinian carnival with its emphasis on the grotesque body, while the machinic nature of the Black Knight's persistence reminds us of Henri Bergson's argument that 'humour is born in moments where the life-force is momentarily usurped or eclipsed by an involuntary manifestation of automatism or reduction of the body to a lifeless machine' (see Stott 2014: 27). But the dialogue is icing on the silly cake as it were, making it clear that we are to regard the scene as comic rather than tragic.

Comic inversion is also central to the scene of Arthur's encounter with the peasants Dennis and 'the woman' as they gather 'filth' in a field. In this scene, Arthur hails what he perceives as an 'old woman' in order to request information about who lives in a nearby castle. He is quickly corrected by the individual who informs him that he is neither a woman nor old. The humour of the scene, however, derives not just from the peasants' surprising lack of obeisance to their king, but from the fact that they turn out to be unexpectedly well-versed in political theory, even to the extent of calling into question Arthur's legitimacy as their ruler. In response to Arthur's assertion that Dennis owes him deference due to his status as king, Dennis launches into an anachronistic Marxist diatribe out of place for both the era (932 AD as we're told in the opening frame) and a peasant field worker addressing nobility:

> 'Oh, King, eh, very nice. And how d'you get that, eh? By exploiting the workers! By 'anging on to outdated imperialist dogma which perpetuates the economic and social differences in our society. If there's ever going to be any progress with the . . .'

Dennis's lecture is then interrupted by another peasant – Jones in drag – who, summoning Dennis to some 'lovely filth', takes note of Arthur, but also fails to recognise him and their shared nationality as 'Britons' or to acknowledge his nobility: 'I didn't know we had a king,' she says. 'I thought we were an autonomous collective.' When Arthur, indignant, asserts again, 'I am your king!' she replies rejecting his authority, 'Well, I didn't vote for you' – provoking a smile from viewers who understand her error: democracy has no bearing on nobility.

Arthur is forced to point this out and, to defend his legitimacy as monarch, to explain that his mandate derives from 'Divine Providence' as the Lady of the Lake gifted him with the sword Excalibur. Rather than impressing Dennis, this provokes only derision, leading Dennis to outline what an absurd premise this is on which to establish authority: 'Listen. Strange women lying in ponds distributing swords is no basis for a system of government. Supreme executive power derives from a mandate from the masses, not from some farcical aquatic ceremony.' Despite Arthur's attempts to silence him, Dennis continues: 'Well, but you can't expect to wield supreme executive power just 'cause some watery tart threw a sword at you!' A textbook example of bathos, Dennis's deflation of Arthur's lofty rhetoric is funny because of its source: an insolent field worker apparently gathering mud or manure – not someone conventionally presumed to be knowledgeable and articulate on issues of governance. The scene ends with Arthur losing his patience and grabbing Dennis, which provokes Dennis's cry, 'Oh! Come and see the violence inherent in the system! Help! Help! I'm being repressed!'

The 'deliberate exploitation of anachronism' (Day 1991: 83) in this scene is construed by Aronstein as being part of the film's overall attack on 'British myths of national identity, monarchy, class, and government at the moment of their supposed origin' (Aronstein 2009: 116) – and, indeed, it is possible to intuit a pointed political subtext to the depiction of filthy peasants gathering filth debating political philosophy with the king they refuse to acknowledge, foregrounding in the process the ways Althusserian ideological state apparatuses including national myth, in concert with more direct repressive measures, work to ensure the docility of the people. Dennis and the woman refuse Arthur's call – refuse to be interpolated as the king's subjects. The political subtext of this scene – which Aronstein links to the film's overall postmodern ethos in which metanarratives of all stripes are challenged – may well be part of the film's cultic appeal. It is important to notice, however, the mechanisms through which these messages are encoded by the film to then be decoded and appropriated by viewers: comic inversion (peasants proficient in political philosophy reducing their less articulate king to physical violence), camp performance (Jones in drag), anachronism (the references to later political theories), sheer absurdity (the gathering of mud) and, importantly, detachable dialogue that becomes shorthand for the entire scene: 'Come and see the violence inherent in the system! Help, help, I'm being repressed!' Individual lines of dialogue thus play a central role in cult enjoyment as they can be redeployed to establish shared affinity for the film in question.

A Silly Place

My suggestion above is that quotability is one important quality of media that often participates in the establishment of cult receptivity – and this would clearly seem to be the case where Monty Python is concerned. With a focus on *Holy Grail*, I would like to consider two other intertwined generic features of the film that also seem to me to be important in constructing its cultic appeal – silliness and self-reflexivity – and then to consider briefly how or why the film might appeal beyond its British context.

Holy Grail, in keeping with much of Monty Python in general, is unabashedly silly – as noted above, it seeks to evoke laughter through absurdity, wordplay, slapstick, grotesquerie and so on – and this may be part of the reason for its neglect by scholars who associate silliness with superficiality, triviality or foolishness. However, while this quality may make it less appealing to those who study cult film, it is I would venture a primary component of its appeal to those who love the film – and I would like to propose that silliness is never as simple or innocent as it may appear as, for adults, it often functions as a form of critique, foregrounding and mocking our expectations. Laughter is elicited by the immediacy of incongruity, but recognition of that incongruity requires anticipation based on prior experience. Put differently, in order to recognise something as a deviation, we need to be conversant with the rule. To explore how silliness functions within *Holy Grail*, let us consider the opening credits and the two scenes with The Knights Who Say Ni.

More 'innocent' than tendentious, to use Freud's terms, the opening credits quickly establish the ethos of silliness that will prevail within the film by foregrounding the unstated expectations that govern opening credits through their repeated violation. To those familiar with cinematic norms, credits typically function as a kind of frame for the film itself. Preceding and/or following the film (or sometimes now interrupting the narrative after a few minutes of action), they are conventionally distanced from narrative content, functioning instead as a kind of 'container' for the film. Like non-diegetic music, the credits are there for the audience, but not the characters. *Holy Grail* upsets these expectations through a sequence of subtitles to the credits that evokes laughter through their mockery of conventional cinematic expectations, and incorporates the credits as part of the film, even as the subtitles insistently foreground the film as constructed artefact, functioning as a form of self-reflexive metacommentary.

The 'trouble' with the credits begins almost immediately as what is apparently a Swedish or Scandinavian subtitle, 'Røten nik Akten Di', is added to the bottom of a frame introducing the Pythons as writers and directors. The phrase is nonsense but, particularly given the 'ø', suggests to English-speaking viewers that it may be meaningful to those who speak Swedish or another Scandinavian language. That the 'Swedish' subtitles are neither Swedish nor translations of the credits quickly becomes apparent, however, as they reveal themselves as a kind of 'Swedish-flavoured English' asking the viewer, 'Wi nøt trei a høliday in Sweden this yër?' and advertising Sweden's 'løveli lakes', 'wøndërful telephøne system' and 'mäni interesting furry animals', including 'the majestik moose'. The subtitles, such as they are, then degenerate entirely as the frame for Costume Designer informs the audience concerning the subtitle author's sister, the Norwegian film star, who was bit by a 'Møøse'. The subtitles, we realise, are not translations at all, but rather a kind of comic monologue competing with the conventional credits for the viewer's attention.

What happens next is that an unnamed 'we' intervenes, halting the credits and assuring the viewer that the subtitles' author(s) 'have been sacked'. But the pseudo-Swedish subtitles continue unabated, so the 'we' apologises again, informing us that '[t]hose responsible for sacking the people who have

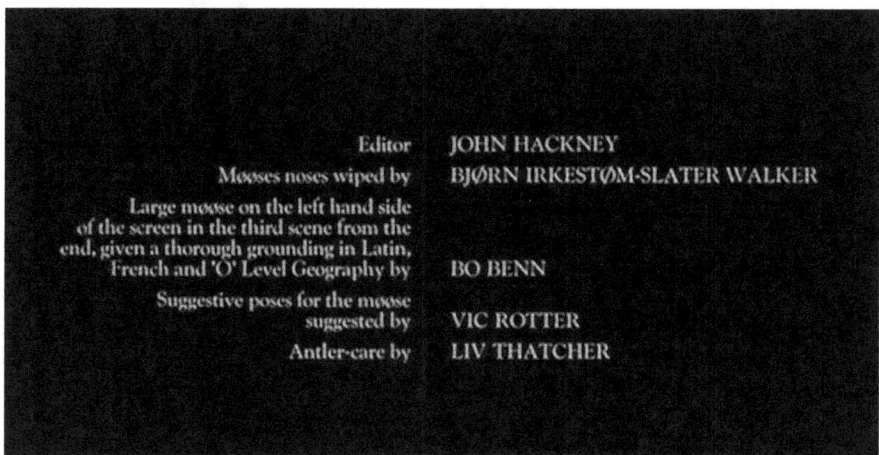

Figure 11.2   Møøse control: *Monty Python and the Holy Grail*.

just been sacked have been sacked'. Sanity appears to have been restored to the credits until one notices that increasingly intermixed with real production positions are those having to do with moose (or 'Møøse'). As with the pseudo-Swedish subtitles, the Møøse positions escalate to the point where the viewer can't miss them and the credits are halted a third time as the viewer is informed that '[t]he credits have been completed in an entirely different style at great expense and at the last minute'. Then, against a seizure-inducing strobing red and green screen and overtop a mariachi music bed, the credits conclude by attributing everything to the ministrations of not moose, but llamas – including 142 Mexican Whooping llamas.

The silly subtitles provoke laughter both through their own inherent absurdity ('A Møøse once bit my sister') and their upsetting of viewer expectations based on prior knowledge of how films function. Indeed, Monty Python's playful approach to the credits enacts a kind of Derridean deconstruction of them, inverting the inside/outside hierarchy, and then calling into question the logic that supports that hierarchy entirely as the line separating what is and isn't part of the film is erased.

While the surprising subtitles of the opening credits provoke laughter by abandoning expectations concerning cinematic conventions, much of *Holy Grail* in general elicits laughter through its parodying of Arthurian romance. Silly scenes throughout, such as the Dennis scene discussed above, poke fun at the seriousness of such legends, and the absurdity is often heightened by the incongruity between the gravitas with which lines are delivered (particularly by Chapman's Arthur) and the ridiculousness of the dialogue and action. Consider for example Arthur's first appearance as he pretends to ride a horse while his servant, Patsy (Terry Gilliam), knocks coconuts together to approximate the sound of hooves. Consider as well the 'Knights of the Round Table' musical number that interrupts the action as Arthur and his knights consider riding on to Camelot. Both scenes surprise the viewer with something unexpected and absurd – the substitution of knocking coconuts for horses, and knights dancing the can-can as they sing ridiculously anachronistic lyrics about eating spam and impersonating Clark Gable.

The playful parodying of Arthurian romance is particularly evident in the scenes in which Arthur encounters the dreaded Knights Who Say Ni. In keeping with quest narratives in general, Arthur and his knights must overcome various obstacles as they seek the Holy Grail. Like the Black Knight who ends up limbless, the Knights Who Say Ni block Arthur's passage and initially appear intimidating – particularly the head knight, played by Palin, who appears double Arthur's size. The sense of danger is also amplified by the ominous soundtrack as Arthur *et al.* move through the forest. Any tension created by the materialisation of the Knights Who Say Ni from out of the mist is, however, quickly undercut by Palin's grating falsetto, wholly out of keeping with his exaggerated size, and the surprising concern of Arthur and his company over having the nonsense word 'Ni' spat at them. The Knights Who Say Ni then demand of Arthur a 'sacrifice' in the form of . . . a shrubbery.

Figure 11.3 Arthur confronts the Knights Who Say Ni: *Monty Python and the Holy Grail*.

Luckily happening upon Roger the Shrubber (Idle), Arthur and his retinue return to the Knights Who Say Ni, only to discover that the terms permitting their passage through the forest have changed. Although the head knight pronounces the shrubbery good, he reveals that they are no longer the Knights Who Say Ni, but are now instead the Knights Who Say Ekke Ekke Ekke Ekke Ptang Zoo Boing and they must give Arthur a new test: not only must he procure another shrubbery, he must also 'cut down the mightiest tree in the forest with ... a herring!' Arthur's incredulous protestation that 'it can't be done' causes the knights to recoil in apparent pain, and it soon becomes apparent that the knights cannot tolerate hearing the word 'it'. Incapacitated by the repeated utterance of the word both by Arthur's party and themselves, the knights do not notice Arthur and his party's escape.

Everything about the two scenes with the Knights Who Say Ni, in keeping with the film in general, is calculated to provoke laughter through sheer absurdity as repeated incongruities undermine the seriousness of the encounters. The head knight's exaggerated size and falsetto defy our expectations concerning physical limitations and correspondence between size and voice. That the nonsense word 'Ni' should function like a curse or harsh epithet – or even cause pain – jars with our sense of the functioning of language – as does the knights' aversion to the word 'it'. That the knights should demand a shrubbery, refer to themselves as the Knights Who Say Ekke Ekke Ekke Ekke Ptang Zoo Boing, or seek to test Arthur by requiring him to cut down a tree with a herring all upset learned expectations concerning the seriousness of such encounters between knights and adversaries in tales of chivalry. The result are scenes that – like the rest of the film – are gleefully silly as they undercut and invert viewer expectations.

Silly scenes like these thus appeal at least in part due to their *irreverence*, which participates in constructing their cultic appeal. As carnivalesque parodies, they consistently poke fun at the solemnity of Arthurian romance, and attack, as Aronstein asserts, 'British myths of national identity, monarchy, class, and government' (Aronstein 2009: 116). Through an 'encyclopedia of comedy – involving gags, slapstick, the grotesque, wordplay, and banter' (Landy 2005: 39), *Holy Grail* punctures the pretensions surrounding myth and nobility, playfully roiling our assumptions concerning national identity, history and character. As Landy suggests of *Flying Circus*, *Holy Grail* arguably appeals to 'young people and disaffected groups for its irreverence toward authority' (ibid.: 36). Rather than silliness as innocent play, this is silliness as light-hearted satire.

Migratory Silliness?

In keeping with Python logic, I would like to end with something perhaps not completely different but at least tangential – and that is the role that national affiliation plays in the construction of cultic appeal. In particular, I'm interested in the question of, beyond simply enjoying a film produced in another country, what it means to appropriate as cult object a film from a different national tradition. Even more specifically: if *Holy Grail* is a film that lampoons British cultural myths, what does it mean to love the film as an American (or other nationality for that matter)?

The minimal available scholarship on American Anglophilia tends to foreground American associations of Britishness with 'high culture' writ large: Masterpiece Theatre, Merchant Ivory films, entrenched aristocracy, tea-time and, of course, James Bond. Joseph Epstein, for example, claims that, '[i]n America, our conceptions of honor, courage, romance, decency – were all imports, all came from English' (Epstein 1997: 3). English culture offered Epstein 'a more heroic world' (ibid.: 18). Jones notes that 'Englishness has long enjoyed high status in American culture' (Jones 2001: 77) and suggests that 'English people are the archetypal upper-class WASPs, a status to which all Americans are assumed to aspire' (ibid.: 78). Speculating broadly on American Anglophilia, Mark Dery suggests that it may be rooted in a contempt for the hypocrisies of American capitalism, which claims to disdain elitism on the one hand while surreptitiously honouring it on the other; white racism; and aspirations to aristocracy on the part of 'aspiring bluebloods' (Dery 2018).

Holy Grail is of course a far cry from *Remains of the Day* (James Ivory, 1993) or *A Passage to India* (David Lean, 1984) or the 'stiff upper lip' of stereotypical British gentry. It is conceivable then that American Anglophiles adopt Python simply because the British do. But I think American cultic veneration of Monty Python is more than a kind of general fetishising of all things British. Precisely because Python's silliness is so deeply invested in the specific context of 1960s and 1970s British culture, the appreciation of the Pythons' humour amplifies what Dery calls the 'borrowed Otherness' of American fans (Dery 2018). In the same way that *Holy Grail*'s subtitles to the credits are funny both because of their intrinsic absurdity and their divergence from the role subtitles are supposed to play, *Holy Grail* is funny both because of the immediate delights of wordplay and slapstick, and because of the way that it defies expectations concerning British myth and character. For the American Anglophile, it is silliness once removed. The knowledge of the American Anglophile is thus rewarded through recognition of those differences. The 'comfortable difference' the American Python fan embraces is thus the exception that proves the rule – to appreciate the parody as parody, one must be conversant with the original. The cultic appeal of silliness is thus inevitably inflected through the lens of nationality.

My argument here has been that quotability, irreverent silliness and a kind of postmodern exploration of the medium of film participate in constructing *Holy Grail*'s cultic appeal. Other scenes from the film, of course, could be considered in relation to these qualities, and no doubt there are additional cultic qualities of the film that deserve commentary. The larger point though is that silliness as performed and consumed by adults is ironically serious stuff as it mocks conventional expectations concerning deportment and maturity. This more than anything may be at the root of cultic veneration of the Pythons: carnivalesque inversion as cultural critique appealing to the culturally disaffected. The cult of Python is a community of laughter that, by embracing silliness, catapults all sacred cows at the standard bearers of conservative culture beyond the castle gates.

Works Cited

Aronstein, Susan (2009) '"In my own idiom": Social Critique, Campy Gender, and Queer Performance in *Monty Python and the Holy Grail*', in Tison Pugh (ed.), *Queer Movie Medievalisms*. Abingdon: Routledge, pp. 115–28.

Carroll, Nöel (2014) *Humor: A Very Short Introduction*. Oxford: Oxford University Press.

Day, David D. (1991) 'Monty Python and the Medieval Other', in Kevin J. Harty (ed.), *Cinema Arthuriana: Essays on Arthurian Film*. New York: Garland Publishing, pp. 83–92.

Dery, Mark (2018) *England My England: Anglophilia Explained*. Amazon Digital Services, LLC [e-book].

de Seife, Ethan (2007) *This Is Spinal Tap*. New York: Wallflower Press.

Eco, Umberto (1985) '*Casablanca*: Cult Movies and Intertextual Collage', *SubStance* 14(2), 3–12.

Egan, Kate (2011) *The Evil Dead*. New York: Wallflower Press.

Epstein, Joseph (1997) *Anglophilia, American Style*. London: The Institute of United States Studies, University of London.

Hebdige, Dick (1979) *Subculture: The Meaning of Style*. London: Routledge.

Hewison, Robert (1981) *Monty Python: The Case Against*. London: Eyre Methuen.

Hoberman, J. and Jonathan Rosenbaum (1991) *Midnight Movies*. Boston: Dacapo Press.

Hunt, Leon (2013) *Cult British TV Comedy: From Reeves and Mortimer to Psychoville*. Manchester: Manchester University Press.

Jones, Katherine W. (2001) *Accent on Privilege: English Identities and Anglophilia in the U.S.* Philadelphia: Temple University Press.

Landy, Marcia (2005) *Monty Python's Flying Circus*. Detroit, MI: Wayne State University Press.

Mathijs, Ernest and Jamie Sexton (2011) *Cult Cinema: An Introduction*. Chichester: Wiley-Blackwell.

Miller, Jeffrey S. (2000) *Something Completely Different: British Television and American Culture*. Minneapolis: University of Minnesota Press.

Smith, Justin (1984). *Withnail and Us: Cult Films and Film Cults in British Cinema*. London: I. B. Tauris.

Sontag, Susan (1964) 'Notes on Camp', *Partisan Review* 31(4), 515–30.

Stott, Andrew (2014) *Comedy*, 2nd edn. Abingdon: Routledge.

Telotte, J. P. (1991) 'Beyond All Reason: The Nature of the Cult', in J. P. Telotte (ed.), *The Cult Film Experience: Beyond All Reason*. Austin: University of Texas Press, pp. 5–17.

Waller, Gregory (1991) 'Midnight Movies, 1980–1985: A Market Study', in J. P. Telotte (ed.), *The Cult Film Experience: Beyond All Reason*. Austin: University of Texas Press, pp. 167–86.

Weinstock, Jeffrey (2015) '*Bubba Ho-tep* and the Seriously Silly Cult Film', in J. P. Telotte and Gerald Duchovnay (eds), *Science Fiction Double Feature: The Science Fiction Film as Cult Text*. Liverpool: Liverpool University Press, pp. 233–48.

12. MEMORIES OF CONNECTING: FATHERS, DAUGHTERS AND INTERGENERATIONAL MONTY PYTHON FANDOM

Kate Egan

In 2017, I began work on the audience research project *Monty Python Memories*. This project's central research tool was an online questionnaire – combining quantitative/multiple-choice and qualitative/free-text questions and answers – asking respondents to share their memories and experiences of encountering Monty Python for the first time and then over subsequent years. The questionnaire was designed to encourage respondents to outline their emergent and enduring fandom for Python, with the first free-text question asking for recollections of their first encounter with Python in any form (the television show, or one of the films, albums or live shows). To my knowledge, this project has since amassed the largest dataset of audience responses to a comedy form/text to date – 6,120 responses from across the world, with a particular concentration of respondents from the US (2,848 responses) and the UK (1,123 responses), but with substantial numbers also received from Canada (409), Australia (264), Germany (144), Sweden (94), France (82), Denmark (76) and Poland (72). I received a relatively balanced number of responses from men and women: 52 per cent men and 46 per cent women, while 71 per cent of the 1,772 participants who responded to the (optional) question about education indicated that they were educated to at least university degree level. The scale of response was assisted by the project's promotion on Monty Python's official website http://www.montypython.com/ and official Monty Python social media outlets on Facebook and Twitter, leading to a dataset which is global in scope and largely representative, because of its recruitment methods, of the memories and experiences of invested, self-identifying Python fans.

The project's focus on the memories and history of experiences of Monty Python fans related to a gap in both existing scholarship on Python and the broader, emergent strand of research on comedy audiences. In 2014, the Monty Python team were reunited on stage at London's O2 arena for the first time in over thirty years. The shows sold out, and a BBC documentary heralded them as the most successful comedy group of all time (*Imagine*, BBC1, July 2014). Despite the passing of more than fifty years, Monty Python's popularity has clearly endured. However, while existing Python scholarship has made significant claims about the core audiences for Python as broadly young, middle class and university-educated (see, for instance, Wagg 1992; Miller 2000; Landy 2005; Brock 2016), these claims have been based either on analysis of Python texts or, in the case of *Monty Python's Flying Circus*, institutional factors relating to the show's initial UK and US reception context of the late 1960s to mid-1970s (the show's target audience, the audience profile of the channel on which it was broadcast or BBC Audience Research reports). While my questionnaire results go some way to supporting the claims of this scholarship, in terms of Python appealing to a predominantly educated audience, the *Monty Python Memories* project's focus on memories and histories of Python fandom allows for a much more detailed consideration of how this appeal has been sustained over the forty-plus years since this initial period of reception, whether it has changed, developed or become qualified, and, if so, in relation to which public and private circumstances.

In contrast, the emerging body of work on comedy audiences has produced excellent and robust research and insights on 'comedy texts and audience practices' (Bore 2017: 8) and 'humor styles' and tastes 'in everyday life' (Kuipers 2015: 19; see also Claessens and Dhoest 2010), but with a predominant focus on the contemporary reception of contemporary comedy texts and forms of humour. The main exception, in some ways, is Sam Friedman's book *Comedy and Distinction*, a ground-breaking empirical study of contemporary comedy taste among attendees of the 2009 Edinburgh Festival Comedy Fringe. Here, Friedman identifies key patterns in comedy preferences for a wide range of both past and present British comedy (from *Last of the Summer Wine* and *Yes Minister* to *Little Britain* and *Stewart Lee's Comedy Vehicle*). His study's primary aim is to consider the utility of Pierre Bourdieu's concepts of habitus and embodied capital when accounting for the 'major fault lines in comedy taste' among contemporary British comedy consumers (Friedman 2014: 43). Most prominently, his findings illustrate that, for a substantial number of his 901 respondents, taste in 'highbrow' or 'lowbrow' comedy relates clearly to respondents' higher or lower cultural capital resources. However, he also argues that his study's results 'suggest important generational differences in comedy taste', and notes that

> older generations, particularly those over 55, tend to have a largely sceptical view of comedy, rejecting the vast majority of new comedians and instead reporting tastes for mainly older, 'lowbrow' comedians. In contrast, taste for 'highbrow' comedy appears to be much more prevalent among those 44 and under . . . one important contributing factor may be the post-1979 aestheticisation of comedy, which has coincided with the cultural socialisation of these younger generations. (Ibid.: 60)

Here, then, Friedman sheds light on potential generational taste fault lines between those born in or before 1964 and those born in or after 1965, with the rise of the British 'Alternative Comedy Boom' of the 1980s – exemplified by such comedians as Rik Mayall, Alexei Sayle and Ben Elton – put forward by Friedman as the key milestone that enabled younger comedy fans to begin to recognise and embrace comedy's 'artistic potential' (ibid.: 87), and thus distinguish their tastes and attitudes to comedy from their parents' and grandparents' generations. For Friedman, this 1980s boom was a crucial moment in shifting the status of British comedy because these comedians 'were united by an experimental approach to comedy that self-consciously attempted to push beyond the "lowbrow" styles that had previously dominated the field', whereas earlier experimenters such as Monty Python and *Beyond the Fringe* 'in statistical terms . . . only made up a small fraction of overall comedy output . . . during the 1960s and 1970s' (ibid.: 19). As with the earlier cited Python scholarship, what Friedman seems to draw on here – when assessing British comedy's contemporary status, cultural hierarchies and impact – is a historical map of comedy and audience preference based on the immediate moment of their production and dissemination. What is not considered here (and in other existing scholarship on Python specifically and on comedy audiences more broadly) is 'the historicity of meaning beyond origins' (Klinger 1997: 112) of enduring comedy like Python – their diachronic reach and impact as they continue to circulate years and decades after their initial reception moment, both in their native countries and internationally, particularly after the rise of home video technologies, the internet and streaming.

Indeed, other *Monty Python Memories* results seemed to challenge and complicate Friedman's findings on generational differences in British comedy taste. For instance, one of the first searches I conducted on the free-text responses in my dataset revealed that one of the most prevalent trends crossing respondents' memories of first encountering Python were mentions of 'Dad' or 'Father', with 1,098 responses mentioning either term at least once in their, generally lengthy, answers, compared to only 576 responses mentioning 'Mother', 'Mum' or 'Mom'. On isolating these 1,098 responses (henceforth referred to as the 'Dad Memories Group'), it became apparent that there was a concentration of younger respondents in this group (particularly in the 18–35 age categories), pointing, crucially, to Python's durability across generations.

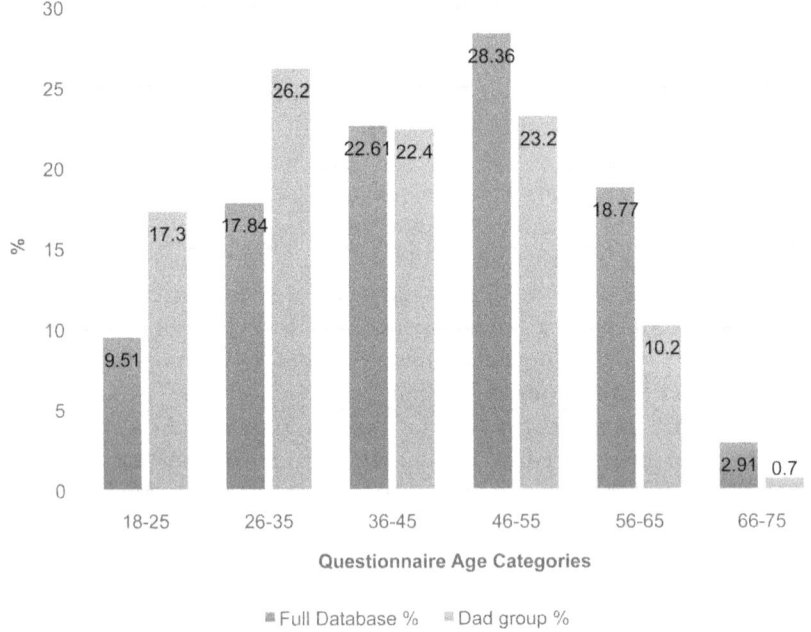

Figure 12.1 The higher percentage of 18–35-year-olds in the 'Dad Memories Group' compared to the *Monty Python Memories* database as a whole.

In addition, there was also a shift in the number of women within this group when compared to the dataset as a whole – specifically, and as illustrated by Figure 12.2, an 8 per cent rise in female responses and a 7 per cent drop in male responses.

The focus on fathers in these Python memories connects, in some ways, with an emerging tradition of work within fan studies focused on familial influence and intergenerational fandom, in studies on, for instance, music fandom (Vroomen 2004), soap opera fandom (Harrington and Bielby 2010), football fandom (Dixon 2013), film star fandom (Ralph 2015), fandom of the *Alien* film franchise (Barker *et al*. 2015) and wrestling fandom (Alcott 2019). All of this work, to differing degrees, has acknowledged the 'role of the family' as 'a recurring social context' in people's accounts of their history of fandom (Barker *et al*. 2015: 43), noting, in particular, how family members can function as gatekeepers, curators, tastemakers or mentors, initiating younger relatives into an engagement with a film, television show, star, sport, novel or music artist. As

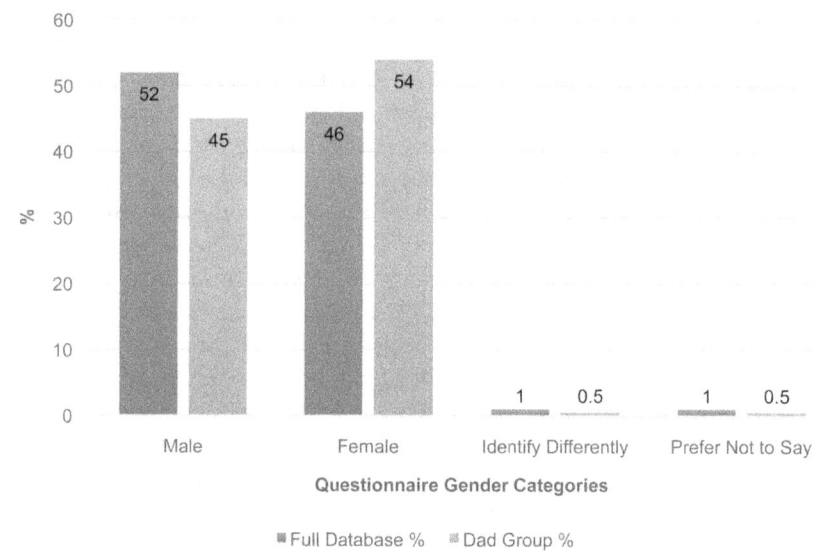

Figure 12.2 The higher percentage of female respondents in the 'Dad Memories Group' compared to the *Monty Python Memories* database as a whole.

acknowledged in Vroomen and Dixon's work in particular, these activities have clear connections to Bourdieu's concepts of cultural capital and habitus – to the ways in which 'cultural knowledge' is 'acquired through family socialisation' (Claessens and Dhoest 2010: 50). However, scholars like Harrington and Bielby and Sarah Ralph have also considered the ways in which these shared investments relate to child and adolescent developmental processes, particularly in considering how forms of media can function in the history of relations between mothers and daughters. For Harrington and Bielby, mothers can operate, in this context, 'as a central figure' in a daughter's 'negotiation into adulthood as mediated through soap opera', facilitating 'adolescent explorations' and providing 'moral guidance' on a daughter's shifting emotional relationships with others through engagement with soap opera's fictional narratives (Harrington and Bielby 2010); while, for Ralph, shared engagement with film stars can 'open up conversations between mothers and daughters about potentially awkward subjects during adolescence', particularly in relation to sexual identity and romance (Ralph 2015: 1).

These existing insights on intergenerational fandom prompt a series of questions, when thinking about the higher concentration of female respondents in the *Monty Python Memories* project's 'Dad Memories Group'. If, as this previous scholarship has indicated, mothers and daughters can use shared media engagements to discuss puberty and romantic and sexual relationships, then what might be the motivations, benefits and consequences of a shared engagement with Monty Python between fathers and daughters? Is this shared investment in Python informed by different forms of emotional engagement and ways of looking at the world? How might this relate to Python's status as sketch comedy, rather than dramatic narrative? These are particularly complex questions, when considering two factors. Firstly, Python's status as an all-male comedy troupe who have been critiqued, particularly since the 1990s, for the sexually objectified roles played by Carol Cleveland in *Flying Circus*, as well as the 'grotesque' and caricatured female characters (the 'Pepperpots') the Pythons have played in drag (Whybray 2016: 172; see also Wagg 1992). Secondly, the fact that respondent attitudes to these more problematic aspects of Python's comedy – and to their relationships with their fathers – will inevitably be complicated by the fact that the respondents are recalling, from the present, memories of Python and their fathers that are located, in some cases, 10–15 years ago (in the early 2000s) and, at the other extreme, 40 years ago (in the mid-1970s or even earlier). Consequently, these recollections of cross-gender relationships around Python will inevitably, as Jackie Stacey has noted, involve complex negotiations between changing 'public discourses' around Python and 'private narratives' relating to their 'own personal histories' and 'the feelings' they have 'about their past, present and future selves' (Stacey 1993: 63, 70). Further to this, the strong focus on paternal influence within these memories of first encounters with Monty Python seems at odds with Python's status as comedy producers fuelled by an anti-establishment spirit, which involved, for Eric Idle, being 'anti-authority, anti-school, anti-teachers, anti-church, anti-mothers, anti-fathers' (cited in Mills 2014: 134) and, therefore, as Robert Hewison notes, revolting against the 'deferential society' that the Python team 'were introduced to by their parents' (Hewison in Jones *et al.* 2009). With this in mind, a further consideration, when analysing these responses, is the extent to which the association between Python and parental influence appears to have impacted on Python's ability to, in Jeffrey Weinstock's terms, retain (or not retain) 'its transgressive edge' (Weinstock 2007: 111).

In the analysis that follows, these questions will be considered through exploration of the discursive repertoires/ways of talking about the association between fathers and Monty Python among the female respondents within the *Monty Python Memories* project's 'Dad Memories Group'. While it should be noted that some of these memories recount activities involving fathers and mixed-gender children (female respondents and their brothers or sisters), the focus will be on the father–daughter relations primarily discussed in these memories, in order to shed light not only on Python's durability across decades but also its surprising status as the focus of a cross-gender form of intergenerational media fandom.

Monty Python Fandom among Fathers and Daughters: Motivations and Circumstances

Responses from women across the 'Dad Memories Group' make reference to the moment their father introduced them to the world of Monty Python, in a number of interlinked ways. Firstly, many respondents recall this paternal introduction in a way that suggests their father wanted to replicate, for their daughter, the conditions under which they had first encountered Python as a younger man. While some respondents note that their father sat them down to watch Python in order to 'pass on the laughter' or 'share the humour', others remark that their father 'wanted me to experience the same feeling of happiness that Monty Python gave to him as a teenager', that he 'decided to show me the first episode he ever saw once he decided I was old enough in middle school', or that he'd 'said he'd been to the cinema to watch it when he was my age about 12/13 and he knew I loved to laugh' (#2177 Canadian, 36–45; #2958 American, 26–35; #962 Portuguese, 18–25; #900 American, 18–25; #2338 British, 18–25).[1] Akin to other studies of intergenerational fandom, the sharing of Python here involves, in many cases, a father 'packaging' it as a 'rite of passage' (Barker *et al.* 2015: 42) that is passed on to the child when they are deemed 'old enough' or when they reach the same age or stage at which their father had first encountered Python. As illustrated in these examples, conditions of replication also extend to showing the same episode first viewed by their father, or of the strong indication being given that the respondent should 'experience the same feeling of happiness' that their father had experienced in his teenage past.

Extending this notion of passing on a family tradition or family experience of Python fandom, a substantial number of American and Canadian respondents also noted that this – almost ceremonial – introduction to Python was informed by their father's British roots. Respondents noted, for instance, that 'my father is English' and 'made me aware of my British heritage', that 'my British Dad was excited to share' Python 'with us as he loved it', and that 'it was very important' to 'my father, a British expat . . . that his Canadian child developed an appreciation for British comedy' (#2885 Canadian, 56–65; #259 American, 46–55; #3618 Canadian, 26–35). Further to this, there is a sense that – for fathers who were broadly first-generation fans who had encountered Monty Python during its initial British or North American circulation between 1969 and 1976 – the importance of passing on 'some of the comedy of his youth' (#2098 Danish, 18–25) also related to the 'specific cultural moment' of 'generational tensions', the breaking up of institutions, and 'the emergence of new forms of globalism' frequently associated with *Monty Python's Flying Circus*'s initial appearance (Landy 2005: 15). As one respondent outlined, for instance,

> many important social issues, stereotypes, tropes, themes, and miscellaneous objects are reflected in the seemingly nonsensical humor of the Pythons.

> However, as my father explained the significance behind these things, many of which were vastly important for his generation, they became more relevant and understandable to me. (#3578 American, 18–25)

There is a sense across these accounts that – at least as presented through reminiscence by their children – this paternal introduction to Python was frequently tied to what Harrington and Bielby have described as the transcendence of familial relationships through shared media engagements. In these examples, introducing Monty Python to their daughters seems to allow fathers to reveal more about themselves as socially and culturally situated people (rather than as just these respondents' fathers), thus providing 'honest insight' into their 'preferences, values and interpretations' (Harrington and Bielby 2010) in order to strengthen the father–daughter bond.

Alongside these packaged and purposeful introductions, many other female respondents recall being introduced to Monty Python by their fathers in a more incremental and diffuse manner, supporting Matt Hills' argument that becoming a fan can frequently 'form part of a routinised, habituated way of interacting with pop culture' rather than always occurring in one 'life-changing, pivotal moment' (Hills 2014: 10). For many of these female respondents, Python is remembered as a constant in their lives growing up. It was 'always on in our house', and, for a Swedish respondent, 'just was there, as soon as I understood enough English to appreciate it'; indeed, many respondents noted that 'I can't remember a time that I didn't know who they were' and that 'I've known about' Python 'for as long as I can remember' (#178 American, 36–45; #801 Swedish, 36–45; #2127 American, 36–45; #3444 American, 18–25).

Informing this sense of Python as a pervasive and quotidian aspect of their childhoods are the frequent references made to other ways Python pervaded their lives, outside of television broadcasts or screenings of home video versions of the shows or films. Firstly, Python's status as a multi-media comedy phenomenon meant that, for some, Python's initial presence in their lives occurred when they skimmed through their father's Python books or when their father played Python albums at home or on tape during family car trips. This meant that the televisual origin of Python's comedy was initially unclear to some; for instance, one respondent recalls that '[i]t was years before I realised who the tape was, or even that the show existed as a television series', while another notes that '*Matching Tie and Handkerchief* was released after my first birthday so I have been listening to it and hearing it recited by family members since I was too small to understand all the words' (#723 British, 36–45; #1842 American, 36–45). Secondly and as illustrated by this last recollection, initial encounters with Python were also frequently initiated by their fathers' consistent re-enacting or quoting of Python sketches or scenes, which, once again, meant that the origin of the recited comedy was initially unclear to respondents. Respondents note, for instance, that 'when I was a child, my father's substitution for a bedtime story was to re-enact various Monty Python skits that he had committed to memory', that 'I think I probably learnt more MP quotes from my Dad's impressions than from the shows themselves', and that 'my dad used to recite them (I particularly remember him doing the Death of Mary Queen of Scots) on long road trips to entertain me . . . I think I probably thought my dad came up with it on his own' (#3578 American, 18–25; #2305 British, 36–45; #742 American, 26–35). What is significant here is the specificity of Monty Python as a form of comedy that is highly quotable and was disseminated via multiple forms of media, from television to albums to books to films. This leads to Python's status, in many of these memories, as a diffuse but constant familial text that permeated the childhood of many of these respondents – at home, in the car, at the dinner table – and often had use-value, for a father, as a repurposed bedtime story or as road-trip entertainment in album form or via re-enactment or quotation. As a consequence, these memories shed fascinating light on key ways in which Python's comedy has maintained its presence and durability beyond its initial broadcast or release, as well as supporting Inger-Lise Bore's insight that quoting comedy 'offers a way to rupture the boundary between the text and our own everyday lives' (Bore 2017: 112).

The focus in many of these accounts on Python as providing a vehicle of communication and entertainment between father and daughter is also a key framework for understanding the importance of a father's association with Monty Python in respondent memories of their developing Python fandom. Whether initial Python encounters had occurred via an introduction or through the consistent presence of Python while growing up, the significance of engaging with Python as children and adolescents was consistently tied, for many respondents, to its status as an investment shared solely or particularly with their father. For many female respondents in the 'Dad Memories Group', Python was 'something we shared', 'my mother and sister didn't "get" the humor, but my dad and I loved it', and 'spending time, sharing something with my dad, that no one else in the family did, was special' (#2168 British, 26–35; #1371 American, 46–55; #1523 American, 46–55). This includes some cases where parents divorced or separated in the respondents' childhood, with one respondent noting, for instance, that Monty Python was the 'one thing we could all bond over' when her and her younger brother visited their father (#2243 Canadian, 36–45).

It could be argued that this establishment of a Python-informed bond between father and daughter might constitute evidence of the impact on intergenerational fandom of what Hannah Hamad has termed 'the reconceived gender norms in parenting that arose from the politically charged movement' of second-wave feminism in the late 1960s and onwards (Hamad 2014: 2). This interpretation needs to be tentative and qualified, however, not only because these memories represent recollections of father–daughter relations that stretch over forty years (covering a great period of change in terms of feminist and post-feminist debate) but also because a shared father–daughter investment in Python, and the frequent marginalisation of a respondent's mother in this investment, doesn't tell us anything about the extent of the mother or father's role in the full range of the 'quotidian practicalities of parenting' (ibid.: 2) – indeed, as indicated, many respondents note that Python fandom was the only connection they had with their father. Despite this, these recollections do seem to chime with certain processes associated with this post-1960s conception of 'new fatherhood', in particular the use of Python sketches as bedtime stories (which could be conceived as a 'quotidian' practicality 'of parenting') and the idea of a father being 'involved with his daughters as much as his sons' (Joseph Pleck cited in ibid.: 10).

Indeed, in many female respondents' recollections of their shared father–daughter investment in Python, there is evidence that this investment has functioned as a key developmental activity equivalent to – but distinct from – the forms of 'negotiation into adulthood' and facilitation of 'adolescent explorations' enabled by shared mother–daughter engagement with soap opera or film stars. This is most clearly illustrated by respondents' detailed accounts of learning, through their father, about comedy and laughter. Memories of this process of learning to laugh with their father are outlined in detail in respondent recollections that recount the process through which they learned, as children, to laugh at Python when their father laughed or 'paid close attention to what was happening' in order to understand why their father was laughing at particular moments (#2639 Canadian, 46–55). The fact that many of these childhood encounters with Python are presented by respondents as access points into distinctly adult comedy – evident in, for instance, one respondent's comment that they 'grew up having memorized some really inappropriate stuff for a ten year old' and another's remembered pleasure at 'sitting with my dad and being allowed to watch grown up telly' (#388 American, 26–35; #2626 British, 46–55) – compounds this sense that sharing an investment in Python with their father ushered them into a space where they could develop their sense of humour through specific paternal mentorship. But, crucially, mentorship of not any form of comedy but one which, for many respondents, was remembered as silly and enjoyable – hence giving their younger selves an access point into the comedy – but also, as indicated, had a distinctly adult allure, through being 'inappropriate', confusing, 'unexpected', 'unusual and different', or because they 'couldn't believe that adults could be so silly and funny' (#1115 American, 26–35; #3562 American, 26–35; #3372 Canadian, 26–35; #2339 Polish, 36–45; #3564 American, 36–45).

The special, and clearly important, ways in which Python enabled an exclusive bond to be built between female respondents and their fathers can also be related to the many vivid memories respondents have of observing or hearing their father's laughter at Python during childhood. The extent to which they loved seeing or hearing their father laugh is emphasised in many of these recollections, and, in turn, the impact and significance of these memories is often signalled through acknowledging that their father rarely laughed or that they'd never seen him laugh so intensely at any other comedy show. As one respondent recalls, for instance, 'it made my father laugh, which, being a hardened military veteran of several campaigns throughout my childhood, was not a regular occurrence, thus anything that made him smile brought me joy as well', while, for another, 'I remember how hard he was laughing. My dad didn't laugh very often at all and when he did, it was a mere chuckle so it made a huge impression on me. He was laughing so hard he was almost crying' (#1610 American, 26–35; #3283 American, 36–45). In line with Harrington and Bielby's argument that intergenerational fandom can assist or feed into a child or adolescent's 'developmental and/or maturational processes' (Harrington and Bielby 2010), such accounts once again foreground the idea that, through discovering and sharing their father's Python fandom, respondents could begin to learn about their father as a culturally situated human being, rather than solely being related to and understood as a parent and father. Further to this, the impression made on respondents witnessing their father 'roaring with laughter' (#405 British, 26–35; #2639 Canadian, 46–55) or 'almost crying' with laughter – a laughter which they ultimately engage with and share – indicates how fathers and daughters can connect affectively and emotionally through shared Python fandom. Here, fathers are remembered as exhibiting and thence sharing expressions of extreme amusement (and thus emotion) with their daughters which, for Sue Sharpe in her study of fathers and daughters, conflict with more traditional conceptions of fathers as needing to avoid emotional engagement with their children in order to adhere to 'the requirements of socially constructed masculinity' and patriarchal conceptions of fatherhood more broadly (Sharpe 1994: 168).

The Gift that Keeps on Giving? The Consequences of Monty Python Intergenerational Fandom

Beyond asking respondents to recall their first encounters with Monty Python, further questions in the project questionnaire asked them to reflect on whether their views had changed since their initial encounter and to give their overall assessment of Python's impact and popularity. The associations between Python and these female respondents' fathers continued to be referred to in their answers to these questions, with discourses of consistency and constancy permeating references to Python's role in respondents' continued bond with their father in adulthood. For many of these female respondents, investment in Monty Python 'continues to be a big bond between me and my dad', 'me and my dad still quote it to each other', and it 'helped me connect with my dad'

(#1839 American, 18–25; #2338 British, 18–25; #3527 American, 18–25). As one respondent succinctly notes, 'it's our thing'; while, for another discussing *Monty Python and the Holy Grail*, 'there is very little common ground between us and so the fact that we can still sit back and roar with laughter over this film makes it perfect in my eyes' (#1026 American, 26–35; #3318 American, 26–35). What is evident in these responses is the use-value of Python in initiating, strengthening and maintaining respondents' relationships with their fathers throughout the life course, giving them, through Python quoting sessions and continued shared viewings, a key 'currency of communication' (Ralph 2015: 14).

Alongside the maintenance of this father–daughter bond, the indelible associations between their fathers and Monty Python have also enabled Python's comedy to function, for these respondents, as a reminder of past memories of shared viewings and shared laughter with their father, particularly for those whose fathers have now passed away. As respondents note, 'I have that amazing memory with him and anything Python reminds me of him and the quality comedy education he gave me', 'it helped me when Dad died', and 'when my father suddenly died in 2005 . . . [our] common interest in Monty Python comforted me – I could refer to the dead parrot sketch and the undertakers sketch and feel my Dad laughing with me even in this sad situation' (#61 American, 36–45; #263 British, 36–45; #1957 Danish, 36–45). Here, 'anything Python'-related, including Python sketches focused on addressing and laughing at death itself, helps respondents hold on to what Jackie Stacey would term 'treasured memories' (Stacey 1993: 64) of their father and the elements of his personality and humour that fed into the exclusive bond they had with their daughters. Not only do memories of Python spectatorship work here to enable the 'memorialising' of 'deceased loved ones' (Kuhn 2002: 44) but also to provide comfort when faced with the loss of opportunity to keep experiencing the shared laughter that served, for many of these respondents, as the foundation of their distinct father–daughter relationship.

The sense that a love for Python is, for these respondents, fundamentally part of who their father is or was (as an individual, beyond his putative status as a parent) is further illustrated by mentions of the fact that, in one case, 'The Galaxy Song' was played at a respondent's father's funeral, that, in another, a respondent and her father danced to 'Always Look on the Bright Side of Life' at her wedding and her thirtieth birthday, and, in many others, that Python films were watched annually by respondents and their fathers on his birthday or at Christmas or Easter (particularly and notably *Monty Python's Life of Brian*). Such activities give a new spin on the idea that, as Barker *et al.* argue, films or other media texts can become part of 'ritualised viewing' practices (Barker *et al.* 2015: 53), with Python's role in a range of family rituals or family life events – including in the form of songs – illustrating its marked utility as a source of (multi-media) comedy that can be drawn on and pervade all aspects of a person's life.

In turn, if Monty Python is shown to be, for many respondents, indelibly associated with their father and the bond they have had with him, it is also presented as something which is now a fundamental part of these respondents' identities too. Respondent answers here returned again to discourses associated with self-development, with many stating that their early encounters with Python had helped to shape, form, or had served as a foundation for their sense of humour. As one respondent stated, 'I owe much of my adolescent character development and sense of humour to them', while, for another, '[i]t opened a huge door for me and I couldn't imagine what my sense of humour would be like if I'd never seen Monty Python' (#932 American, 46–55; #2709 Canadian, 18–25). Discourses of constancy and consistency also characterised these responses, in terms of their reflections on repeated encounters with Python's comedy over the years. The words 'always' and 'still' are repeated constantly throughout these accounts; for instance, respondents note that 'I have always found' Python 'hilarious, no matter how many times I watch', 'I still feel great joy when I watch the programmes and the films', and 'Python still makes me hurt laughing' (#131 American, 18–25; #491 British, 36–45; #708 British, 36–45). In these examples, respondents engage in what Harrington and Bielby, drawing on developmental psychology, term 'autobiographical reasoning'. Here, respondents present a sense of continuity in their Python fandom, outlining how Python's continued capacity to amuse respondents, and produce the same kind of intense, physically impactful laughter experienced as a child, illustrates 'continuity in the self over time' and 'personality coherence from infancy to adulthood' (Harrington and Bielby 2010). Indeed, this sense of constancy and consistency is prevalent even in the group of female respondents who note that, looking back, aspects of Python's comedy can be read as sexist or dated. As one respondent notes, '[i]t is interesting that I retain such fond memories, even as I look back to what now reads as sexist'; for another, 'some of the programmes now look a little dated and parts are a bit sexist' but 'that aside the silly humour and more sophisticated humorous way of looking at life still stands up in our modern society'; while, for another, 'I still love it I'm just more aware of how sexist this time was' (#28 Belgian, 46–55; #1615 British, 36–45; #701 Canadian, 46–55). In these examples, then, there is clearly a pull and negotiation – when reflecting on their contemporary relations to Python – between, in Jackie Stacey's terms, 'private narratives' of their history of consistent Python fandom and its association with past memories, and a contemporary 'critical awareness' of the dated aspects of Python (Stacey 1993: 63, 65), which are frequently bracketed off, in these responses, from Python's pleasurable silliness or 'more sophisticated . . . way of looking at life' or are put in context by being seen as reflective of the time in which Python was made.

219

Another key illustration of the impact of Python's continued presence in these respondents' lives is that a substantial number noted that they have either passed on, or intend to pass on, their Python fandom to their children, replicating the processes enacted by their fathers and passing on the family tradition in a manner akin to Dixon's insights on football fandom and family influence. Respondents note, for instance, that 'I'm loving that my kids are now old enough to *begin the process all over again*!', and that 'my daughter enjoys it *as much as I did*, because the humor references general experiences that most everybody shares' (#3797 British, 46–55; #263 British, 36–45; #1553 American, 36–45; my italics). This second example refers to a characteristic that has long been seen as a core component of Python's comedy, something which has enabled Python to travel and succeed outside the UK in a way that has not been achieved by other forms of British comedy. In line with this respondent's comment that their comedy 'references general experiences', Jeffrey Miller has accounted for Python's success in the US, for instance, by noting that Python 'largely avoided topical satire that named specific names and/or issues; instead, it focused on institutions of authority familiar to both national cultures – the church, the military/police, the legal system, governmental bureaucracies' (Miller 2000: 131–2). While this broad applicability has its limits – with, as noted earlier, a number of female respondents acknowledging that, looking back from the present, Python can be seen as having problematically sexist elements – it also appears, in many cases, to have propelled Python's circulation and impact not only internationally but also through time and generations.

Many respondents also vividly conveyed the sense that they carry Python around with them, through their ability, like their fathers, to know and recite every word of particular Python sketches and films. As one respondent notes, 'I have since expanded my repertoire and I can proudly quote several Monty Python productions backwards and forwards'; for another, 'it's so wonderful to have all of their comedic skits etched into my brain'; while, for another, 'some skits are just written on my bones at this point. I feel like they are old family friends' (#3873 American, 26–35; #1497 American, 46–55; #1842 American, 36–45). Once again, and illustrating Barbara Klinger's argument that 'dialogue' can 'define the means' by which media texts 'circulate culturally' (Klinger 2008), the marked quotability of Python's comedy output is shown to be key to its durability and continued presence in the life cycles of these respondents, evocatively illustrated by the comment, from one respondent, that Python's sketches have now come to be 'written on my bones' after years of circulation through childhood into adulthood.

In line with the earlier respondent's comment that they 'owe much' of their 'adolescent character development' to Monty Python, respondents also demonstrate, in their responses, how their initial introduction to and engagement with Python served as 'crucial' in their 'adult identity-formation and self-definition'

(Barker *et al.* 2015: 62). For one respondent, for example, 'the stream-of-consciousness quality of it appeals to me. I have Asperger's and my brain is all over the place. I feel less alone when I watch anything Pythonesque. Somebody up there gets me'; for another, 'I can't think of my adolescent years and coming of age without Monty Python. They helped me discover who I am and where I "fit"'; while, for another, 'I was always a weird kid, who grew up into a weird adult who looks at life in a different way than most, and I gained a love for the Monty Python humour into my adulthood' (#2585 American, 46–55; #1698 Canadian, 36–45; #1722 Canadian, 46–55). For these respondents, then, embracing Monty Python, through the mentorship of their father, was about embracing difference or distinctiveness and then coming to terms with this, by allowing this engagement to help them work out 'where I "fit"', including, in some cases, recognising that, through their father's mentorship, they had become a fan of something that was conventionally associated with male comedy fans. In these cases, some respondents reported that, as a youngster, they were often the only female in their peer groups who knew or were invested in Python, or that they recall pleasure in standing out from other girls through their investment in Python's adult comedy. For instance, as one respondent recalled, 'I remember being a Brownie in girl scouts. They asked each of us to share our favorite TV program. While the other girls mentioned *The Brady Bunch* or *The Partridge Family*, I proudly said, "Monty Python"' (#1230 American, 46–55).

Many female 'Dad Memories Group' respondents also reflected on how their enduring engagement with Python had impacted on their ways of seeing the world. As one female respondent put it, 'personally: their humour is stimulating my brain – my fantasy, my imagination, my curiosity. Monty Python has given me another way of looking at the world' (#1957 Danish, 36–45). For many, Python's comedy was seen to have multiple levels within it that not only encouraged repeat viewing and fed into its appeal as 'adult' comedy, but which also enabled respondents' relations with Python to grow and develop as they moved through different life stages. As one respondent notes, 'I think that I always liked their humor and nonsense, but I get their philosophical and social criticism ("we are all individuals!", the peasants in *Holy Grail*) more as an adult and appreciate that level of their humor' (#1429 Israeli, 26–35).

Indeed, relations to Python may develop for these enduring female fans due to the depth and layered nature of the comedy content itself, but can also shift in line with respondents' changing relations with their fathers. As one respondent notes, for instance, '[a]s a teen I related to the rebellion they offered by skirting the rules of decency in polite society (as a pastor's kid I could relate to toeing that fine line)' (#3885 American, 36–45). This respondent's reference to relating to Python as a tool of rebellion against (or criticism of) the religious aspects of their upbringing during adolescence is also mirrored in a number of other responses which note that their engagement with Python (and, in particular, *Life of Brian*) impacted on their worldview. For one respondent, this film made 'me re-think my religious beliefs and why we believe', while, for another, 'I was raised in an evangelical Southern (US) Baptist family and never took to religion. Monty Python was the first truly (and innocently) funny take on the story of Jesus I had come across' (#3020 American, 36–45; #3564 American, 36–45).

In these examples, then, becoming a Python fan remains an 'anchoring event' serving as a 'touchstone for a continuing set of beliefs about the world' (Pillemer 1998: 65–83), which, as with the first Monty Python generation represented by many of these respondents' fathers, involves an engagement with the anti-authoritarian aspects of Python's comedy. As in these cases, however, this is an engagement which can lead to respondents' criticism of the same familial and paternal context through which they were introduced to Python in the first place. Such paradoxes and complexities illustrate the value of attending, in detail, to people's memories of enduring comedy fandom, and particularly the kind of durable, transnational, pervasive, culturally eclectic, polysemic and multi-medial comedy represented by Monty Python.

CONCLUSION

In some ways, the recollections of initial encounters with Python discussed in this chapter seem to point to processes which Jeffrey Weinstock has identified as informing the long-term circulation of *The Rocky Horror Picture Show* – where, through a new status 'as an inherited rite of passage', the 'necessity of viewing' an originally daring and countercultural text moves from 'subcultural demand to general cultural imperative', from an 'edgy' to a mundane and 'normal' act (Weinstock 2007: 112–13). In this respect, paternal encouragements for daughters to watch the same episodes and experience the same pleasures as those first encountered by their youthful fathers could be seen to stymie and restrict the shaping of these daughters' comedy tastes and engagement with humour. While the recollections analysed in this chapter to some degree support such readings, there are two key discursive trends repeatedly crossing the responses which illustrate how enduring comedy consumption can shed new light on 'how young people, past and present, engage with popular culture and media as part of the process of growing up' (Kuhn 2002: 238), and, in turn, how they build and maintain meaningful familial relationships that cross both gender and generation.

Firstly, the fact that an investment in Python served as the (in many cases) singular or primary element in many of the father–daughter relationships discussed and recalled by these female respondents provides a new intergenerational perspective on the social uses and functions of comedy and, crucially, Giselinde Kuipers' important argument that humour is primarily 'a form of communication that is embedded in social relationships' (Kuipers 2015: 7). Despite the dated nature of some of Python's comedy (from the perspective of present-day reminiscence), the diversity and polysemic nature of Python's output (silly but adult, absurd but socially critical, irreverent but philosophical) has clearly enabled quotations and particular sketches to endure and to serve, for these respondents, as vehicles of communication which maintained father–daughter relationships while, paradoxically, transcending them by foregrounding, for daughters, their father's status as a distinct person. Secondly, and in contrast to Weinstock's argument that the take-up of a text like *Rocky Horror* by younger generations has little to do with the assertion of 'transgressive individuality' (Weinstock 2007: 111), engagement with Python, in examples discussed across the chapter, has enabled respondents to embrace a sense of themselves as different, distinct or as standing out from their gender or peer group in different contexts, and to, in other cases and in relation to Python's anti-authoritarian or socially critical dimensions, critically assess and reflect on aspects of their own social worlds and familial backgrounds.

In these respects, such cross-gender intergenerational forms of Python fandom can, arguably, be read less as a form of co-option of daughters into the comedy tastes of older generations, and more as continuing textual encounters which, in varying ways, have enabled the 'expansion of self-experience' and 'knowledge' about these respondents' selves (Hills 2014: 11), their familial and social relationships, and their ways of seeing the world, both humorously and critically.

Note

1. Throughout the chapter, in-text references to quotations from project questionnaire responses give the ID number of the response, the nationality of the respondent and the age range of the respondent (e.g. #46 British, 26–35).

Works Cited

Alcott, Thomas (2019) 'Not Putting Away Childish Things: The Importance of Childhood in the Audience Reception of Professional Wrestling Stars', *Participations: Journal of Audience and Reception Studies* 16(1), 3–29.

Barker, Martin, Kate Egan, Tom Phillips and Sarah Ralph (2015) *Alien Audiences: Remembering and Evaluating a Classic Movie*. Basingstoke: Palgrave Macmillan.

Bore, Inger-Lise Kalviknes (2017) *Screen Comedy and Online Audiences*. Abingdon: Routledge.

Brock, Alexander (2016) 'The Struggle of Class against Class Is a What Struggle? *Monty Python's Flying Circus* and Its Politics', in Juergen Kamm and Birgit Neumann (eds), *British TV Comedies: Cultural Concepts, Contexts and Controversies*. Basingstoke: Palgrave Macmillan, pp. 51–65.

Claessens, Nathalie and Alexander Dhoest (2010) 'Comedy Taste: Highbrow/Lowbrow Comedy and Cultural Capital', *Participations: Journal of Audience and Reception Studies* 7(1), 49–72.

Dixon, Kevin (2013) 'Learning the Game: Football Fandom Culture and the Origins of Practice', *International Review for the Sociology of Sport* 48(3), 334–48.

Friedman, Sam (2014) *Comedy and Distinction: The Cultural Currency of a 'Good' Sense of Humour*. Abingdon: Routledge.

Hamad, Hannah (2014) *Postfeminism and Paternity in Contemporary U.S. Film: Framing Fatherhood*. New York: Routledge.

Harrington, C. Lee and Denise D. Bielby (2010) 'Autobiographical Reasoning in Long-Term Fandom', *Transformative Works and Cultures* 5. <http://dx.doi.org/10.3983/twc.2010.0209> (last accessed 20 August 2018)

Hills, Matt (2014) 'Returning to "Becoming-a-Fan" Stories: Theorising Transformational Objects and the Emergence/Extension of Fandom', in Linda Duits, Koos Zwaan and Stijn Reijnders (eds), *The Ashgate Research Companion to Fan Cultures*. Farnham: Ashgate, pp. 9–22.

Jones, Bill, Alan G. Parker and Ben Timlett (dir.) (2009) *Monty Python: Almost the Truth – The Lawyer's Cut*. London: Bill and Ben Productions.

Klinger, Barbara (1997) 'Film History Terminable and Interminable: Recovering the Past in Reception Studies', *Screen* 38(2), 107–28.

Klinger, Barbara (2008) 'Say It Again, Sam: Movie Quotation, Performance and Masculinity', *Participations: Journal of Audience and Reception Studies* 5(2). <http://www.participations.org/Volume%205/Issue%202/5_02_klinger.htm> (last accessed 7 November 2018)

Kuhn, Annette (2002) *An Everyday Magic: Cinema and Cultural Memory*. London: I. B. Tauris.

Kuipers, Giselinde (2015) *Good Humor, Bad Taste: A Sociology of the Joke*. Boston, MA: De Gruyter Mouton.

Landy, Marcia (2005) *Monty Python's Flying Circus*. Detroit, MI: Wayne State University Press.

Miller, Jeffrey S. (2000) *Something Completely Different: British Television and American Culture*. Minneapolis: University of Minnesota Press.

Mills, Richard (2014) 'Eric Idle and the Counterculture', in Tomasz Dobrogoszcz (ed.), *Nobody Expects the Spanish Inquisition: Cultural Contexts in Monty Python*. Lanham, MD: Rowman & Littlefield, pp. 125–36.

Pillemer, David B. (1998) *Momentous Events, Vivid Memories*. Cambridge, MA: Harvard University Press.

Ralph, Sarah (2015) 'Using Stars, Not Just "Reading" Them: The Roles and Functions of Film Stars in Mother–Daughter Relations', *Celebrity Studies* 6(1), 23–38.

Sharpe, Sue (1994) *Fathers and Daughters*. London: Routledge.

Stacey, Jackie (1993) *Star Gazing: Hollywood Cinema and Female Spectatorship*. London: Routledge.

Vroomen, Laura (2004) 'Kate Bush: Teen Pop and Older Female Fans', in Andy Bennett and Richard A. Peterson (eds), *Music Scenes: Local, Translocal, and Virtual*. Nashville, TN: Vanderbilt University Press, pp. 238–53.

Wagg, Stephen (1992) 'You've Never Had It So Silly: The Politics of British Satirical Comedy from *Beyond the Fringe* to *Spitting Image*', in Dominic Strinati and Stephen Wagg (eds), *Come on Down? Popular Media Culture in Post-war Britain*. London: Routledge, pp. 254–84.

Weinstock, Jeffrey (2007) *The Rocky Horror Picture Show*. London: Wallflower Press.

Whybray, Adam (2016) '"I'm Crushing Your Binaries!" Drag in Monty Python and Kids in the Hall', *Comedy Studies* 7(2), 169–81.

INDEX

ABC, *Wide World of Entertainment* programme, 8
absurdism, 23–38
  in animation, 95
  Gilliam's visual, 109, 117
  The Goon Show (radio show), 42
  joyful spirit of, 31–2
  ordinary people in bizarre situations, 30–1, 34, 41, 51–2, 67, 162
  and Richard Lester, 127
absurdist theatre, 23–38, 128
Academy Awards, 191
Adam Adamant Lives! (TV series), 29
Adams, Douglas
  The Hitchhiker's Guide to the Galaxy, 173, 176–7, 180
  The Meaning of Liff, 176
The Addams Family (TV series), 100, 135
The Adventures of Baron Munchausen (Gilliam, 1988), 9–10
advertising, 102, 104
'Albatross' sketch, 144–8

The Album Version of the Soundtrack of the Trailer of the Film of Monty Python and the Holy Grail (1975), 7
Alexander, J. J. G., *Medieval Illuminators and Their Methods of Work*, 108
Alexander, Jonathan J. G., 113–16
Altamont Free Concert, 83, 133
Althusser, Louis, 199
'Always Look on the Bright Side of Life', 79, 88, 218
America
  Anglophilia, 204
  audience, 8, 192
  counterculture, 92
  cult of Python in, 75–6
  fans, 213, 220
American Film Institute, star award, 10
Americanisation, 129–30
And Now for Something Completely Different (MacNaughton, 1971), 8, 111–12

227

animals, 141–54
  cultural understandings of, 143
  eating animals: the albatross, 144–8
  pets: the cat, 148–51
  selection for comic effect, 142, 147
animated foot, 1, 25, 27, 41, 43, 87, 97–8, 103
animation, 12, 91–106
  Conrad Pooh (character in), 100–1
  as interlinking elements, 127
Another Monty Python Record (1971), 7, 86–7
'Anything Goes' (episode 42), 76
Archer, Neil, 14, 15, 88, 107–8
'Argument Skit' (episode 29), 32
Aristotle, 157, 174
Aronstein, Susan, 14–15, 112, 199, 203
Arthur Ewing's 'musical mice' act (episode 2), 86, 87, 143–4
Arthur 'Two Sheds' Jackson (character), 86
Associated-Rediffusion, 92
associative relations, 96–7
At Last the 1948 Show (TV series), 5, 9, 24, 88
Auden, W. H., 101
audience expectations upset
  'Hell's Grannies' (episode 8), 136
  incongruity, 145–6, 158
  Monty Python and the Holy Grail (Gilliam and Jones, 1975), 200–5
  Monty Python's Flying Circus (TV series), 127–8
  music, 84
  televisual and cinematic conventions, 194
Audience Research Reports, 3
audience response, initial, 3, 208
Aufenanger, Jörg, 177
'autobiographical reasoning', 219
The Avengers (TV series), 29
Avery, Tex, 102

The Babadook (Kent, 2014), 190
'Baby, It's Cold Outside' song, 163
BAFTAs, 10–11, 24
Bagpuss (TV series), 30
Bakhtin, Mikhail
  carnival, 12, 45–6, 126, 183, 198, 205
  The Dialogical Imagination, 174
  'laughing truth', 32
  Rabelais and His World, 33, 45
Barclay, Humphrey, 92
Barker, Martin, et al., 218–19
Barthes, Roland, 177
Bassey, Shirley, 79
Basu, Laura, 51–2
Baudrillard, Jean, 184
Bazin, André, 175–6
BBC Audience Research reports, 208
BBC management, 2–3, 6, 7, 166
BBC radio, 29
BBC Written Archives, 85
BBC1, 1
The Beatles, 63, 83, 126
  films, 127
  Magical Mystery Tour (1967), 29
Becker, Ernest, 43
Beckett, Samuel, 26–8, 31, 33–4
  Happy Days, 25
  Murphy, 26–7, 32
  Not I, 96
  Waiting for Godot, 27
The Bed Sitting Room (Lester, 1969), 127
'Beethoven's Mynah Bird' sketch (episode 21), 87–8
Benko, Steven, 166
Bennett, Alan, 42
Bentine, Michael, 92
Bergman, Ingmar, 108
  The Seventh Seal (1956), 112–13, 118
Bergson, Henri, 175, 198
  Laughter, 33

Berlant, Lauren, 167–8
'betwixt and between', 116–17
Beyond the Fringe (revue), 42, 63, 93, 126, 209
'Bicycle Repair Man' sketch (episode 3), 129–30
Bielby, Denise D., 211, 214, 217, 219
Biographic Studio, 92–3
'The Bishop' (episode 17), 35
Bishop of Southwark, 51
Black Knight (character), 39, 49, 196–8, *197*
Blackboard Jungle (Brooks, 1955), 135, 137
'Blackmail' (episode 18), 33, 77, 134
Blake, William, 137
blasphemy, 166–7
Bobker, Danielle, 158
Bonzo Dog Doo-Dah Band, 83, 126
book covers, 7–8
Bordwell, David, *Figures Traced in Light*, 115
Bore, Inger-Lise, 215
'borrowed Otherness', 204
Bosch, Hieronymous, 113
Botticelli, *The Birth of Venus*, 103
Bourdieu, Pierre, 208, 211
Bradbury, Malcolm, 26
The Brand New Monty Python Bok, 7–8
Brandt, George, 27–8
Brazil (Gilliam, 1984), 10, 36, 184, 185
Bresson, Robert, *Lancelot du Lac* (1974), 49
Breugel, Pieter, 113
Brexit, 163–4
British 'Alternative Comedy Boom', 209
British Board of Film Censors, 135
British class system, 39–56
  American Anglophilia, 204
  animation, 32, 103

brass-band music, 82
female characters, 14
and Gilliam, 92, 95
Monty Python and the Holy Grail (1975), 199, 203
Monty Python's Life of Brian (1979), 159
'Upper Class Twit of the Year' sketch, 133–4
'Working-Class Playwright' sketch, 125
British culture – 1960s, 125–38
  'borrowed Otherness', 204
  counterculture, 24–5, 57–8
  satire, 93–4
  second-wave feminism, 215–16
  surrealism, 28–30
Brock, Alexander, 67, 127
Bronzino, *Allegory of Love with Venus and Cupid*, 103
Burgess and Maclean, 85

Calvino, Italo, 176, 177, 179–80
Cambridge Circus (revue), 92
Cambridge University Footlights, 4, 41–2
Camelot (Logan, 1967), 112, 118
Camille, Michael, 116–17, 118–19
camp, 14–15, 83, 189, 199
'Camp Square-Bashing' sketch (episode 22), 14–15
Camus, Albert, 26
Canadian Broadcasting Company, 8
Canadian fans, 213
Canby, Vincent, 183
Cannes Film Festival
  Grand Prix 1983, 9
  Meaning of Life, 184
cannibalism, 6
carnival, 12, 45–6, 126, 143, 198, 205
Carroll, Nöel, 175, 195
Carruth, Hayden, 44
Carry On films, 42, 112

Carter, Angela, 46–7
Casino Royale (Huston et al., 1967), 112
Cassity, Kathleen J., 166
Catholic Church, 41
censorship, 94, 131, 166, 192
Chapman, Graham, after Python, 10
'Cheese Shop' sketch (episode 33), 78
Cheng, William, 168
   'Taking Back the Laugh: Comedic Alibis, Funny Fails', 166
children's television, 30
Childs, Peter, 26–7
Clampett, Bob, 102
The Clangers (TV series), 30
Clark, Petula, 85
classical music, 86–8
Cleese, John
   after Python, 9–10
   desire to leave, 7
   Fawlty Towers, 36
   first meeting with Terry Gilliam, 92
   Life of Brian, 167
   origins of Monty Python, 4
   Q5, 5
   'Rhubarb Tart' song, 88
   'Sermon', 185
   So, Anyway. . ., 155
   on Terry Gilliam as outsider, 108
Cleveland, Carol, 14, 212
Cliff, Andrew, 192
Cold War anxiety, 129–30
Colonel (character), 69–70
comedy as social critique, 24–5, 30, 33, 35–6, 93–4, 128, 199, 203
'community of laughter', 195
The Complete and Utter History of Britain, 4, 63–4, 110–11, 119n
'Confuse-A-Cat' sketch (episode 5), 144, 149–52
consumerism, 134
Cook, Peter, 42, 83, 85, 137, 182
Coote, Lesley, 107–8

counterculture, 25, 82–3
cruelty, 160, 174, 175–7, 185
Crumb, Robert, 92
'Crunchy Frog' sketch (episode 6), 144
cult film, 173–86
cult of Python, 189–206
   in America, 75–6
Cutler, Ivor, 29
'The Cycling Tour' (episode 34), 85

Da Vinci, Leonardo
   The Last Supper, 103
   The Mona Lisa, 103
'Dad Memories Group', 209–26, *210*, *211*
Dadaism, 83, 126
Dad's Army (TV series), 62
Daily Telegraph, 25
Dark Shadows (TV series), 135
Davies, Philip, 52
Day, David D., 50, 107–8
De Wolfe Music Presents: Monty Python's Flying Circus (CD), 75–6
'Dead Parrot' sketch (episode 8), 48–9, 69, 141–2
death, 39–56
Death of Stalin (Iannucci, 2018), 185
Death playing chess (character), 112–13
Deb, Sopan, 54
Debord, Guy, *The Society of the Spectacle*, 130
'Decomposing Composers' song, 87
dehumanisation, 43, 45
Department S (TV series), 29
Derrida, Jacques, 201
Dery, Mark, 204
Diringer, David, 114
Disney films, 96–7, 102, 118
Disney's 'Nine Old Men', 96
disruptive metamorphosis, 98–100
Dixon, Kevin, 211, 220
Do It Yourself Cartoon Kit, 92–3

Do Not Adjust Your Set (TV series), 4, 5, 24, 92, 126
  songs, 79
Dobrogoszcz, Tomasz, *Nobody Expects the Spanish Inquisition*, 13
Doctor in the House (TV series), 4
Donnelly, Kevin, 126
'Don't Sleep in the Subway' song (episode 19), 85
Dryden, John, 95–6
Duncan, Russell, 126, 129
Durante, Jimmy, 'I'm the Guy Who Found the Lost Chord', 88
Dürer, Albrecht, *Knight, Death and the Devil*, 113
Dürrenmatt, Freidrich, 36

Eagleton, Terry, 185
  The Meaning of Life, 174–5
Ealing comedies, 42, 92
Ebert, Roger, 183
Eco, Umberto, 194–5, 196
Edinburgh Festival, 63
Edinburgh Festival Comedy Fringe 2009, 208–9
Edwardian and Victorian photographs, 98–9
Ehrenreich, Barbara, 177–8
Emery, Dick, 42
EMI Films, 9, 63
Encyclopaedia Britannica, 3
Epstein, Joseph, 204
Eric Idle Sings Monty Python (live recording), 76
'Eric the Half a Bee' song, 31, 77, 80
Erik the Viking (Jones, 1989), 10, 184, 185
escalation, 35
Esslin, Martin, *The Theatre of the Absurd*, 26
Eton, Peter, 59
existentialism, 44
  alienation, 130–1
explosions, 59–65, 68, 70

Facebook, 207–8
'Fair Play for Paintings' strike, 103
The Fairly Incomplete and Rather Badly Illustrated Monty Python Song Book, 77
fandom
  familial, 210–26
  family rituals, 218–19
  as family tradition, 220
  fathers and daughters, 213–17
  female, 207–26
  generational taste in comedy, 208–10
  intergenerational, 207–26
'Farewell to John Denver' song, 80
Fawlty Towers (TV series), 10
  Cleese, John, 36
Fear and Loathing in Los Vegas (Gilliam, 1998), 10
Feldman, Marty, 5, 10
female characters, 212
  'Pepperpot' characters, 14
Fierce Creatures (Schepisi and Young, 1997), 10
Firmin, Peter, 30
A Fish Called Wanda (Crichton, 1988), 10
Fisher King (Gilliam, 1991), 10
'Flying Fox of the Yard' (episode 29), 33
'Flying Lessons' (episode 16), 87
'Flying Sheep' (episode 2), 134, 138, 144
FM radio, 76
folk traditions, 86–7
Forstater, Mark, 111–12
Four Lions (Morris, 2010), 51
'Four Yorkshiremen' sketch, 9
Fox, Paul, 3

French, Karl, 184
French, Philip, 184
'French Lecture on Sheep Aircraft' sketch (episode 2), 144
Freud, Sigmund, 190–1, 196–7, 200
  Jokes and Their Relation to the Unconscious, 33, 166
Friedman, Sam, *Comedy and Distinction*, 208–9
From Spam to Sperm (BBC1 documentary), 80
The Frost Report (TV series), 4, 5, 24, 92, 127

'gag-that-builds', 97, 99–100
Gent, James, 24
German accents, 62, 66, 68–9
German television, 3, 9
Get Out (Peele, 2017), 190
Gibron, Bill, 160, 167
Gilbert and Sullivan, 42
Gilliam, Terry
  active artwork, 46
  after Python, 10
  American Python, 91–2, 95
  Animations of Mortality, 104–5
  Beware the Elephants, 116
  'Christopher's Punctured Romance', 92
  The Cocktail People, 92
  The Crimson Permanent Assurance short feature, 181, 184
  films, 36
  first meeting with John Cleese, 92
  as impish God, 91–106
  'I've Got Two Legs' ditty, 78
  on Jones, 11
  manuscripts illustrations, 109–10
  as outsider to the Pythons, 108–9
  satiric animation, 91–106
  theme tune, 82
  see also animation
Gilray, James, 92

glam-rock attire, 83
God, 49
Godfrey, Bob, 92, 92–3
Goldstone, John, 109
The Goodies, on *Top of the Pops*, 82
The Goon Show (radio show)
  absurd and bizarre, 25
  absurdism, 42
  'The Affair of the Lone Banana', 60, 61–2
  Crazy People, 58
  'The Dreaded Batter Pudding Hurler (of Bexhill-on-Sea)', 59–60, 61, 62
  explosions, 59–61
  'Foiled by President Fred', 60–1, 62
  innovations of, 12
  Milligan, Spike, 5
  'Napoleon's Piano', 61, 62
  Nazi master weapon, 62
  'The Phantom Head Shaver', 61
  politicians, 61
  sea travel, 61–2
  and the Second World War, 57–63, 65–6, 68, 70
  surrealism, 92
  'Tales of Men's Shirts', 61–2, 64
The Goons Show (TV broadcast), 62
'Gorilla Librarian' sketch (episode 10), 144, 152
Gothic horror, 43–4, 53, 134–5
Grierson, John, *Nightmail*, 100–1
Griffin, Dustin, 93–5, 104–5
Guardian, 164
Guiffre, Liz, 84

Hamad, Hannah, 215
HandMade Films, 9
happy endings, lack of, 128, 162–3, 191
Hardcastle, Gary C., *Monty Python and Philosophy*, 13
Harper's magazine, 185

Harrington, C. Lee, 211, 214, 217, 219
Harrison, George, 9, 63, 166
  friendship with Eric Idle, 137
  Rutland Weekend Television, 83
Harry Enfield and Chums (TV series), 42
The Harry Enfield Television Show (TV series), 42
Harryhausen, Ray, 100
Harty, Kevin J., *Cinema Arthuriana: Essays on Arthurian Film*, 107, 119n
Heath, Edward, 85
Hebdige, Dick, 190
'Hell's Grannies' (episode 8), 35, 83, 135–7, 138
Help! publication, 92
Hemmings, David, 132
Henderson, Michael, 41–2
'Here Comes Another One' song, 80
'The Hermits' sketch (episode 8), 130–1, 138
Herzog, Hal, *Some We Love, Some We Hate, Some We Eat*, 144, 147
Hewison, Robert, 3, 192, 212
  book covers, 7–8
  Monty Python: The Case Against, 6–7
Hills, Matt, 214
History of the BBC 'Monty Python at 50' website, 3
Hobbes, Thomas, 157
Hoberman, J., *Midnight Movies*, 193
Hoffman, Donald, 42, 49–50
Hogarth, William, 92
'Hollywood Arthuriana', 112, 119n
Hollywood Production Code, relaxation of, 135
Hollywood Reporter, 181, 183
horror films, 43–4, 53, 134–5
  monsters as metaphors, 190–1

How to Irritate People (TV programme), 4
'How to Recognise Different Types of Trees from Quite a Long Way Away' (episode 3), 28
Howarth, W. D., 27, 33–4
human-animal relationships, 143, 148–53
Humanistic, 30–1
humourlessness, 167–8
Hunt, Leon, *Cult British TV Comedy: From Reeves and Mortimer to Psychoville*, 193
Huxley, Aldous, *The Doors of Perception*, 137
hypocrisy, 160

'I Bet You They Won't Play This Song on the Radio' song, 80
'I Like Traffic Lights' song, 80
identity politics, 94
'Idiot in Society' sketch (episode 20), 133
Idle, Eric
  'Always Look on the Bright Side of Life', 54
  anti-establishment spirit, 212
  and counterculture, 83, 126, 138
  friendship with George Harrison, 137
  on *Life of Brian*, 51–2
  Meaning of Life, 185
  as 'musical' Python, 76
  'Python'-adjacent projects, 9–10
  Spamalot, 36
If . . . (Anderson, 1968), 132
illuminated manuscript illustrations, 113–14
'I'm (Still) So Worried' song, 11
'I'm So Worried' song, 11, 77
I'm Sorry I'll Read That Again (radio show), 88
songs, 79

Imaginarium of Doctor Parnassus (Gilliam, 2009), 10
Imagine (BBC documentary), 208
incongruity, 155–71
Innes, Neil
  as family tradition, 89
  as secret Python, 81–2
  sound design of *The Holy Grail*, 82–3
  TV shows, 29
  'When Does a Dream Begin', 81–2
intergenerational fandom, 207–26
interlinking elements, 127
inversion, 77, 136, 137, 196, 198–9, 205
Ionesco, Eugene, *Rhinoceros*, 25
Isherwood, Christopher, 29
'It's a Man's Life in the Army' (episode 4), 70
'It's a Tree' sketch (episode 10), 127
'It's' man (character), 2
'It's the Arts' sketch (episode 6), 86
'I've Got Two Legs' ditty, 78
Ivor the Engine (TV series), 30

Jabberwocky (Gilliam, 1977), 10, 119n
Jenss, Heike, 129
Jesus and Brian: Exploring the Historical Jesus and His Times via Monty Python's Life of Brian, 166
'John Cleese and Eric Idle: Together Again at Last.For the Very First Time' tour, 9–10
The John Peel Show (radio show), 29
Johnston, Ollie, 96, 97, 99
joie de vivre éclatante, 174, 179, 179, 184
Jones, Terry
  Absolutely Anything, 10
  about *Beware the Elephants*, 116
  after Python, 10
  Chaucer's Knight: The Portrait of a Medieval Mercenary, 110

contemporary perspecive on *Life of Brian*, 51
  about Eric Idle and music, 76
  history programmes, 36, 110
  last work, 11
  The Meaning of Liff, 176
  playing the organ naked, 86
  Q5, 5
  as scholar, 110–11
  Simply Absurd (Radio 4 documentary), 25
  theme tune, 82
  Who Murdered Chaucer?: A Medieval Mystery, 110
Journal of Film and Religion, 166
Just the Words transcription books, 85
Juvenal, 43–4
juvenile delinquency, 135–7

Kafka, Franz, 34–6
Kafkaesque, 34, 36
Kant, Immanuel, 145–6, 158
Keaton, Buster, 111, 113
KERA, 8
Kitt, Eartha, 85
Kovacs, Ernie, 92
Kracauer, Siegfried, 174
Kray Brothers, 132
Krutnik, Frank, 12, 12–13
Kuipers, Giselinde, 51, 222–3
Kurosawa, Akira, 108, 112
  Throne of Blood (1957), 113
Kurtzman, Harvey, *Help!* 92

Lady Chatterley trial, 131
Landy, Marcia, 12, 193–4
  'affluent society' and media, 128–9
  animals, 143, 152
  Monty Python's Flying Circus, 192
  Python and the war, 64
  serious art and nonsense, 86
  sketches and canonical works, 77
  TV techniques mocked by MPFC, 3

language and word games, 31–2, 128, 179, 194, 203
Larsen, Darl, 78, 83, 84–5, 112, 118
'laughing truth', 32
laugh-track, 153
Le Guin, Ursula K., 176
The League of Gentlemen (TV series), 29
Lester, Richard, 63, 127
'Lethal Joke' sketch (episode 1), 63, 64–6, 69
Levine, Amy-Jill, 15
Levy, Brian, 107–8
Levy, Don, *Herostratus* (1967), 130
'light entertainment', 2, 24, 76, 78, 81, 83, 85
'Light Entertainment War' (episode 42), music in, 81
'Literary Football Discussion' sketch (episode 11), 130
Little Britain (TV series), 42
'logic of the absurd', 146–8
London Weekend Television, 110–11
Lovelace, Earl, *The Dragon Can't Dance*, 45
'The Lumberjack Song' (episode 9), 14–15, 79, 84

McCarthy, Soren, 184
MacInnes, Colin, *Absolute Beginners*, 129
McLuhan, Marshall, 129
McNally, Neil, 184
MacNaughton, Ian, 82
Mad magazine, 92
Maffesoli, Michel, 175
'Make tea not love' slogan, 136–7
Małecka, Katarzyna, 43
Man Who Killed Don Quixote (Gilliam, 2018), 10
Mannheim, Karl, 180–1
marginalia, 117

'Marriage Guidance Councillor' sketch (episode 2), 28, 129, 132
Martin, George, 63
Marxism, 50
'Mary Recruiting Office sketch' (episode 30), 70
Mathjis, Ernest, 182, 184
  Cult Cinema: An Introduction, 192–3
mechanisation, 130–1
'Medical Love Song' song, 80
Mendik, Xavier, 184
Menippean satire, 32
meta-humoristic tendencies, 128
meta-theatre, 162–3
#MeToo, 163
Meuwese, Martine, 109–10, 113, 114–15, 117–18
  'The Animation of Marginal Decorations in "Monty Python and the Holy Grail"', 108
Michelangelo
  The Creation of Man, 103
  David, 94, 102
Midnight Cowboy (Schlesinger, 1969), 132
'midway' experience, 101–4
Miller, Jeffrey S., 8, 220
  Something Completely Different: British Television and American Culture, 193
Miller, Jonathan, 42
Milligan, Spike, 5, 10, 12, 24
  war service, 59, 61
Mills, Richard, 83, 126, 126–7, 137, 138
Ministry of Silly Walks, 47
mockumentaries, 189
modernist alienation, 130–1
Molière, 33–4, 35
Monty Python: Almost the Truth (Lawyer's Cut), 11

Monty Python and the Holy Grail (Gilliam and Jones, 1975), 8
Black Knight, *197*
contrasted with *The Rocky Horror Picture Show*, 193
credits, 200–2
division of labour between Jones and Gilliam, 108–10, 118–19
as illuminated manuscript, 115–16
intergenerational fandom, 218
Jones as director, 114–15
killer rabbit of Caerbannog, 144, 152
The Knights Who Say Ni, 202–3, *202*
as a medieval manuscript, 107–23
migratory silliness? 203–5
mockery of authority, 194–9
'The Monster of Aaargh', 117
møøse control, *201*
music in, 79
'The Quest for the Holy Grail', 117–18
quotability, 195–6
on-screen 'book of the film', 118
'Season Animation', 117
sexuality and gender, 15
silly subtitles, 200–2
social hierarchy and death, 49–50
sound design, 82–3
'The Tale of Sir Galahad', 117–18
'The Tale of Sir Launcelot', 117–18
W. G. Grace as God, 96, 117
Monty Python Live at City Center (1976 album), 7
Monty Python Live at Drury Lane (1974 album), 7
Monty Python Live at the Hollywood Bowl (1982), 9
Monty Python Live (Mostly): One Down, Five to Go, 3, 9, 11, 13, 40, 76–7, 208

The Monty Python Matching Tie and Handkerchief, (1974 record), 7, 8, 214
'Background to History', 81, 83
Monty Python Memories audience research project, 207–26
Monty Python Speaks
'Always Look on the Bright Side of Life', 88
Life of Brian, 160
origins of Monty Python, 5
sound design of *The Holy Grail*, 82–3
Monty Python website, 4–5, 207–8
Monty Python's Big Red Book, 7
Monty Python's Contractual Obligation Album (1980), 11, 80
'Decomposing Composers' song, 87
'Rock Notes' news sketch, 83
Monty Python's Flying Circus (1970 record), 7
Monty Python's Flying Circus (TV series)
and 1960s British (popular) culture, 125–40
and counterculture, 131–5
and the Second World War, 57–73
'Albatross' sketch, 144–8
'The All-England Summarise Proust Competition' episode, 81
'The Ant, an Introduction' episode, 78, 80, 89, 132–3, 144
'Anything Goes,' 76
'Argument Skit,' 32
Arthur 'Two Sheds' Jackson (character), 86
Arthur Ewing's 'musical mice' act, 86, 87, 143–4
'The Attila the Hun Show' episode, 133, 135
'Beethoven's Mynah Bird' sketch, 87–8
'Bicycle Repair Man' sketch, 129–30

INDEX

'The Bishop' sketch, 35
'Blackmail,' 33, 77, 134
'The Buzz Aldrin Show' episode 132
'Camp Square-Bashing' sketch, 14–15
'Cheese Shop' sketch, 78
'Confuse-A-Cat' sketch, 144, 149–52
'Crunchy Frog' sketch, 144
'The Cycling Tour' sketch, 85
'Dead Parrot' sketch, 48–9, 69, 141–2
'Don't Sleep in the Subway' song, 85
'Flying Fox of the Yard,' 33
'Flying Lessons,' 87
'Flying Sheep', 134, 138, 144
'French Lecture on Sheep Aircraft' sketch, 144
'The Golden Age of Ballooning' episode, 85
'Gorilla Librarian' sketch, 144, 152
'Grandstand' episode, 27, 32
'Hell's Grannies', 35, 83, 135–7, 138
'The Hermits' sketch, 130–1, 138
'A Horse, a Spoon and a Bucket' (suggested title), 144
'How Not to Be Seen' episode, 84, 136
'How to Recognise Different Types of Trees from Quite a Long Way Away' sketch, 28
'Idiot in Society' sketch, 133
'Intermission' episode, 85, 133
'It's a Living' episode, 85, 133
'It's a Man's Life in the Army,' 70
'It's a Tree,' 127
'It's the Arts' sketch, 86
'It's the Arts (or: the BBC Entry to the Zinc Stoat of Budapest)' episode, 144
'Lethal Joke' sketch, 63, 64–6, 69

'The Light Entertainment War' episode: music in, 81
'Literary Football Discussion' sketch, 130
'The Lumberjack Song', 14–15, 79, 84
'Man's Crisis of Identity in the Latter Half of the 20th Century' episode, 130
'Marriage Guidance Councillor' sketch, 28, 129, 132
'Mary Recruiting Office sketch,' 70
'The Mouse Problem', 131
'Mr. and Mrs. Brian Morris' Ford Popular' episode, 87
'Mr Hilter/Minehead By-election' sketch, 63, 67–9
'The Naked Ant' episode, 144
'New Cooker' sketch, 34–5, 45
'The Nude Organist' episode, 84
'Nudge Nudge' sketch, 77, 132
'Owl Stretching Time' episode, 144
'The Poet McTeagle' sketch, 131, 138
'Poets' sketch, 127
'Psychiatrist' sketch, 78–9
'Psychiatrist Milkman,' 33
'The Royal Philharmonic Orchestra Goes to the Bathroom' sketch, 86
'Secretary of State Striptease' sketch, 134
'Sex and Violence' episode, 87, 132
'The Toad Elevating Moment' (suggested title), 144
'Undertakers' sketch, 6–7, 6
'Upper Class Twit of the Year' sketch, 47–8, 133
'Vox Pops on Politicians' sketch, 133
'Whither Canada?' episode, 1, 64, 86
'Working-Class Playwright' sketch, 125, 134, 138
'You're No Fun Anymore' episode, 60, 78

237

Monty Python's Life of Brian (1979 album), 7
Monty Python's Life of Brian (Jones, 1979), 8–9, 155–71
  anti-Semitism, 164
  'Big Nose', 164
  blasphemy, 166–7
  'cave man' jailers, 159
  family rituals, 218
  Harrison, George, 63
  mob rule, 159–60
  music in, 79
  'ordinary bloke' in bizarre situation, 30
  phallocentric Roman names, 159
  Pilate's speech impediment, 159
  rape, 164
  sexuality and gender, 15, 164
  social hierarchy and death, 51–3
  'stoning' sequence, 158–9
  transgender, 164
Monty Python's Personal Best Bits compilations, 91
Monty Python's Previous Record (1972), 7
Monty Python's The Meaning of Life (1983 album), 7
Monty Python's The Meaning of Life (Jones and Gilliam, 1983), 9, 173–88
  absurd and the poetic, 177–9
  body fluids and food, 182–3
  bureaucracy, hyperbole and waste, 179–83
  Cannes Film Festival, 184
  'Christmas in Heaven', 81, 84
  The Crimson Permanent Assurance short feature, 81, 180–1
  death comes to dinner, 53
  deliberate cruelty, 175–6
  ending of, *186*
  'Every Sperm Is Sacred', 81
  'everyday trivia', 178–9
  fish tank, 144, 175–6, 177
  'Galaxy Song', 81, 218
  hyperbole and waste, *183*
  joie de vivre éclatante, *179*
  'The Middle of the Film', 178–9
  'The Miracle of Birth', 177
  'Mr. Creosote', 182–3
  'Penis Song', 81
  philosophy, 174–7
  rituals, 177–8
  Roman Catholic song and dance, 175
  songs, 80–1
Moorcock, Michael, Jack Cornelius novels, 29
Moore, Dudley, 42, 78, 85, 87–8, 182
Morreall, John, 157–8, 162
  Taking Laughter Seriously, 167–8
'The Mouse Problem' (episode 2), 131
'Mr Hilter/Minehead By-election' sketch (episode 12), 63, 67–69
Muggeridge, Malcolm, 51
mundanity, 28, 34–5, 44–5, 54, 79, 101, 147, 222
The Munsters (TV show), 135
music, 75–90
  allusions and in-jokes, 84–5
  background, 82, 85
  brass-band music, 82
  classical, 86–8
  fashionable, 82–3
  non-diegetic, 78–9, 200
  songs brief and incongruous, 79
  songs exclusive to albums and live shows, 80
  theme tune, 82

Nazi master weapon, 64–6
Neale, Steve, 12, 12–13
Netflix, 11, 13
'Never Be Rude to an Arab' song, 77, 80
'New Cooker Sketch' (episode 14), 34–5, 45

New York Times, 183
Nicol, Bran, 31
Noggin the Nog (TV series), 30
Not Only But Also (TV series), 88
Nothing But the Best (1964), 134
'Nudge Nudge' sketch (episode 3), 77, 132

Occidental College, 108–9
Orton, Joe, *Entertaining Mr Sloane*, 128
Osborne, Robert, 183
Othering, 41
Oxbridge, 41–2, 44
Oxford Revue, 4, 41–2

Palin, Michael
  after Python, 10
  bureaucracy, 180
  dancing in the cheese shop, 78
  Death of Stalin (Iannucci, 2018), 185
  fashionable music, 82–3
  Holy Grail, 117, 118
  'It's' man (character), 2
  on Jones and love of films, 111
  on Jones as scholar, 110
  Life of Brian, 160
  Meaning of Life, 180
  Q5, 5
  theme tune, 82
  travel programmes, 36, 185
  on watching *The Canterbury Tales*, 113
Palmer, Jerry, 146–7
pantomime, 42, 45, 46–7
Parkes, Taylor, 40, 44, 53, 76
Parrot Sketch Not Included – 20 Years of Monty Python, 10
Parry, Hubert, 'Jerusalem,' 84, 89
Pasolini, Pier Paolo, 108, 112, 177, 179–80
  The Canterbury Tales (1972), 113
  Salo (1975), 182

pastiche, 81–2, 112
'Pepperpot' characters, 14
Performance (Cammell and Roeg, 1970), 134
permissiveness, 125–6, 131–3, 182
'Philosophers' Song', 80
philosophy, 174–7, 184–5
'photomontage', 95
Pinter, Harold, 27–8, 31, 33–4
Pirandello, Luigi, 26, 178–9
  Eleven Short Stories, 178
  Six Characters in Search of an Author, 26, 178
Pirsig, Robert, *Zen and the Art of Motorcycle Maintenance*, 176
Plato, 157
Poe, Edgar Allan, 'The Masque of the Red Death', 53
'The Poet McTeagle' sketch (episode 16), 131, 138
'Poets' sketch (episode 17), 127
Pogle's Wood (TV series), 30
political cartoons, 101
'political correctness', 155–71
Pop Art, 25, 29
Pop Matters magazine, 161
Pope, Alexander, 'The Rape of the Lock', 43–4
Postgate, Oliver, 30
power dynamics, 149–52, 155–71
'presentist' approach, 163–5
The Prisoner (TV series), 29
The Producers (Brooks, 1968), 112
Profumo affair, 131
psychedelia, 40, 126–8, 133, 137–8
'Psychiatrist Milkman' (episode 16), 33
'Psychiatrist' sketch (episode 13), 78–9
Psychomania (Sharp, 1973), 136
Public Broadcasting Stations (PBS), 8, 10–11
Pulitzer Prize for Literature, 191
Pyle, Howard, 113

Pynchon, Thomas, 179, 179–80
'Python Night' (BBC1, 9 October 1999), 80
Pythonesque, 7, 23, 26, 34, 36, 127, 162, 166, 179, 221
The Pythons: An Autobiography by the Pythons, the Flying Circus, 4, 5

Q5 (TV series), 5, 24
The Quietus (website), 76
quotability, 194–6, 214–15, 220

Rabelais, François, 32, 33
radio sound effects, 59
Radio Times magazine, 51
Ralph, Sarah, 211
Randall, Lilian M. C., *Illustrations in the Margins of Gothic Manuscripts*, 109–10
Rebel Without a Cause (Ray, 1955), 135
'The Record Shop/First World War Noises' sketch, 8
Reinsch, Paul N., *Python beyond Python*, 11, 14
Reisch, George A., *Monty Python and Philosophy*, 13
reversal, 100, 101, 155–71
'Rhubarb Tart' song, 88
Richards, Keith, 137
Ripping Yarns (TV series), 10
rituals, 177, 184
The Rocky Horror Picture Show (Sharman, 1975), 178–9, *179*, 180, 193, 222–3
Rodin, Auguste, *The Kiss*, 102–3
Rogers, Clodagh, 85
The Rolling Stones, 137
Romeo, Demetrius, 84
Rosenbaum, Jonathan, *Midnight Movies*, 193
Rosenstone, Robert A., 107

Ross, Alison, 33
Rothko, Mark, 31
Round the Horne (radio show), 42
'The Royal Philharmonic Orchestra Goes to the Bathroom' sketch (episode 11), 86
Ruling Class, The (Medak, 1972), 133
Running, Jumping and Standing Still Film (Goons short film), 63
Russell, Ken, *The Music Lovers* (1971), 87
Rutland Weekend Television (TV series), 82
episode 4, 'Rutland Weekend Whistle Test', 83
songs, 79
The Rutles, 83, 126
All You Need Is Cash mockumentary, 136

satire
American fans, 220
Americanisation, 129
and animation, 91–106
attack on the powerful, 36
British class system and death, 39–54
Chapman and Cleese, 24
female characters, 14
The Frost Report (TV series), 4, 127
Humanistic, 30
language and word games, 31–2, 134
Menippean, 32
Monty Python and the Holy Grail (1975), 203
Monty Python's Life of Brian (1979), 156, 160–1, 166
music, 82–7
power dynamics, 158
religious, 9
The Ruling Class (Medak, 1972), 133

and the Second World War, 62–3, 65, 69
TV formats and genres, 33
'Working-Class Playwright' sketch (episode 2), 125
satire boom, 12, 63, 126, 131
Satre, Jean Paul, 26
La Nausee, 44
scatological humour, 3, 26–7, 32, 86
Schopenhauer, Arthur, 145–6, 158
Second World War, 63–70; see also *The Goon Show*
The Secret Life of Brian (TV documentary), 51
Secret Policeman's Ball (1979), 78
'Secretary of State Striptease' sketch (episode 20), 134
'self-definition', 220–2, 223
self-reflexivity, 199–203
Sellers, Peter, 42, 182
The Servant (Losey and Pinter, 1963), 134
Sexton, Jamie, 182
  Cult Cinema: An Introduction, 192–3
sexuality and gender, 14–15, 87, 131, 164
Shakespeare, William, 33
  tragedies, 191
  Twelfth Night, 45, 46–7
Shand, Neal, 24
Sharpe, Sue, 217
Sherrin, Ned, 85
'shock of the new', 93
A Show Called Fred (Goons TV series), 63
Siegel, Joe, *The Cocktail People*, 92
silliness, 189–206
  Cutler, Ivor, 29
  Do Not Adjust Your Set (TV series), 24
  'Eric the Half a Bee' song, 31
  fandom, 219

Gilliam, Terry, 92
Hoffman, Donald, 42
hyperbole, 182
joie de vivre éclatante, 184–5
Monty Python and the Holy Grail (1975), 50, 107, 119
music, 76
premiere episode of MPFC, 2
Simonelli, David, 137
Simply Absurd (Radio 4 documentary), 25
Singer, Aubrey, 3
'Sit on My Face' song, 80, 89
Smith, Justin, 14, 195
  Withnail and Us: Cult Films and Film Cults in British Cinema, 193
social hierarchy see British class system; power dynamics
social unrest, 103, 131–5
Some of the Corpses are Amusing website, 85
Sontag, Susan, 31, 189
Sousa, John Philip
  'The Liberty Bell' march, 1, 84, 87, 93
  'Washington Post', 78, 88
South Park (TV show), 91, 95
Spamalot (musical), 9, 10, 76–7, 162–3
Spanish Inquisition, 41, 53–4
Stacey, Jackie, 212, 218, 219
Steptoe and Son (TV series), 81
stereotypes, 15, 35, 164, 204, 213–14
Stewart, Patrick, 164
storybooks, 118
Stott, Andrew, 191
'stream-of-consciousness approach', 127
'Summarising Proust' song, 77
Summer of Love, 136–7
surrealism, 23–38, 83, 85, 92, 126–8
  of animation, 95
  automatism, 127
  of imagery, 93

Svankmajer, Jan, 102
Sweet Charity (stage play), 112
Swift, Jonathan, 104
'Swinging London', 63, 132
Swinging Sixties, 132, 134

'tableau gag', 97–9
Talbot, Hudson, 113
Tarkovsky, Audrey, *Sculpting in Time*, 115
Taylor, Joan E., *Jesus and Brian*, 13
Teddy Boys, 135, 137
The Telegraph, 166, 184
Telotte, J. P., 194
'tendentious joke', 166, 196–7
Thames Television, 4–5
Theatre of the Absurd, 23–38, 128
This Is Spinal Tap (Reiner, 1984), 189
This Time for Keeps (Thorpe, 1947), 88
Thomas, Frank, 96, 97, 99
Time Bandits (Gilliam, 1980), 10, 184
Tomlinson, Fred, 81
Took, Barry, 5
Top of the Pops, 82
Topliss, Iain, 101
Towlson, Jon, 131
transgender, 164 *see also* sexuality and gender
Trevelyan, John, 94
Trotsky, 85
12 Monkeys (Gilliam, 1995), 10
'Twentieth Century Vole' sketch (episode 6), 132
Twitter, 207–8
2D cut-out animation, 92
2D cut-out collages, 91
2D stop motion, 92–3, 99, 105

'Undertakers' sketch (episode 26), 6–7, 6
Universal, 179
Up the Chastity Belt (Kellett, 1971), 85

'Upper Class Twit of the Year' sketch (episode 12), 47–8, 133
Upward, Edward, 29
  The Railway Accident and Other Stories, 29
'utterances', 174, 175, 182

Varon, Jeremy, 130
Vassall incident, 131, 134
Verkaik, Robert, 2–3
Vietnam war, 92
violence, comic
  absurdism, 26–8
  animation, 93, 98–9, 103
  carnival, 12
  counterculture, 132, 134
  'Hell's Grannies' (episode 8), 135–6
  Hewison, Robert, 3
  Monty Python and the Holy Grail (1975), 15, 194–9
  Monty Python's The Meaning of Life (1983), 176–8, 182
visual literacy, 97
Voltaire, 157
'Vox Pops on Politicians' sketch (episode 21), 133
Vroomen, Laura, 211

Wagg, Stephen, 12
Waller, Gregory A., 193
Wallflower Press, 'Cultographies' series of books, 193
Warner Bros, 102
Warner's four modes of metamorphosis, 98
Waters, John, 189
Watkins, Peter, *Privilege* (1967), 130
We Have Ways of Making You Laugh (TV series), 92, 116
'We Love the Yangtze' song, 80
Weiner, Robert G., *Python beyond Python*, 11, 14
Weinstock, Jeffrey, 212, 222–3

West, Patrick, 184
Whitfield, B. Lynn, *Python beyond Python*, 11, 14
Whybray, Adam, 14
Wild One, The (Benedek, 1953), 132, 135, 136
Wilmut, Roger, 3, 63
  'escalation sketch', 13
  'format sketch', 13
  Just the Words transcription books, 85
  programme title, 5
Wilson, Benji, 25

Wilson, Colin, *The Outsider*, 130
Wind in the Willows (Jones, 1996), 10
Witchfinder General (Reeves, 1968), 134
'Working-Class Playwright' sketch (episode 2), 125, 134, 138

Yellowbeard (Damski, 1983), 10, 185
Young, Jimmy, 92, 116
youth audience, 93
youth culture, 135–7

Zeman, Karel, 101, 102

EU representative:
Easy Access System Europe
Mustamäe tee 50, 10621 Tallinn, Estonia
Gpsr.requests@easproject.com

www.ingramcontent.com/pod-product-compliance
Lightning Source LLC
Chambersburg PA
CBHW071835230426
43671CB00012B/1972